Dear Reader:

The book you are about to read is the latest bestseller from St. Martin's True Crime Library, the imprint *The New York Times* calls "the leader in true crime!" Each month, we offer you a fascinating account of the latest, most sensational crime that has captured the national attention. *The Milwaukee Murders* delves into the twisted world of Jeffrey Dahmer, one of the most savage serial killers of our time; *Lethal Lolita* gives you the *real* scoop on the deadly love affair between Amy Fisher and Joey Buttafuoco; *Whoever Fights Monsters* takes you inside the special FBI team that tracks serial killers; *Garden of Graves* reveals how police uncovered the bloody human harvest of mass murderer Joel Rifkin; *Unanswered Cries* is the story of a detective who tracked a killer for a year, only to discover it was someone he knew and trusted; *Bad Blood* is the story of the notorious Menendez brothers and their sensational trials; *Sins of the Mother* details the sad account of Susan Smith and her two drowned children; *Fallen Hero* details the riveting tragedy of O. J. Simpson and the case that stunned a nation.

St. Martin's True Crime Library gives you the stories *behind* the headlines. Our authors take you right to the scene of the crime and into the minds of the most notorious murderers to show you what really makes them tick. St. Martin's True Crime Library paperbacks are better than the most terrifying thriller, because it's all true! The next time you want a crackling good read, make sure it's got the St. Martin's True Crime Library logo on the spine—you'll be up all night!

Charles E. Spicer, Jr.
Senior Editor, St. Martin's True Crime Library

STILL ALIVE ...

When the chilling psychological profile came back from the FBI, police called a news conference. The killer, Detective Moore believed, would turn out to be a white man in his early thirties with above-average intelligence and considerable social skills.

Then the FBI report raised the curtain on the dark side of the killer and created a probable scenario of what happened that horrible night when he charmed Joan Rogers and her daughters into making the the sunset cruise. He had coldly planned the murders from the very start, when the three innocent victims happened to cross his evil path. "That was probably one of his fantasies," said Moore.

He raped and drowned the women for the pure thrill of it, the sheer enjoyment of terrorizing his victims and watching them suffer. Worse yet, the FBI reached the gruesome conclusion that the three were probably still alive when they were dumped overboard, tied and bound to forty-pound cement blocks.

DEATH CRUISE

Don Davis

St. Martin's Paperbacks

DEATH CRUISE

Copyright © 1996 by Don Davis.

Cover photographs courtesy of Hal Rogers.

ISBN: 0-312-95786-6

Printed in the United States of America

St. Martin's Paperbacks edition/April 1996

10 9 8 7 6 5 4

For Debbie and Donna

AUTHOR'S NOTE

This work could not have been written without a number of people who went far out of their way to help. Their assistance surpassed anything I could have imagined. Some asked that their names not be published, and I have respected their wishes. To everyone who made time for a stranger with a lot of questions, I owe a great deal of thanks. With the exception of using fictitious names for the Canadian rape victim and her friend, everything in the book comes from personal interviews, public records, news reports, and background briefings. At times, information given by various people concerning the same event did not match and had to be reconciled by the author.

Special thanks go to Chief A. B. Hatcher and Detective Gino Hotchkiss of the Madeira Beach Police Department; Detective Sergeant Glen Moore of the St. Petersburg Police Department; David Parry and Ron Eide of the Office of the Public Defender of the Sixth Judicial District; Fred Zinober, Lee Atkinson, Steve duQuesnay and the staff at Tew, Zinober, Barnes, Zimmer, & Unice; prosecutors Bruce Bartlett, Doug Crow, Jim Hellickson, Glenn Martin, and Robert Lewis of the Office of the State Attorney, Sixth Judicial District; investigators Scott Hopkins and Steve Porter; Jo Ann Steffey, Mozelle Smith, and Betty Dale Curtis; Barbara Sheen Todd and Wayne Mock, and court stenographers Michelle Luckinbill and Lette Brauer.

Salutes also to the helpful reporters who covered the complex story, particularly Jim Chapman of the *Ft. Wayne Journal-Gazette*, Bill Yelverton at the *Tampa Tribune*, and Tom French and Craig Pittman at the *St. Petersburg Times*. Ray Sullivan and Barb Oakman at the *Lima News* and Judy Bunner of the *Willshire Times-Bulletin* also provided timely help.

In Ohio, thanks also go to Jim and Colleen Etzler, Ed Glossett, Dan Norris, and Phil Pohlman, the kids at Crestview High, and the friends of the Rogers family who took time to speak with me.

The project would have been impossible without the help of two people who endured the tragedy and shared their homes and memories with me, asking nothing in return. I'm in debt to Detective Cindy Cummings in Florida and Hal Rogers in Ohio.

As always, the weight of weaving this manuscript from a bunch of disjointed words into a book fell upon Robin Elayne Murphy Davis, my primary editor, best friend, and wife.

—D. A. D.

1

Florida is a warm magnet for Canadians. They flock to the sunshine by the tens of thousands, filling hotels, thronging to restaurants, pumping millions of dollars into local economies from Jacksonville to Miami to Tampa. They are known as Snowbirds because their southerly migratory patterns swell in numbers when winter temperatures plunge in the Great White North.

The influx lies at the soul of a love-hate relationship with Florida residents, who want the Canadian tourists' economic benefits but would just as soon do without their slow-paced lifestyle.

"It's the goddamn Canadians, Bob," moaned one caller to a talk show.

"So what's new?" responded the host.

"Got behind nineteen of them in traffic, Bob."

"Yep."

"All of them were in Hyundais, Bob. Never got out of third gear."

The Snowbirds are also derided as being so tight with a dollar that a standard joke among waiters is that the main difference between Canadians and canoes is that canoes sometimes will tip. It is also jokingly said that ten thousand Canadian visitors can boost the local economy by a total of $450.

But that is all said with more than a bit of tongue in cheek, for without the Snowbirds the Florida economy would suffer instant, great losses. Therefore, they are welcomed with open arms and cash registers, and everything possible is done to make their stays enjoyable, including attention by the police in various municipalities. For if something bad happens to a Canadian tourist, word quickly filters back to Toronto or Montreal, affecting decisions on vacation destinations. On Mother's Day in 1989, something very bad indeed happened to one Canadian tourist and the result would hang like a worrisome dark cloud over the Tampa-St. Petersburg area for five long years before it was finally resolved.

Gayle Arquette, a chestnut-haired, strikingly beautiful girl from Ontario, was on vacation, taking a welcome break after graduating from college and before assuming a new job as a social worker. Accompanied by her friend, Linda Lyle, also a vibrant, good-looking young woman in her early twenties, Gayle fled Canada on holiday, lured by the spring sunshine and the mythical draw of Florida as a fun and exciting place for the young. Daytona Beach, made famous by the movie and song *Where the Boys Are*, is located on the Atlantic Ocean side of the state, but Gayle and Linda had no doubt that a pair of pretty girls could find a social life on Florida's west coast.

If one views Florida as shaped like the open palm of the right hand, then the thumb hanging slightly apart from the mainland, separated by the vastness of Tampa Bay, is Pinellas County. The urban metropolis of Tampa is on the eastern side of the bay, and St. Petersburg is at the lower western side. Along the coast, stretching north from St. Petersburg, is a long, thin line of beach communities flanked by water on both sides and linked to inland Pinellas County by a series of bridges.

About halfway up the peninsula are the quaintly named beachfront towns of Treasure Island and Madeira Beach, and it was in a "Mad Beach" condominium that Gayle and Linda settled for their Florida stay. The water came almost to their front door, as the Gulf of Mexico stretched open and wide toward the setting sun. Shopping was plentiful, particularly among the quaint shops of the Boardwalk, a collection of specialty shops, restaurants, and boat businesses clustered along weathered piers that hang out over the water along 128th Avenue, facing the watery cut between Mad Beach and Treasure Island known as John's Pass. And cute guys seemed plentiful, whether riding colorful jet skis, loafing about the beachside bars, or soaking up tans on the beach.

In fact, Gayle and Linda agreed to go fishing with two young men they had met on one of their strolls along the Boardwalk. First, however, Gayle needed to complete a special task. She spent much of Sunday, May 14, 1989, preparing Mother's Day dinner for her mother, aunt, uncle, and Linda. The weather was pleasant and they joked about the difference in temperature between May in Ontario and May along the Florida Suncoast.

When the meal was done and the dishes cleaned, the girls waved goodbye to the adults and headed out for their evening, walking over to their first stop, a 7-Eleven convenience store on Gulf Boulevard, the town's main street, to pick up a six-pack of beer about 9:30 P.M.

In the parking lot of the store sat a large, dark-colored trucklike vehicle that Gayle would recall as something like a Jeep Cherokee, Isuzu Trooper, or Ford Bronco—one of those four-wheel-drive, all-terrain jobs. It wore Florida plates.

The driver struck up a laughing conversation with the girls, whom he had guessed were visitors, and soon determined they were from Canada. He was a big guy in his mid-thirties, standing about five feet, nine inches tall and weighing about two-hundred pounds. He was well tanned and had reddish blond hair cut short and a pale mustache of the same color. He quickly extended his hand and introduced himself as Dave Posner, saying he knew a lot about Canada because he once had lived in upper New York State. The voice was light and personable, the manner polite.

There was a note of seriousness, almost concern, in his voice as he asked them why they were out alone in this area. This particular stretch was considered a high-crime locale, he warned, and they should be very wary about talking to any strangers, including himself. When told they were on their way to meet a couple of guys at Fisherman's Wharf, Dave offered them a ride in his truck.

The ride up Gulf Boulevard was brief, but the time seemed to pass even faster because of Dave's steady chatter about the water and the excitement of living in coastal Florida. Arriving at the restaurant, he made a courteous offer, accompanied by a bright smile. Linda got out of the vehicle and walked away, but as Gayle was exiting, she mentioned that she was interested in doing some fishing. Dave replied that he had a 30-foot boat and would be happy to take them out tomorrow for a cruise around the area and to let them try their luck for a deep-water catch.

Gayle quickly accepted for both of them, certain that Linda would want to come along. Dave said that was terrific, and he would meet them tomorrow about 2 P.M., because it took about two hours to get from his house, across Tampa Bay, around the tip of Pinellas County and up to John's Pass. He pointed in the darkness toward the Boardwalk and a pier at the very end. Be at Don's Dock at two, he said.

Gayle was excited about the prospect of a ride out on the open water, but Linda was just as adamant that she would not be coming along. There was something about that Posner guy she didn't like, and Gayle should not meet him either, she warned. Nonsense, argued Gayle, he's just a nice guy, and anyway, he's so *old*, probably almost in his forties. Come on, Linda, she pleaded, come along. Absolutely not, Linda replied, and that was that.

Linda stuck to her decision the next day after lunch and Gayle finally walked to the Boardwalk by herself. She did not see the dark truck parked anywhere, but made her way along the line of shops, examining T-shirts and gifts, looking at the nautical decor of the stores, such as the model shark tangled in a net over a doorway. Large boats were tied up awaiting their scheduled departure with a load of tourists, and people were buying bait. A clutch of sleepy pelicans lay asleep at the edge of the water, their long bills tucked beneath their wings, looking like large balls of feathers.

Shielding her eyes against the bright sun, she finally caught sight of Dave riding near the boat dock, alone in a boat that was faded blue on the outside and white inside. It seemed to her to be an older model, all boxy angles, more of a fishing boat than one of the sleek fiberglass powerboats that sliced through the water in front of some big outboard engine. She also noticed that the boat wasn't thirty feet long as he had boasted, but a stubby seventeen-to-twenty footer. He saw her about the same time and spun the wheel, bringing the boat to bump against the fenders of the pier, and Gayle stepped quickly aboard. Dave wanted to know where Linda was, and a somewhat embarrassed Gayle explained that her friend had decided not to come for the ride. She thought she saw a flash of disappointment in his eyes, but he gave her only a bright smile as she settled into one of the two pedestal seats at the front of the boat. With a slight push of the throttle, the boat's inboard-outboard engine rumbled louder and they moved beneath the John's Pass bridge, heading for the Gulf.

But as soon as they cleared the protection of the land, the pointed bow of the boat began to slap hard into the waves as rough weather somewhere far away churned the normally placid Gulf waters. So instead of pushing into deep water, Dave turned the boat and gave Gayle a tour of the sandy white Pinellas County beaches.

For more than six hours, they talked as he pointed out things of interest beyond the sandy ribbon of shoreline. He had made three sandwiches, because he had expected Linda to accompany them, and they shared the odd one. There was no beer or any alcohol aboard, but he did have a thermos filled with icy water. The AM-FM radio in front of her did not work, but otherwise Gayle felt totally safe and at peace as she spun around in the swivel seat, sinking comfortably into the worn upholstery as the sun toasted her. When she faced the stern of the boat, there was a completely open area before the engine cover and a pair of flanking squarish, boxlike things stretched from side to side across the back. A dark blue canvas canopy was laid back and lashed down around the stern. Once, looking curiously at the engine, she saw it was painted yellow and the word Volvo was stamped across the top. Dave baited her hook and helped teach her how to fish in deep water. He pulled up a wire crab trap to demonstrate for the landlubber Canadian how crabs were snared for restaurants.

She learned a lot about her husky host as the hours passed. He lived with his mother in Bradenton, or some town that began with a B, and he owned an aluminum company. He explained that salt water was the corrosive enemy of boats, and he regularly would pull his free of the water by using a web of pulley davits. And, almost shyly, he admitted that he had trouble in relationships with women. He smoked, but did not drink.

As the sun began to duck lower in the sky, Dave returned her to the dock about 6:30 P.M., saying that the trip had been fun, and he had another idea. You've seen the water by daylight, but a sunset over the Gulf, out in a boat, is a different experience entirely. He said he had to clean the boat a bit, and that she should go along and have some dinner. Grab your camera and come on back and I'll give you a sunset cruise. Oh, yes, he added: See if Linda would like to come along.

Back at the condo, Gayle had a quick bite to eat, said hello to her relatives, and told them about her day running up and down the coast. She tried to persuade Linda to join her for the evening part of the adventure, but Linda once again held firm. She wanted nothing to do with that Posner guy. Gayle said she was reading him all wrong.

It was two hours before sunset when Gayle, wearing jeans and a T-shirt over her two-piece bathing suit, returned to the Boardwalk at 7:30, arriving at Don's Dock without Linda and having to make apologies for her to Dave. This time, she was certain that Dave was upset. Still, he shook off the rejection well enough and the boat was soon churning away from the dock and heading under the bridge, swinging south to Treasure Island, where they stopped, the boat gently rocking in the waves, while they spent time fishing.

As the darkness began to fall, he pulled in the anchor and put away the fishing gear, cranked the engine and pointed the bow of the boat straight toward the setting sun. He stopped to allow her to take photographs of the sunset, then she took a picture of Dave and he snapped one of her.

"You're a nice-looking lady," he said, betraying nothing more than a compliment.

"Thank you," she replied. "Thank you."

The boat headed west again, toward the sun hovering orange on the horizon, its final rays toasting their faces. Soon, they had passed through the usual cordon of other boats and were sailing alone.

Gayle accepted Dave's offer to pilot the boat, and slid into the right-hand driver's seat and clasped the worn, spongy black material that wrapped the steering wheel. Her fingers felt the slickness of duct tape that patched one worn section of the tattered foam rubber. Somewhere in the distance, she heard a bell buoy clanging, almost in alarm.

When Dave, standing behind the chair, leaned close to show her how to work the throttle and wheel and to help weave the boat through the paths of crab traps, she started to have her first doubts. She was out on a boat, far from shore, with a big man that she hardly knew and there was no one around. The lights on shore looked like dim matches burning a million miles away.

She gathered her nerve and told him that it was too dark now and that she wanted to go home.

"Come over here," Dave said, his big shadow looming in the darkness. "I want to give you a hug." She refused.

He wanted her to sit on his lap, and whispered that he thought she was a foxy lady. Gayle's reaction was one of immediate fright, but her resistance was futile. She began to scream.

Dave grabbed her hand and easily pulled her toward him, mocking her. "Do you think somebody is going to hear you?" he asked.

"You lay one hand on me and I'll charge you with rape," Gayle threatened in panic. His firm grip forced her to her knees.

"You are going to have sex with me," Dave ordered.

"There's no way around it. What are you going to do? Jump over the side of the boat?"

Still she struggled against him. "I said I don't want to," she pleaded. "I'm a virgin. Leave me alone!"

The man she knew as Dave Posner began giving orders, holding her firmly and painfully as he took off his pants and forced Gayle to perform oral sex on him.

Disgusted, she hoped the fellatio would satisfy him, but she was wrong. The worst was yet to come aboard that tiny floating prison in which she was being held captive.

Dave grabbed a towel and spread it on the open floor. Gayle alternately sobbed and screamed while he peeled off her shorts.

He grew furious at her constant screams and yelled back at her. "Shut up! Shut up! If you don't shut the fuck up, I'm going to tape your mouth. You want me to tape your mouth?" He made a move as if to get a roll of tape, and she tried to bring herself under control. There was no weapon visible, but Gayle knew that with his size, Dave would have no trouble making her do anything he wanted and perhaps killing her if she was too much trouble.

He agreed with her assessment, and in a reasonable tone, asked, "Is sex worth losing your life over?"

Crawling atop Gayle, he fondled her, removed her tampon, spread the terrified woman's legs, and had vaginal intercourse with her, all the while commenting that she "had a fucking nice pussy."

Gayle Arquette was as frightened as she had ever been in her life as the man finally ejaculated inside her. Then he flipped her onto her stomach but failed in an attempt to have anal intercourse. Finally, spent, he pulled away, handed her the thermos of water, and ordered her to douche.

Meanwhile, Dave staggered to the side of the boat and

vomited overboard. Gathering himself, he ignored her to attend to some urgent business. He opened her camera and ripped out the film that contained his image, then used a cloth to wipe away any possible fingerprints from the camera and his victim's sunglasses.

With his weeping prisoner still huddled in the middle of the boat, Dave turned on a spotlight to locate channel markers and began steering the boat back toward shore. Occasionally, he would lean over the side and throw up again.

As the lights of land approached, representing safety for Gayle, Dave asked an incredible favor. "I know you are going to report me," he said. "But before you do, give me a chance to tell my mother. She's a little old lady and she'll die if she has a policeman arrive at her door."

Gayle naturally promised that she would do as he said. She would have promised anything, just for the opportunity to escape from that boat. Finally, she saw the lights at John's Pass, and in minutes Dave maneuvered the boat close to shore, edging it through the soft surf on the Treasure Island side of the pass. There would be no hard wood deck beneath her feet when she got out of the boat this time, and when the engine began to idle and the boat slowed to a halt, Gayle hesitantly climbed over the side. The water was cold on her legs. He let her leave without incident, telling her almost solicitously to "watch your step" as she waded to safety on the shore.

As Gayle hurried up the sandy road toward Gulf Boulevard, she could hear the inboard Volvo engine purring away into the night.

The embarrassment was simply too much. She had been careless, and despite being warned by Linda, had gotten herself into a dangerous situation. She could not think straight, but she walked into the condo about

10:30 P.M., ran a hot tub of water, and slowly sank into it to let the heat wash away her shock.

She kept the secret for a whole day, fearing that her revelation would ruin her mother's birthday. Finally, as night fell, she confided in Linda.

Officer Tammy Nixon of the Madeira Beach Police Department was driving along the 800 block of Gulf Boulevard at 11:16 P.M. on Tuesday, May 16, when Linda Lyle flagged her down. She explained to the police officer that a friend of hers had been assaulted the day before, but had been afraid to report it.

Linda took Nixon to the condo, and then the officer ferried both of the Canadian girls up the street to police headquarters where Gayle began to tell her story. Later, she was taken to the Pinellas County Health Department in St. Petersburg for a rape test, although no one doubted for a moment that the girl had been assaulted.

She and Linda gave police a detailed statement that enabled them, with the use of a Smith & Wesson Identikit, to put together a composite sketch of the man who called himself Dave Posner. He was a man in his late thirties about five foot nine inches tall and some two hundred pounds, with reddish blond hair cut short. He had a mustache and wore a slouch hat to protect his balding head, and on the day he raped Gayle Arquette, he had worn a bright green shirt with some sort of mesh around the bottom. He lived with his mother, owned his own aluminum business, and was from some town that started with the letter *B*.

The report was then distributed on a routine basis to other law enforcement agencies. The crime was described, along with the description of the assailant and the boat.

It was very little, but about all that could be done.

Five years later, Madeira Beach Police Chief Archie "Bert" Hatcher, a former head of homicide detectives in

Tampa, said it was the worst kind of crime to try and solve. Two people meet at random and one perpetrates a crime on the other aboard a boat. The victim is from a faraway city and would be unlikely ever to see her attacker through an accidental meeting. The rapist could be from anywhere along the crowded Florida coast and boats that are blue and white number in the thousands. Tracing such a boat that vanished into the night was impossible after giving it a forty-eight-hour head start.

Not surprisingly, there was no arrest.

Gayle Arquette returned to Canada and got on with her life.

Dave Posner, however, satisfied with the success of his hit-and-run rape, began making other plans. On Sunday night, May 14, he had taken his wife out for an early dinner to celebrate their first wedding anniversary, and after returning home, had driven alone over to Madeira Beach, where he'd had the chance meeting with Gayle Arquette and her friend. The day after his anniversary, he had forced the Canadian to submit to sex on his boat, and felt confident that he had gotten away with the crime.

Chief Hatcher was wrong on one point. Gayle would see Posner again, many years later, when the rapist went on trial—under another name—for murdering three other women during one single, deadly boat ride. Gayle's vivid testimony about what happened to her on a dark and terrifying night in a small boat off the Florida coast would be a pivotal piece of evidence that would help send the man who assaulted her to the electric chair.

2

Two weeks after the brutal rape of Gayle Arquette, investigating officers had run into a blank wall. There were no new witnesses, no fresh clues, no calls from other police departments, no stroke of luck, and no arrest. Gayle returned to Canada and the Tampa Bay area returned to normal.

The temperature was again knocking on the mid-nineties, as the middle of summer approached, and nightly lows were in the comfortable seventy-degree range. Early risers drinking their coffee and scanning the *St. Petersburg Times* on Sunday, June 4, would read that a touring company of the Bolshoi ballet was performing up in Clearwater and the Florida agricultural authorities were demanding that a shop in Tampa stop selling three-inch-long Madagascar hissing roaches as exotic pets. The international scene was dominated by the bloody attack of the Chinese army on demonstrating students in Beijing's Tiananmen Square.

Mariners setting out for a day on the water could look forward to almost ideal conditions during the early part of the day, with winds out of the south at ten miles per hour and gentle seas running at about two feet. It was a good day to get the boats out before late afternoon, when there was a chance of the usual summer thundershowers. For the crews of three separate pleasure boats, however, the day would end about midmorning as they made individual, macabre discoveries.

The first radio call came into the Coast Guard station at 9:20 A.M., from a man aboard the sailboat *Amber Wave*, which was located near Piney Point. He reported that something that appeared to be a human body was floating in the water, adding with ominous certainly, "It looks like murder."

A swift nineteen-foot Coast Guard inflatable boat sped to the scene with three people aboard. Normally, only two people would be in the rescue craft, but the possibility of a body in the water meant the addition of an extra set of lifting arms might be necessary.

And, indeed, there was the body of a young woman floating near Piney Point. The pale buttocks protruded through the surface of the water, but the head and torso were angled sharply down. The Coast Guard team tried to pull the corpse aboard, but were unable to shake it free of whatever anchored it. Finally, after wrestling with the problem for thirty minutes, they sliced through a yellow nylon rope that was knotted around the neck of the victim, allowing the entangling weight below the water to fall free. They pulled it aboard and arranged it into a body bag, sickened at what they found. The victim had been tied hand and foot, was nude from the waist down, and had several layers of duct tape wrapped around her head and neck. There was no doubt that this was the result of a hideous murder, and police would be waiting at the pier for the boat's return.

No more than ten minutes after the recovery of the body, the sailboat *Suzy* tuned to the Coast Guard radio band and placed a call for help. The *Suzy* was two miles east of The Pier, at the edge of St. Petersburg, and reported a body in the water there, too.

The Coast Guard boat delivered the first body back to the large dock of the Bayboro Harbor Coast Guard station at 10:24 A.M., then rushed to the new scene, not far from where the first victim had been found. This time the body came aboard easily, but presented no less of a shock when it was laid onto the body bag at 11:10 A.M. It was another woman, nude from the waist down, tied hand and foot, duct tape wrapped around the mouth and chin and a yellow nylon rope knotted at the neck. At the other end of the rope was a heavy cinder block, the thirty-five-to-forty-pound type builders use to construct houses.

The similarities were immediately apparent to the boat crew, which noticed that this victim, in her frantic struggle for life, somehow had managed to free one of her hands and tug down the silver tape that had been choking her. The Coast Guard crew held soft conversations while they worked, saying they hoped that the women were not alive when they went into the water. But the evidence before them, that one had put up a struggle, made it hard to believe otherwise.

By now, a second Coast Guard boat had been hauled into service, for no sooner had the earlier rescue craft dashed off for its new assignment than the base radio crackled with still another message. People aboard the pleasure boat *Charlie Girl* had a report of a grim but familiar nature by now. There was a body in the water about two miles from The Pier.

The Coast Guard crew found the scene very unsettling when they had the third body aboard at eight minutes after noon. Once again, the victim was a female, nude from the waist down, tied hand and foot, with a yellow nylon rope looped around her neck and lashed to a big cinder block that served as an anchor.

The women were placed side by side on the dock as the Coast Guard officers gave the task over to the waiting band of law enforcement personnel that had gathered.

They had the unenviable task of examining the bloated, water-damaged bodies in order to launch the investigation into what had happened to bring such violent death to the three women. It was a hard thing to do, even for people accustomed to dealing with homicides on a rather routine basis.

Under Florida law, a member of the Office of the State Attorney responds to a major murder scene to provide legal guidance, if needed, to the investigators. On this bright Saturday, that duty fell to Doug Crow, an assistant state attorney with a blistering reputation for putting bad guys in prison. He hovered at the far edge of the crowd of investigators, but even one hundred yards from the bodies, the scene to him was grotesque. "It was difficult just to be in the area," he recalled later. The violence of the deaths affected him. The three women had obviously been murdered by a vicious killer or killers whom police needed to catch quickly. The person or persons responsible had already murdered at least three people and, thought Crow, probably would kill again. Having drawn the case, he decided not to hand it off to another prosecutor. Doug Crow would stay with this one, and knew in his gut that it probably was going to be a roller-coaster ride. He had no idea at the time just how long it would actually take before he could put this one down.

To the investigating cops, the three bodies represented what they dislike the most—a mystery. There were no signs of identification, the currents could have moved the bodies around the bay for several days before they were discovered, and even the exact cause of the deaths was unknown. Just who *were* these people whose bodies had been pulled from Tampa Bay in the tiny space of three hours?

To complicate matters, when the Coast Guard went out to retrieve the final two bodies they also discovered a thirty-two-foot boat rocking abandoned in the calm seas.

Did the women come from that boat? The police had it towed to dock for investigation.

It is a given fact in criminology that most murders are solved within the first seventy-two hours after the crime is committed. That is when blood samples can be taken, evidence gathered, crime scene tests meticulously conducted, when perhaps even a murder weapon can be found and a suspect arrested. That holds true when the murder takes place in a room somewhere, not when the victims are thrown into the deep channels of Tampa Bay. After being in the water for so long, many of the vital elements of forensic science would be washed away. It was agreed that this one was not going to be completed in a mere seventy-two hours. About the only thing that happened during that period of time was that the police determined the abandoned boat had nothing to do with the murdered women, apparently ending up in the same vicinity by the very currents which had deposited the three bodies there.

But police work also teaches officers of the law that steady, plodding routine can usually yield results. Time passes, and things come together. When starting out with a first-class mystery, it is better to stick close to the book.

After recovery, the first stop was to ferry the bodies to the medical cxaminei so autopsies could be performed and investigators could at least get a handle on what might have happened to the unidentified women. It would not be much, but it would be a great deal more than they knew at present.

As the body bags were sealed and transported, divers from the Hillsborough County Sheriff's Office arrived at the scene of the first discovery, donned their fins and tanks, and plunged into the water. It was the first of many, many police efforts that would yield no new information.

And of course, there was one other group of people at the scene—news reporters. Normally cops and the media maintain a cordial, but adversarial, relationship. But as with so many other things in this case, that fact would not hold true. Before everything was said and done, the media would be co-opted by the police, surrender some of its independence, and play a major role in actually trying to solve the crime. That change started small, as the first stories ended with a plea for anyone having any information about the deaths to contact the Hillsborough County Sheriff's Office at 247–8660 or the St. Petersburg Police Department at 893–7511. Later, the new link being forged between the police and the press would grow more and more complex.

Autopsies are awful but necessary tools for the people who investigate crime. More than once, a dead body has provided the clue needed to apprehend the murderer, almost as if it were pointing a finger from beyond the grave. Medical specialists who conduct the post mortems steel themselves against the evidence of violence that is placed before them and concentrate on making note of every little detail. A fiber found beneath a fingernail, holes made by an ice pick discovered under thick hair, a flattened bullet plucked from a heart, or the label of a blouse can have immense significance when the case comes together. Perhaps, investigators hoped, the careful study of the bodies of these three women would provide some idea of their identities and lead investigators to whoever killed them.

That was not to happen on the three cases numbered 1890685, 1890686, and 1890687 by the medical examiners, although the information gleaned by the autopsies would at least help the police start the arduous process of getting to know the murder victims.

The language of science can be simultaneously clear

and horrific, but the impersonal precision is necessary when police read the reports, looking for avenues of investigation, and when lawyers take the documents into a court of law. Therefore, the external examination of one of the victims read like this:

"The body is that of a well-developed, well-nourished white female, measuring sixty-seven inches in length and weighing one hundred twenty-five pounds. There is a yellow nylon rope with a slipknot around her neck, the other end of the rope is attached to a concrete block. The hands are bound together behind the back with a clothesline-type rope and the ankles are bound together with a yellow nylon rope. A black barrette accompanies the body. The body is clad only in a pullover black sleeveless shirt, Tropical Heat brand, size medium. The body is extremely bloated and exhibits general skin slippage and marbling. The scalp is covered with long blond hair which is loosely adhered to the scalp. The eye color cannot be determined. There is a silver-colored post earring in the superior aspect of each earlobe, and a silver-colored ring in the interior aspect of each earlobe. Natural teeth are present and in good condition. Shallow superficial abraded depression is noted around the neck. The chest, abdomen, and back are unremarkable except for decomposition. Genitalia, adult female. There is a silver, narrow, colored ring on the left ring finger and a cloth ring on the right ring finger. The cloth ring is purple with green and white stripes. No scars or other identifiable marks."

Another of the victims was found to be five foot six and weighing 113 pounds. She had long, wavy brown hair and wore a Pinwheels brand blouse, size medium, over a dark turquoise bathing suit top. The yellow rope was wound around her neck, with the other end tied to a concrete block, and a piece of silver duct tape was stuck to the left side of her neck. The clothesline rope was around the right wrist, and a loop also was at the opposite end, although not tied to an arm. She wore a pair of gold post earrings, a gold ring with two gold-colored hearts on it on her right ring finger, a gold ring with a clear stone on the left little finger, silver rings on both the left index finger and the left ring finger, and a gold ring with an oval white stone on her left middle finger.

The third victim measured five feet, four and a half inches, weighed only ninety-five pounds, and had brown hair of a medium length. She wore a Mister Noah beige pullover shirt with no sleeves, and of the six buttons down front, the top two were undone. A diagonally-striped green, white, and pink cloth bracelet, similar to a ring worn by the other victim, was on her arm. Her ears were pierced twice on the right and once on the left. Duct tape was wrapped around the lower part of the face and neck, the hands were tied with clothesline, and the ankles were bound with yellow nylon rope. The slipknot in the yellow rope around her neck had been pulled so tightly by the weight, which was not recovered by the Coast Guard, that the measured diameter was a mere three inches.

None of the victims had any scars or identifying marks and there were no fresh needle marks. The decomposition was such that it was impossible to tell that one of the victims was a child.

The thorough study left investigators with precious little. There were no names, of course, but that was to be expected in the opening hours of the investigation. More troubling was that the medical examiner could not determine an exact cause of any of the deaths due to the damage done while the bodies were submerged for three days. There was no trace of any beating and the water washed away any possibility of determining if a rape had occurred. It was impossible to determine even whether they were alive or dead at the time they went into the water, although it looked as if one had managed to struggle free of the rope binding her hands before she died.

As far as clues, the similarities between the bodies provided some direction. All were white females. All were nude from the waist down, but still wore blouses and tops. All three had pierced ears and apparently enjoyed wearing jewelry. All were discovered in the same terrible positions, lashed to weights that had pulled them under water.

3

Hal Rogers was getting anxious. It was already Sunday, which meant Monday and possible problems were just a few sweeps around the clock face away. The girls were due back today, but he had not heard a word from them for several days. On Monday, his wife Jo had to be back at work and one of his daughters, Michelle, was due to start summer school. They had telephoned a few days ago to let him know they arrived in Tampa, but he had heard nothing since.

A slender, rather quiet man and a hard-working dairy farmer, he had not accompanied his family on the trip. A combination of rainy weather that flooded the land and delayed planting, his responsibility for taking care of the cows, and his efforts to dissolve the farm partnership with his brother John required that Hal mind the home front in Van Wert, Ohio, a little agricultural community near the Indiana state line.

The fact that Jo, Michelle, and Christe gave hours to the farm every day was more than apparent to him. He had been working hard the whole time they had been gone, more than a week. It long ago dawned on him, as he walked out into the soft, warm rain to milk the cows and put up silage, that perhaps the busy days of early summer had been the wrong time for his best helping hands to take a vacation.

Hal had intentionally stayed out of the trip. It was the first real vacation for the three of them, and they deserved the break. When they asked his advice, he replied that it would be better if they planned it on their own, so that if a problem arose, they would know how the original schedule had been laid out. "I told them to take their time, go see what you want to see," he would recall later. Just don't bother wasting time on anything you might be able to see around here.

According to Jo's telephone calls and a single postcard, things apparently had proceeded on schedule, through Epcot Center, the MGM Studios, the Kennedy Space Center, and Silver Springs. Jo had dropped him a postcard on May 30 from outside of Orlando, right in the middle of Florida and home to Disney World.

Her extremely neat handwriting had stacked the address like building blocks. The card was a photograph of two vintage automobiles—a Cord convertible and a Rolls Royce Phantom II—on display at Silver Springs, and bore a fifteen-cent Buffalo Bill stamp.

"Stayed the nite at Titusville," she had written the previous evening, May 29. "Leaving for Sea World then Disney World tonite for three nites. Weather is hot and humidity is very high (98 %). Kids having a great time, dragging me everywhere, seeing Silver Springs. Went on glass bottom boat ride. Better go, have to get Christe out of bed. Love ya—Take care—don't work too hard."

Hal could find no indication of alarm in that cheerful note, but still returned to his chores on Sunday with an uneasy mind. Michelle's boyfriend, Jeff Feasby, had called several times asking if they had telephoned yet. Michelle had called Jeff from their motel room in Tampa on Thursday, June 1, with Christe and Jo making a happy racket in the background. Everything seemed fine then, Jeff said, and he had expected them to leave Florida early Saturday morning, with the goal of making it back to Ohio in a single day, or at most, arriving home on Sunday evening.

Jeff's questions fed Hal's growing feeling of discomfort. As he went out to feed the cows on Sunday night, the 1986 Oldsmobile Calais that Jo had driven to Florida was nowhere in sight. "I wanted them home," he would recall years later. "I missed 'em."

The police forces of two metropolitan areas—Tampa and St. Petersburg—were stymied, and the investigation had only just begun. Anyone hoping for a quick identification saw that possibility vanish swiftly with the passing hours.

No local women had been reported missing, leading to the conclusion that the three victims had been from out of town, probably tourists, which meant they could have been from anywhere. People travel to Florida from throughout the world, drawn by the sunshine, the beaches, and the huge list of major entertainment attractions. The last thing the cops wanted was a triple murder of tourists. Florida, particularly down in the Miami area, was already getting a reputation as a danger zone for tourists, and another major crime involving visitors would only add more fuel to that firestorm.

What they could do in the first few days of investigation, they did. Fingerprints were taken from the bodies and compared to those in a vast databank maintained by the FBI. The results were negative.

The possibility that the three were hitchhikers was seriously examined. One group of three women had been seen on U.S. 19, north of St. Petersburg, waving a sign that they were bound for Miami. A second threesome had been seen near the junction of interstates 4 and 275. Police could find neither group.

The telephones were beginning to ring with a monotonous regularity as people called in with tips, some interesting and some outrageous. But none of the dozens of tips could be ignored. Each claim required careful examination, a process that added to the growing number of work hours being put in by the police.

Another positive move was to use the media to distribute descriptions of the victims, their clothing, and their jewelry. They decided to hold a news conference and allow reporters to examine—and let photographers take pictures of—some of the jewelry found on the victims, an unusual step because that meant the police were disclosing evidence. However, a newspaper report could be picked up by a wire service and transmitted nationwide, increasing the number of possible witnesses who may know something. At this point in the investigation, any possible help was welcome.

Monday
June 5

Monday morning dawned at Hal-Jo-Ro Dairy Products to find Hal Rogers tending the cows and farm with the help of only one hired hand. It was back-breaking labor. But his mind wasn't really on the intensive effort demanded by his business.

He kept looking from the milking barn toward the driveway, hoping to see that Oldsmobile cruise up and deliver his wife and a larking pair of teenage daughters. He always checked the driveway in the mornings because Jo worked the midnight shift for a company in Indiana, and he wasn't comfortable until she arrived home safely.

She had once hit a deer on the long road home, and had almost clipped another. Hal always got antsy when Jo was late.

Trying to put things in a best-case scenario, he imagined that something had attracted the curious eyes of his family on and they had just stopped off to examine it. But darker thoughts began to crowd in, unwanted and unbidden.

The day passed in eerie silence at the dairy farm, and in the afternoon, Hal began working the telephone again. He called relatives and learned they had not heard from the girls. He called Jeff again and was told that Jeff had received a short postcard from 'Chelle, teasing him about looking like a monkey in the Jacksonville Zoo. He called Jo's employer, Peyton Northern, and discovered she had not been in touch there, although she was due back to work immediately. Still, he hesitated about calling the police. Had Jo telephoned while he was out milking in the barn? What if he started bugging the cops and then Jo and the girls drove up just a day late? He'd feel like an idiot.

Hal Rogers went to bed Monday night in an uneasy state of mind. After tossing and turning for hours, he concluded that he had better call the police and file a report that the girls were missing. He shuddered to think that they might have been involved in an automobile accident.

**Tuesday
June 6**

Another day with nothing. Police were confident that something would turn up soon, for three women couldn't just be killed and disappear as if they had never been on the planet. They had names. They were people. Somebody, somewhere would soon know that they were missing and raise an alarm. More tips were telephoned in, and each was checked as police supervisors added more officers to the case to handle the workload.

It was difficult, however, to wait patiently when there was another question in the mix. Not only did the women have to be identified, but police wanted to find out who killed them and prevent another potential murder. Someone who killed three people at one time in such a cruel way bore all the marks of a very dangerous individual. If the murderer walked away from this crime, he probably would kill again.

Proceeding with the logical proposition that the victims most likely were not from the area, police distributed a flier about the missing women to a motel and hotel owners' association. Unless they had stayed with relatives who had not reported them missing, they probably had checked into a rented room. The problem was that in the Tampa Bay metro area there were tens of thousands of rentable accommodations. Instead of scanning each individual unit in the more than two dozen localities that comprise the area, perhaps a motel worker would notice something strange and report it.

They also began trying to solve the puzzle of how the bodies ended up where they did. As a coast guard spokesman noted, they could have floated in from anywhere, possibly dropped within inches of each other or miles apart.

Police contacted a professor at the University of South Florida who was able to construct a computer program to chart the swirls and eddies and tides of the bay in order to guess where the bodies had gone into the water.

This was an important question, for it established jurisdiction, a subject that was becoming more tangled by the day. The bay is surrounded by Tampa and Hillsborough on the east; St. Petersburg, the biggest city in Pinellas County, was to the west. Someone had to take charge of the investigation to prevent the various agencies from tripping over each other. In order to streamline the probe and avoid a turf battle, a conference was called in Tampa between the major investigative agencies involved. The conclusion, after hours of discussion, was that since two of the bodies were found within the St. Petersburg city limits, and since it was not known where the actual crime had taken place, the St. Pete Police Department would be the lead unit.

The idea was to avoid petty bickering about areas of responsibilities and to concentrate on going after the bad guy.

Still, it was not going to be easy, no matter who had the reins. Time was moving rapidly, putting more distance between the killer and his dreadful deed.

As the Florida sun went down Tuesday night, police still did not know the names of the three women who had been slain.

In Ohio, Hal Rogers telephoned his in-laws, but Jo's parents had not heard anything. He was getting irritated at the girls for not telephoning anyone. Rogers went about his chores, carrying a sack of worry on his slender back. At least, he thought, he would have heard something from the police if his family had been involved in a traffic accident. No news is good news. When the sun went down Tuesday, the driveway still yawned emptily at him.

Nearby, on a farm outside Convoy, Ohio, Jo's brother Jim and his wife, Colleen, were concerned. She had been at a swap meet and couldn't keep her mind on any bargain. He had been at work in the wet fields, similarly preoccupied. If Jo would have run into difficulty, she would have called somebody. But no one had heard a thing.

Wednesday
June 7

Hal awoke and looked outside. No Jo. No Michelle. No Christe. Clearly worried, he took care of the dawn chores around the dairy. Cows milked and fed, and still no sign of the girls, he concluded that something definitely was wrong. He was no longer thinking about a traffic accident. A more macabre menu of possibilities had haunted his dreams. Had someone robbed them? Had they been knocked unconscious? Had they picked up a panhandler or run into some "backwoods hillbillies" while driving through the South?

He glumly called the Ohio Highway Patrol to advise them that his wife and daughters were two days overdue in returning from a Florida vacation. The highway patrol referred him to the Van Wert County Sheriff's Office, which was headed by family friend Stan D. Owens. In such a close-knit community as Van Wert, Owens was immediately interested because he had seen the Rogers family endure some pretty hard times recently and hoped this was not an extension of the earlier problems.

The police told Rogers that they had no reports on Jo, Michelle, and Christe, but that they would circulate the missing persons report and see if any major accidents had occurred on the roads between Florida and Ohio. Rogers thanked Owens and continued dialing, talking to the highway patrol offices all the way down to Tennessee.

Looking back on those hard hours, Rogers said by then he had begun to fear the absolute worst. "Somebody had done something to them," he said. "That was the way my mind was working." All he wanted at the moment was for word that they were alive.

Fearing that he might have to make a sudden trip, Hal went to the bank in Willshire and drew out seven thousand dollars in cash. He did not have a credit card and thought he might have trouble writing a check in a strange town. Cash, he knew, would get the job done. He tucked one thousand dollars into his wallet and, reflecting the low-crime attitudes in that part of the Midwest, thought nothing of putting the remaining six thousand into a bank bag that he placed in his truck.

Thursday
June 8

At the Days Inn at Rocky Point, located on the Courtney Campbell Parkway that stretches between Tampa and upper Pinellas County, a maid going about her routine noticed something strange. For a week, maids had been visiting Room 251 daily and nothing ever changed. The beds had not even been slept in, and female belongings were scattered about, but maids dusted around them. Remembering the reports she had seen concerning three women who had been found murdered, she decided to talk to her manager.

Sergio Ortiz agreed with her concern and telephoned Tampa police. The officer who responded was told the room had been rented on June 1, exactly one week earlier, by a woman who signed in as Joan Rogers. A desk clerk said she had checked in about noon on that day without incident, having made an earlier reservation. Other motel workers would recall that two teenaged girls were waiting in her car.

Homicide detectives quickly sealed off the room and set up shop in an adjacent one, as they notified St. Petersburg police of the development. By early Thursday afternoon, teams of technicians from both departments were scouring the motel room, from the ceiling to beneath the carpet.

* * *

It was the break for which police had been waiting. After following dozens of fruitless leads, they actually had something with which to work. Joan Rogers had signed in with a name and address. They telephoned Ohio and contacted the Van Wert County Sheriff's Office.

Still, a tentative identification was not solid enough. Proof was needed. So authorities in Ohio sent down dental records, fingerprints, and photographs of Joan, Michelle, and Christe Rogers. Unfortunately, in doing so, they had contacted Hal Rogers for permission to get the records and pictures. His worst nightmare seemed to be coming true. Something *was* wrong.

Friday
June 9

Forensic odontologist Kenneth Martin made a positive report on the dental work. Fingerprints lifted in the motel room matched those sent down from Ohio.

At 10:45 A.M., a St. Petersburg detective placed a call to Sheriff Owens in Ohio to inform him that the identifications were firm.

Hal Rogers was standing in his driveway when a stranger drove up, stopped by the edge of the road, and approached. The young man identified himself as a newspaper reporter. "Those three bodies down in Florida have been identified as your family," he said. The reporter wanted a comment. Hal went inside his home without saying a word, crushed, finally knowing that his wife and two daughters were dead.

Jenny Etzler was alone at home when she answered the door to find family friend Stan Owens standing there. The ashen-faced sheriff broke the horrible news that her daughter and two granddaughters were dead. Owens's

sad duty wasn't yet complete, for as he drove away from
the Etzler home, he spotted two tractors coming down
the road, with Bill Etzler and his son, Jim, behind the
wheels. Owens swung his sheriff's car in behind the tractors and followed them back to the house. When they
had dismounted and were standing in the barnyard, he
repeated the news that the girls had been murdered. Colleen Etzler, Jim's wife, got the heartbreaking news in a
doctor's office where she worked in Decatur, Indiana.

4

Room 251 at the Days Inn on Rocky Point Island at 7627 Courtney Campbell Causeway suddenly became the focus of an intense police investigation. The large motel complex faces the water of Tampa Bay and the coastline across the traffic-laden road. Skinny palm trees line a courtyard swimming pool and grainy beach sand is tracked into the registration area, game room, and bar by barefoot visitors.

But Jo Rogers was vacationing on a budget, so the room she rented did not face onto the more attractive areas of the motel. Instead, flanked by rooms 249 and 253, its door opened onto a concrete walkway overlooking a sun-baked rear parking lot, scrub brush, and a distant glimpse of bay water. Still, it must have seemed as different as another world for Jo and her daughters, when compared to the spartan existence they lived on the Ohio dairy farm.

The room was standard issue for a midprice Florida motel. It was immaculately clean, had a television set on a long dresser table, a large mirror, several bright lamps, a small table with two soft chairs, two plump double beds, thick drapes, and a blessed air conditioner to chase away the terrific summertime heat and humidity.

Police who searched the room found an assortment of women's clothing, bathing suits, a roll of exposed film, and luggage. The beds were still made and had not been slept in, according to the motel maids. There was no indication that anyone was preparing to check out, and no sign at all of a struggle or foul play. Forensic experts began sweeping the room for even the most minute items that might help illuminate the situation, but it became immediately obvious that whatever happened to the three victims took place elsewhere.

When developed, the final frame of the discovered film showed Michelle sitting in the motel room. A copy was shown to Hal Rogers in Ohio and he confirmed that it was his oldest daughter in the picture, putting a final certainty to the identification process.

Still missing, however, was the car. Detectives reasoned that if indeed the women had been dumped overboard, then the logical place for them to have gotten into the boat in the first place was probably the boat landing ramp located 2.8 miles to the west, directly down the causeway. A patrol car was dispatched to the scene, a wide parking lot on the north side of the busy highway, bordered by the road on one side and water on the other.

Tampa patrolman Mitchell Wilkins quickly found a 1986 blue, two-door Oldsmobile Calais sitting empty in the bright sun. The Ohio tag was 230–TCU. A quick radio check showed that it was registered to Joan M. Rogers from Van Wert County. One of the front seats was tilted forward, indicating that someone had exited from the rear seat, which led to the conclusion that at least three people had last ridden in it. Peering into the locked vehicle, the policeman could see a folded highway map, a book of crossword puzzles, a partially eaten candy bar, and two decks of playing cards on the seats. From the mirror dangled a little air freshener with the stamp, BORN TO PARTY. In the back of the car was a folded sunscreen. When spread out, it would show the words that motorists count on for assistance: NEED HELP, PLEASE CALL POLICE. The car was impounded and searched for evidence.

Finally, the police had something firm to go on. From Hal Rogers, it was learned that the vacation began on May 26, and that Jo and her girls checked into the Days Inn at Rocky Point on June 1, disappearing a short time after, only to be found murdered and floating in the bay a few days later.

The task force of officers and detectives working the case grew almost daily, sometimes numbering more than forty people, and set out to reconstruct the victims' trip, step by step. For somewhere along the way, Jo, 'Chelle, and Christe Rogers met the person or persons who killed them.

And following up on the idea that the offer of a boat ride was involved, questioning police discovered that a large dark vehicle, like a Ford Bronco or Chevy Blazer, pulling a blue and white boat on a four-wheeled tandem-axle trailer, had been seen in the motel parking lot about the time the Rogers were last there. That fact was woven into the official reports, but meant little at the time because of the inexact description of the vehicle, and many boats in Florida are blue and white.

When the search was complete, a number of new facts were known, primarily the identification of the victims and the data gathered from a handful of witnesses. A week into the case and the face and name of the killer or killers was still unknown. "We've never had a murder like this before," Detective Sergeant Bill Sanders of the St. Petersburg Police told the *St. Petersburg Times*. "At this point we don't have any leads or suspects."

A homicide detective assigned to the case flew from Florida to Ohio to coordinate with police authorities on that end, even as Sheriff Owens in Van Wert made a peculiar statement to reporters. "There is absolutely no indication of any involvement of anyone in this area," he declared.

Who said there was?

JOAN M. ROGERS
MICHELLE L. ROGERS
CHRISTE E. ROGERS

WILLSHIRE—Joan M. Rogers, 36, and her daughters, Michelle L. Rogers, 17, and Christe E. Rogers, 14, all of here, died June 1 or June 2 in Florida.

Their bodies were found floating in Tampa Bay. The St. Petersburg police department is considering the deaths homicides.

Mrs. Rogers was born Nov. 12, 1952, in Van Wert County, the daughter of Wilhelm and Virginia Reed Etzler. Her parents survive in Convoy. On Oct. 16, 1971, she married Hal Rogers, who survives.

Mrs. Rogers worked at Peyton Northern in Bluffton, Ind. She was a member of Zion Lutheran Church in Schumm and was a 4-H leader.

Survivors also include one brother, James Etzler of Convoy.

Michelle L. Rogers was born Feb. 22, 1972, in Van Wert, the daughter of Hal and Joan Etzler Rogers. Her father survives at home.

She would have been a senior this year at Crestview High School in Convoy. She was a member of Zion Lutheran Church in Schumm and Future Farmers of America, in which she held the office of sentinel. She was also a member of a 4-H club.

Christe E. Rogers was born Oct. 6, 1974, in Van

Wert, the daughter of Hal E. and Joan M. Etzler Rogers. Her father survives at home.

She would have been a freshman this year at Crestview High School. She was a member of Zion Lutheran Church in Schumm. A cheerleader, she was a member of Crestview Band Flag Corps, Wren Girls' Softball Team and a 4-H club.

Survivors of the two teenagers also include maternal grandparents, Wilhelm and Virginia Etzler of Convoy; paternal grandparents, Wayne and Irene Rogers of Van Wert; paternal great-grandfather, Espy Rogers of Van Wert; and paternal great-grandmother, Estella Trimble of Van Wert.

Joint services for Mrs. Rogers and her two daughters will be at 10:30 A.M. Tuesday at Zion Lutheran Church, Schumm, Revs. Gary Luderman and Kurt Bickel officiating.

Burial will be in Zion Lutheran Church Cemetery.

Friends may call 2 to 9 P.M. Monday at Alspach-Gearhart Funeral Home, Van Wert.

The unusual triple obituary in the *Lima News* was a classic piece of newspaper work that covered all the bases, saying everything that needed to be said. It did not say everything that could have been said, leaving the less polite details to the news columns.

And there was abundant coverage, both in print and on television, of the Florida murders and the shock wave of astonishment, disbelief and outrage that swept through the small farm community in which the three victims had spent their entire lives.

"It's just so sad," said waitress Susan Reynolds at the Village Restaurant in Willshire. In an area where everybody knew everybody else, such a tragedy would leave an indelible scar. Friends remembered holding the girls in their arms as infants, remembered how hard Joan worked, remembered the fun things in an attempt to banish the bad.

The funerals were held jointly on Tuesday, June 13, in the dark brick Zion Lutheran Church, which had stood solidly on a windswept rise at the intersection of Schumm Road and Route 26 since 1913 and was rooted to the community by its official English-German name of the Evangelical Lutheran Zion's Kirche. Pesky reporters and camera crews kept a distance from the mourners. The Rev. Gary Luderman, pastor of Zion, and the Rev. Kurt Bickel, who had married Jo and Hal, officiated at the three-casket service attended by three hundred people as light filtered through the stained glass windows of the chapel.

"You may be asking yourselves now, 'Where was God? Where was God when Joan and her daughters were crying out in pain, when these terrible things were happening to them in Tampa Bay?' " Luderman told the mourners. "God was with them. They were not going toward death, but toward life."

The church bells began to chime as the mourners filed out behind the caskets, following the grim procession across the street to a brief burial ceremony. The graves that had been dug beneath a large tent were set in pairs. Michelle and Christe would be buried in the top set, Jo in one of the plots at their feet. The fourth site was empty.

Even when it was done, some of the friends and relatives lingered at the graves, as if reluctant to pull away from their last contact with the people that had just been laid to their final rest, as if still disbelieving that such an atrocity could have been committed upon such harmless, innocent country folk.

"Why did this have to happen?" sobbed Terry James. "Why did this have to happen? What did they do to deserve this? Why did they have to die this way? They were such good people. They never hurt anybody.''

Things like vile triple murders were seen as events that took place elsewhere, in lawless metropolitan areas. It wasn't supposed to happen so close to home.

"After the funeral is all done and everyone goes home, that's when the people really begin to grieve. Now the reality sets in," Luderman observed. "Now friends and family members have to put their lives together in an entirely different way than it was before. Life goes on, but it's never the same after this.''

Students and teachers from Crestview High felt haunted by the experience. It was as if death had a special claim on their school that summer. Two weeks before Michelle and Christe were killed, popular senior Amy Barker was fatally injured when a large truck smashed her car. Two weeks after the deaths of the Rogers girls, a male student died in a motorcycle accident. For a school in which the size of a class seldom rose above sixty students in a single grade, the losses were devastating.

But even more devastating was the sight of a single shaken human being: Hal Rogers. He felt as if his body was there at the services, but he was not. The caskets had not been opened, and although "it felt right," he wasn't really certain if the right body lay in the right grave. He had to be content that the authorities had made the correct identifications.

From the moment he had learned they were dead, his mind went blank and he walked in a fog. Even today, he remembers little of those dreadful days. "Until long after the funerals, I didn't know shit," he admits.

He plunged into the never-ending work at the farm, thankful that it was so demanding he had no time to think, and began to drink heavily, uncaring, trying to wash away the emptiness in his life. Friends consoled,

relatives shared the grief, and people who simply felt
sorry provided sympathy for him as he withdrew behind
his darkly-tinted eyeglasses that kept the world at bay.
No one really knew what Hal Rogers was going through,
because he himself did not know. Days, months, and
years would pass before he could deal with the tragedy
and begin to normalize his sundered life.

The media gave him no relief. Boxy television trucks
parked out on Ainsworth Road and aimed cameras at the
white house. Reporters streamed to the place in hopes of
getting an interview. He learned to lie to them, to tell
them that Hal Rogers had just left and wouldn't be back
for hours. The media spotlight, however, is a fickle thing,
and after a few weeks of strong coverage, alienating almost everyone in Van Wert County and trampling on the
privacy of Hal Rogers, the spotlight drifted to fresher
stories.

When his eyes focused in the mornings, perhaps after
a night when he would count twenty-four empty beer
bottles on a table before him and not even remember
whether he had gotten drunk at home or at a club, Rogers
would sometimes see a small desk calendar that he kept
in his house, the black type on a white page staring at
him from a yellow backing. He could never bring himself
to tear off the page that read Tuesday, June 13, 1989, the
day of the burials. He kept it through the years, as if by
not turning the calendar, he could forever lock Jo, Michelle, and Christe to him.

Missing from the Lima newspaper's obituary that sup-
posedly listed all the relatives of the deceased was one
specific name, that of a man who could not attend the
funeral. Everyone in the country knew the secret, but why
mention such a dreadful thing on a day already drenched
in sadness?

When a St. Petersburg detective arrived in Ohio to look

into the family background, he did not have to look far to find something quite unsettling.

The relative not at the funeral was John Rogers, the brother of Hal. John was sitting in prison serving a stiff sentence for the rape of a young woman. He accepted a plea bargain that dropped a multiple-count charge that he had raped his own niece, Michelle, repeatedly.

Also raising the detective's suspicions was the fact that, just before he entered prison, John Rogers had spent several weeks in Florida, in and around the Tampa area, a short time before the murders. Then there was the matter of anonymous notes investigators found during the John Rogers rape case that threatened that a mother and two daughters would "swim under the sea" because they "told."

The Florida police could not let such a set of similarities roll past unnoticed, particularly when almost everybody they interviewed in Van Wert County was openly wondering if John might have had something to do with the tragedy.

5

John Rogers was serving a seven-to-twenty-five-year term in the Chillicothe Prison's sex offender program as a result of his sadistic and brutal fantasy life.

Court papers document the crime that sent him to prison as involving an eighteen-year-old woman named Laura, who moved into John's trailer as a rent-paying roommate in November 1987. One night a few months later, on Valentine's Day, February 14, 1988, she returned to the brown and white trailer after taking her boyfriend home to nearby Ohio City, and discovered something peculiar.

John, thirty-one, a muscular ex-Marine, had remained in the rear bedroom while Laura and her boyfriend were visiting, and he was still there when she returned to the mobile home. But set up in the kitchen, pointing toward the living room, was a video camera on a tripod.

Laura testified that after trying to make a telephone call, she moved toward the door as if to leave, only to be knocked to the floor by John, who was holding a knife. He quickly blindfolded her and placed her in the living room of the small dwelling, turned on the video camera and an audio tape recorder and forced her, at knifepoint, to perform a sexual carnival, including fellatio and anal intercourse. At one point, he even clamped a pair of handcuffs onto his rape victim and forced her to call him "master" during the taped attack.

When he had finished his brutal assault and released her, the shaken Laura drove to the Van Wert County Hospital, arriving in the emergency room at 3:30 A.M. Medical personnel took a look at her injuries and called police. Officers arrived to interview her at 4:01 A.M., but the terrified young woman would not cooperate. She would not identify her attacker or describe what had happened to her.

Within a month, she had a change of heart, went to the authorities, and filed a complaint of rape against her former landlord, John Rogers.

Two detectives drove out to the Rogers' dairy farm the next morning, the start of a bright and sunny day, and found the suspect washing tanks in the milking barn. Since several other people were around, they asked to speak to John privately in his trailer. The detectives did not bring along a search warrant and had to ask his permission to enter the trailer. He granted it and the three of them sat down around the small kitchen table. Detective Ralph Eversole and Chief Deputy Frank Bowen explained the purpose of their visit, read John Rogers his Miranda rights and had him sign the document containing his constitutional guarantees.

While they talked, the officers noticed a brown briefcase in the living room and asked Rogers what was in it. Tax papers, he replied, and they asked that he open it. The briefcase had a three-dial lock, and Rogers said that the combination was some version of his birthday, but he could not remember the numerical sequence. He tried twirling the knobs a few times, but the case remained locked.

Then Rogers told the detectives that he still had work to finish outside. A conveyor belt had broken and he needed to feed the cows, so he asked if they would let him do the repair job, then they could return to the trailer and continue the questioning. The police, reared in farm country, knew the incessant demands of running a dairy operation. John told them that Hal, his brother and co-owner, was out of town and he had to do most of the work himself. They all went outside, and as the detectives stood beside a fence, John Rogers walked to the silo and began working. It took him about thirty minutes to fix the chain to the auger, and at one point one of the policemen offered to help.

Hal Rogers would recall later that the half hour interval spent outside was important. He said that while John was working on the conveyor, John managed a whispered conversation with his niece, Michelle, telling her to go into the trailer, open the briefcase, and remove the contents. Her father said she tried to do as she had been told, but could not make the lock work.

Sure enough, when the detectives and John returned to the trailer, the briefcase was still tightly closed and the cops were growing more curious about its contents. Still operating without a warrant, they could not confiscate it themselves, but they could ask him to open it. One policeman found a screwdriver and handed it to Rogers, who quit playing with the combination, slid the blade into the lock, and popped it open.

The contents of the briefcase immediately changed the entire investigation from being just a talk with a suspect. The discovery of such evidence elevated it to a serious criminal case. Hal Rogers wasn't even home, but his tidy farm world was about to explode in his face.

In the case was a forty-five-minute videotape, five photographs of a bound, blindfolded, and seminude young white woman, whom police assumed was Laura, and a number of audiocassettes. There were no tax papers.

The police placed John Rogers under arrest. When they played the videotape, they discovered a recorded documentation of the assault on Laura. "I thought I had seen and heard a lot of things in a year in Vietnam, but when I heard that woman's screams on that tape, saw what John Rogers was doing. . . . I hadn't seen it all," said a furious Charles Kennedy, the Van Wert county prosecutor.

Police soon returned to the trailer armed with search warrants for the building, the area around it, and John's blue-gray automobile. They quickly rounded up a trove of sexually explicit material—ultragraphic skin magazines, more refined publications such as *A Visual Dictionary of Sex*, a Red Accent tripod for a camera, boxes of VCR and audiotapes, a microcassette recorder and a TEAC reel-to-reel recorder, handcuffs and their key, and a miscellany of things they could not even name. In court papers they were listed under categories such as "three vibrators and two rubber doohickies."

John Rogers soon hired an attorney and had an alibi. He had never seen the stuff in the briefcase, he said, and although he owned a briefcase that was similar, the one the detectives found was not his. When he had last seen Laura on the night in question, he had been sipping wine when she left with her boyfriend, John Rogers claimed. He left a short time later, drove to a friend's house for a few minutes before midnight, then went over to the town of Bryan, where he talked with his sister and was seen by a witness.

Yes, he said, he had purchased a VCR camcorder for $943, but had returned it to the store before Laura said she was assaulted. He denied any knowledge of the rape and disdainfully said the handcuffs found in his kitchen cupboard also were not his. Those had been made in Taiwan, he pointed out, and "I like to buy American-made products."

It made little difference. Not only was Laura accusing him of the assault, not only had police discovered that his trailer and car were loaded with sexual material and gadgets, but the seminude, handcuffed, and blindfolded woman had been identified. It was not Laura at all. The victim in that set of photos, with her tearful voice recorded on a tape while she was being raped, calling her attacker "master," was Michelle Rogers, the teenaged niece of John Rogers. He denied recognizing her in the photographs.

A seven-count indictment was handed down by a grand jury in the Court of Common Pleas against John F. Rogers, claiming he had raped his niece as well as his roommate, Laura.

The court documents show that between June 1, 1986, and November 30, 1987, John forced Michelle to have sex with him a number of times. She was only fourteen when her uncle began his vicious attacks.

The first occurred in the summer of 1986, when he coaxed Michelle to come inside his trailer home and give him a back rub. While that was going on, he asked the young girl to insert medication into his anus, which she did. Then he forced her to have intercourse with him, the charges read.

A month later, he had her perform another daytime back rub that once again turned into forced vaginal intercourse.

Michelle stonily kept the secret of forcible sex with her Uncle John. She did not confide in her mother, her father, her sister, any of her relatives, or anyone at school. She carried the dark burden alone. The attacks ceased until the next summer, 1987.

John's trailer home was only about fifty feet from the double-wide where Michelle lived with her family. A stand of young pine trees separated the two residences.

Legal documents paint a grisly picture of John sneaking into Hal's home through the narrow hallway that led to Michelle's tiny bedroom and finding her asleep on her waterbed, alone. He dragged her from bed, blindfolded the girl, and held a knife on her as he hauled her back to his trailer, pulling her by her dark hair. Once inside his place, he forced her to perform fellatio and endure vaginal sex against her will. Audiotapes were made. Photographs were taken.

That same summer, he raped her on the floor of her home after finding her asleep on the couch. On still another occasion, he made her undress before the camera and took pictures as he assaulted her. The documents claimed the attacks on Michelle continued until November 1987, about the time Laura moved into the trailer with him.

The child may have sensed some reprieve, but she maintained her strict silence. A relative would later guess that Michelle had reasoned if she did not tell anyone, then she would be treated as "the same old Michelle" when she was around them. It was a terrible burden for the teenager to bear, smiling on the outside and shaken to the core of her soul on the inside. She told no one.

Hal and Jo Rogers had been in Columbus on a business trip when John Rogers was arrested. When they found out what had happened, it was as if a bomb had gone off in their world. Hal simply could not imagine his brother violating the family bond, crushing his trust, and Michelle wasn't talking, other than to finally admit what had happened once the pictures in the briefcase came to light.

Hal and Jo were shocked into immobility. They did not know who or what to believe. Incest and forcible rape were not things that were discussed in Ohio farm families. Was it true? It was much easier to believe what the cops were saying about Laura, a stranger, than what they were saying about Michelle, their own daughter.

John and Michelle had never been close. Their outward relationship, their public persona, had been one of frequent fighting. Hal Rogers said his brother John, who "didn't know when to shut up," constantly picked on the girl, and Michelle would eventually get mad and strike out verbally or physically at her uncle. There was no love lost between the two. This might explain why.

Certainly if what the police claimed was true, wouldn't Michelle have told them sooner? Why wouldn't she talk openly about it now?

Hal Rogers was boxed into a tight corner. He had promised to help his brother, but had never expected that John would rape Michelle. But when time came to post a ten-thousand-dollar cash surety bond so John could remain free until sentencing, it was Hal, his brother and business partner, who came up with the needed money. That, without a doubt, made Michelle even more fearful of her precarious position within the family.

"I told him I would help him before I learned what the whole big story was. Once I give my word, I don't back down unless somebody lets me out. People don't understand it, but that's just the way I am," he explained.

Weeks passed as Hal remained confused about what to do, who to believe. Finally, he realized the submissive personality of Michelle made her an easy target for the more forceful personality of his brother. Her resistance would go only so far in such a situation, he reasoned, then she would withdraw and give up and wait for a brighter day tomorrow. He had seen that behavior throughout her life, and he was finally convinced that his daughter—although she still refused to discuss the incidents with him—was telling police the truth.

One afternoon he put a hand on each of her shoulders and told her that he believed her story. Always a man of few words, he looked deeply into the eyes of his daughter and saw tears welling up in them. "John will never come back here," he promised. "He won't hurt you again."

It was the end of the line for the brothers. John was ordered by the judge not to see the family or visit his trailer, so he moved to Michigan to stay with his parents until the case was settled. Hal began to dissolve the partnership, severing all ties to his brother.

When 1989 rolled around, knowing he was most likely going to be behind bars for a long time, John decided to take a final Florida vacation. John, accompanied by his new girlfriend, Deborah, his mother Irene, and his grandfather Espy, drove Irene's 1989 Chevrolet Caprice for a Florida stay that lasted almost six weeks. His mother had a trailer home in the village of Ellenton, near Tampa, and a number of family members had settled in the area. While out on bond, and with cash in his pocket from the farm buyout, John filled his free time by taking the soft-spoken Deborah on a whirlwind tour of the state's fun attractions, hitting Disney World, Busch Gardens, and the Kennedy Space Center.

He returned in March when an attorney advised him that a final hearing date was approaching. Michelle had been subpoenaed on March 24 to appear in common pleas court four days later as a witness. If she went on the stand the ball game was over for John Rogers. Chances were slim that a jury would listen to the testimony of Laura and the pretty, vulnerable Michelle and not throw the book at the man who assaulted them. It was time to make a deal.

On April 11, 1989, Van Wert authorities accepted a plea bargain that would exempt Michelle from the horror of having to testify in open court about the incestual rape, while at the same time put John Rogers behind bars. John pleaded no contest to the single charge of the rape of

Laura, and was sentenced to serve seven to twenty-five years.

The additional charges of raping his niece were dropped. In legal terms, it was spelled out that "all other charges relating to crimes" against Laura and Michelle "shall be dismissed without prejudice." The deal originally had been for John to plead guilty, but court papers show a last minute twist was made to the deal. The "guilty" was scratched out at the last minute in the records and the hand-written "no contest" entry substituted.

The family split went deep. For some inexplicable reason, Irene Rogers, Hal and John's mother, firmly believed Michelle had lied and that the pictures showing her granddaughter seminude, bound, and terrified had been unjustly planted as evidence against her son.

"John did not rape Michelle," she insisted in an interview with the *Tampa Tribune*. "Michelle and her mother made everything up. They did it. Didn't you ever hear of fifteen- and sixteen-year-old girls making that stuff up?"

Earlier, prosecutor Kennedy had brushed away an attempt by Irene Rogers to submit into evidence a second videotape. She maintained it showed some man wearing a disguise, not John, committing the crime. Kennedy said it looked as if a copy of the original tape had been amateurishly doctored, and ignored it.

Of a more serious nature were alleged threats that John and Irene Rogers said Irene was receiving. One claimed that unless John accepted a plea bargain, his nieces' heads would "look like pumpkins." Another threatened Irene's life. A third scrawled message warned that "2 children 1 mother that should not have told, now they swim under the sea with heavy shoes." John protested that he didn't know who was sending the notes, and anyway, they referred to his other two nieces and their mother, who lived in Michigan, not to Jo, Michelle, and Christe. Police eventually disregarded the anonymous warnings.

"Every mother sides with her son," shrugged Hal Rogers.

John's removal from the scene avoided the terrible possibility that Michelle would have to take the witness stand and publicly accuse her uncle of repeated sexual assaults. While it would have put John in prison, it also would have exposed her to a painful, humiliating grilling beneath the court and media spotlight. Her friends would know everything! That was more than a teenaged girl could possibly bear.

Instead, some relief from that horror was arranged by offering John a plea bargain.

Finally, she could start putting the nightmare behind her. The month after John Rogers went behind bars, Michelle, her mother, and sister left the farm for a Florida vacation.

When the tragic news was announced that all three had been murdered, prosecutor Charles Kennedy's first instinct was to pick up his telephone and call the prison at Chillicothe to make certain that John F. Rogers was still incarcerated. He was.

Authorities in Ohio and Florida soon concluded that no matter how bizarre the links between the two crimes seemed, the events were unconnected.

Michelle had escaped one hell only to be overcome by another.

6

The State of Ohio is one of contradictions, with its population of about eleven million people primarily packed into large urban centers, such as Cincinnati, Cleveland, Toledo, and Columbus, and a number of second-tier cities such as Canton, Akron, and Dayton. The Buckeye State once boasted great manufacturing centers that spread goods to the world through major ports on Lake Erie and had a substantial impact on American history by producing eight men who became presidents of the United States. Athletes such as golf great Jack Nicklaus and track star Jesse Owens, major authors such as Harriet Beecher Stowe and James Thurber and scientific pioneers like Thomas Edison, Orville Wright, and astronaut Neil Armstrong all sprouted from Ohio roots.

One common thread among the families of Ohio is a tie to fundamental values and a determination to work hard to succeed.

Beyond the big cities in the northwestern part of the state, the land changes from the rugged Allegheny Plateau in the east to gently rolling plains that eventually spread across the Indiana state line and on through the entire Midwest. It is fertile land, rich in minerals and water and dirt that can grow anything. From horizon to horizon, it is farm country.

Halfway down an Interstate 75 axis from Toledo in the north, on Lake Erie, to Dayton, lies the town of Lima. Sixteen miles west-northwest of Lima, State Route 309 joins the broader U.S. 30, which crosses the Little Auglaize River into Van Wert County. Some twenty-nine miles to the west lies the Ohio-Indiana border, with the towns of Van Wert and Convoy the last Ohio stops on the road.

Originally settled in the middle of the nineteenth century, the people who live in the area have not generally followed the same migration patterns from farm to city as in many other areas. The ancestral stock is primarily German and, as Hal Rogers would observe, "You're either a Schumm, Etzler, Dietz, or something and if you don't drink beer, you're not from around here."

Hal Rogers and Joan Etzler were members of families who had been in the area for years, and their roots were deep in the fertile dirt of Van Wert County.

Wayne Alfred Rogers, a farmer in Ridge Township, was twenty-two years old, and his wife, Irene Trimble, from Union Township, was nineteen when they gave birth to their first child, Hal Eugene Rogers, on April 4, 1952. They would have two more sons and one daughter. On November 12, 1952, Joan Mae Etzler was born to thirty-three-year-old Convoy farmer Wilhelm Albert Etzler and his wife, Virginia Mae Reed, twenty-eight. She was their second child, and first daughter. Both Hal and Joan were born at the Van Wert County Hospital. Their daughters would be able to trace their local ancestry back over at least four generations of people who had worked the Van Wert County soil, an interesting and stable family chain in an age of rapid movement and migration.

The Wayne Rogers farm was located on Ainsworth

Road in the southern part of Van Wert County, close to the little town of Willshire, which sits so close to the Indiana border that, just by turning a corner in town, a person can enter another state. The Etzler farm was in the northern tier of the county, three miles south of the town of Convoy.

In the middle part of the century, school districts within Van Wert County underwent a reorganization caused by the twin pressures of money and basketball. Each community seemed to have its own school system and, since basketball is considered the ultimate sport in the Midwest, the teams were extremely competitive. When the time finally arrived for the little school districts to combine because finances were stretched too thin for so many schools to offer redundant services, the basketball rivalries helped determined the new combinations of school districts. Neither academicians, alumni, nor students wanted to see their alma mater swallowed by their basketball court rivals, even if uniting small schools made financial sense. The result was a gerrymandering of districts and Hal Rogers found himself attending school not just a few miles away in Willshire, but far up the road at the Crestview Junior-Senior High School in Convoy.

That meant he rose early to do chores around the farm, then got on a yellow bus for the long ride to Convoy. He was a farm kid in every respect, his body lean and tight with elastic, whipcord muscles, and his personality withdrawn and quiet, speaking only when he had something to say. He took life so seriously that he would later say, "I was born old."

It was in school that he first met Joan, whose full name was pronounced Jo-Ann but was clipped by friends to just Jo.

She was a slender, active and pretty girl blessed with a personality that could charm anyone. At home, the farm work was done by three large men—her father, her uncle, and her brother, Jim. There was no need for her to plunge into the dirty work of farm life, and, Jim would say, "She knew enough about it to stay away." Actually, the men were a bit skeptical about the quality of her help, remembering how she once drove the riding mower smack into a tree.

Freed from most of the hard work, she was able to be a rather happy-go-lucky girl. As a kid, Jo liked to dress up her dogs and wheel them around in a baby carriage, play with an endless supply of cats, and wander around a barn filled with lambs. As a teenager, she was fashion conscious and her mother taught her how to sew her own clothes.

At school, the vivacious Jo plunged into a busy activity schedule. She played the clarinet and the cello in the school orchestra, chose softball and bowling as her sports, and attended afternoon meetings of 4-H and Y-Teens. At home, she learned to cook and filled the house with rock and roll music from a stack of 45-rpm records.

Also at school, proving the axiom that opposites attract, the quiet Hal Rogers and the effervescent Jo somehow fell into the same orbit. "I thought she was kind of dingy at first, and she had to learn that I wasn't as much of an asshole as she first thought. She always said I was a party pooper." By the time he graduated in 1970 (she would take her diploma in May the next year), their life course had already been set.

The same year she graduated, they were married on October 16, 1971, by the Rev. Kurt Bickel in Convoy, who vouched on the wedding certificate that neither bride nor groom was "an habitual drunkard, imbecile or insane and is not under the influence of any intoxicating liquor or narcotic drug." With the blessing of the church and their families, the two teenagers set out on their own, living on Hal's salary at the Kresge Company and Jo's income at the G. C. Murphy Company.

But poverty was going to be a temporary thing, if Hal and Jo Rogers had anything to say about how they lived. "We didn't want to be poor and she always had the faith that we could do it," he said. They were willing to sacrifice the present in order to have a better future.

Things were very bleak at first, and they scraped by under tough conditions. Money was tight, as with most newlyweds. Hal recalled that at one early home, he had to wrap plastic around the outside of the house to keep pictures from blowing off the walls. If the temperature was zero on the fields outside during the frigid Ohio winter, it was minus ten degrees in their upstairs bedroom. There was no running water.

Still, their parents never interfered with their lives and the newlyweds learned to lean on each other. Hal, working at a new job, was continually awed when he came home exhausted and found his pregnant wife waiting for him. "She was a good-looking woman," he said. "She was my anchor."

He was working a night shift on February 22, 1972, and was not going to get home until 3:30 A.M. the next morning. Missing the shift would have meant missing money in a paycheck, so when Jo realized she was about to give birth, she called her family to get a ride to Van Wert County Hospital. The young couple's first child, a daughter, was born at 11:10 P.M., weighing only four pounds, ten ounces. Jo was nineteen years old.

They named the girl Michelle Lee, breaking the two-generation use of the middle name of Mae for women on Jo's side of the family. The baby was healthy, had reddish brown hair and a lopsided little smile. Her brilliant eyes were the most remarkable thing about her—dark brown irises surrounded by sclera that were as blue as a robin's egg instead of the normal white. Although Michelle lost weight after birth, she was taken from the hospital almost immediately, against doctor's orders, because Hal and Jo did not have insurance. Jo stayed with her family and Hal went back to working two jobs, up at 10 A.M. every day and not arriving home until well after midnight.

Things were changing rapidly for the young couple. While Jo was still in the hospital, Hal bought their first piece of land, a place near his parents' farm where they could put a trailer and start being homeowners instead of renters. Within a few days, they had a new baby and a homesite that would allow them to continue their plan to return to farming, working for themselves.

For seven years, Hal would average about fifty-four hours of work a week, and Jo would work at jobs that included waitressing to bring in money. Her days of being the carefree teenybopper, popular at school and not required to do dirty-fingernail work on the family farm, faded into the bleak reality that her life was going to require hard work. "We toughed it out and saved," Hal said. Together, they moved toward their goal of being self-sustaining, but even as they put a trailer onto their dirt patch and moved in, Hal was losing the precious chance to watch his first child grow. In 1974, they invested in a new combine, an expensive piece of equipment that many farmers could not afford. When it came time to harvest, Hal would go for days without sleep, as he mounted the cab of the combine to reap the fields of Van Wert County on a custom, contract basis.

That same year, Michelle learned to walk at the age of fourteen months. She had never crawled, but would draw her right leg up to her tummy and push along the floor like a snail. Then one day, she was standing up and took her first step. It was as if she was in a hurry to get on with her life.

Jo became pregnant again in 1974, and at 12:30 A.M.

on October 6, a six-pound, seven-and-a-half-ounce baby girl was born. They named her Christe Eugenia, and she came home wearing the same baby gown that her sister had worn. Eugenia was a female version of Hal's middle name, Eugene. Jo would often wonder why they had given Christe her husband's middle name, but had not bestowed her middle name of Mae onto their first child. Perhaps it was because Hal had wanted his second child to be a boy, and by giving Christe the spin-off masculine name, she would become a surrogate one.

At a time when many young people of their age in America were protesting the Vietnam War and becoming socially and sexually active in a rapidly changing world, Hal and Jo Rogers had already settled down. They did not mind being young parents, figuring that when the girls entered their twenties, they would only be in their forties with plenty of time left to enjoy life, travel, and grandchildren. They were optimistic about the way things were going, and did not feel that their own youth was slipping away with the passing seasons.

Indeed, they were an integral part of the extended family scattered around the county. They would get together with the Etzler family several times a year up in Convoy, and their trailer was only a mile from Hal's parents and siblings. It was common for them to share the holidays with relatives.

The big step for them came when Hal and Jo bought the two-hundred acres of family land where the Rogers family had grown up. His parents relocated to Michigan, and in 1978, Hal and Jo moved into the double-wide, white mobile home with black shutters on Route 1, Ainsworth Road, near Willshire. There was a single barn on the land and a pair of tall grain silos that loomed over them like huge missiles poised to fly somewhere. Looking up at those giant storage bins, Hal and Jo could have no doubt that they had cast their lot with the land. When one of his younger brothers, John, was discharged from the Marines in 1980, he took up residence in a white and brown single trailer next door and bought a small equity in the farm, in exchange for not having to pay rent or maintenance costs.

The days started early, even if one of the babies awakened them during the night. Everyone was up at 5:30 each morning to start the day's milking and feeding cycle. Seeds had to be planted, land had to be tilled, and crops of corn and soybeans demanded constant attention.

A short time later, Hal and John pooled their money on a fifty-fifty basis to buy some cattle and branch into dairy farming. Since they could not spare time from the operation, Jo took Michelle for a ride to Pennsylvania and purchased the more than seventy head of cattle needed to start the dairy.

Still, with the resiliency of youth and the knowledge of exactly who they were and where they were heading, Hal and Jo seemed to observers to have made a fine adjustment to their demanding lifestyle. "They were always happy, but always tired," one friend remarked.

An interesting phenomena began taking place within the family as the kids began to grow. Michelle seemed to have her mother's dark good looks but her father's quiet personality, while Christe inherited Jo's bubbly schoolgirl personality. And it became clear that Hal, with some time to spend with his family now that he did not have to rush off to a factory every day, loved Michelle, but adored Christe. While Jo was at work and Michelle at grammar school, he would head for the fields hand-in-hand with the delighted Christe, who would sit behind him and sing as he tilled the fields on his tractor. When she tired of that, she would sit in the shade of a tree, coloring in a book, while her father worked nearby. On a lazy Sunday afternoon, when Hal might fall asleep on the sofa, little Christe would crawl atop him, curl up like a kitten on his chest, and also drift off to sleep. It was a lifelong habit, a bond they would always share. "We knew each other," he would later recall with simple clarity.

Michelle loved farm life. Getting up early and doing chores before school was not a problem, and getting to play among the calves and cows, learning the rhythm of nature were her favorite things. Even when she was in kindergarten, she would bounce out of bed to help milk the cows before going to school. As a teenager, to the consternation of her younger sister, she was so satisfied to be around the farm that she put off getting her driver's permit for another year after she turned sixteen. Working on the farm was her fun, and the little red Honda scooter Hal bought her provided wheels aplenty as far as she was concerned. She would rather fix a car than drive one, and one of her school projects was repairing a gasoline lawn mower engine. "She was always clean, but wasn't afraid of grease or dirt," observed Karen Weck, one of her friends.

Michelle was a pretty girl, slender like her parents, with dark brown hair reaching past her shoulders, and her eyes could flash either anger or merriment. Her natural, farm-fed good looks did not require much makeup and she usually wore only some eye shadow and faint lipstick. A good friend described her as "just a down-to-earth, jeans and T-shirt girl." The one exception was the dazzling array of earrings and rings she wore. "The girl loved her jewelry," remembered a friend.

The words most used to describe Michelle were "demure and quiet." Her school achievements were low key and unspectacular. Instead of athletics, or some area in which she might shine as an individual, she joined groups like the Parliamentary Procedures Team, 4-H, and the Future Farmers of America. The dairy team of which she was a member gained the ranking of twenty-first out of 140 such teams throughout Ohio.

Paul Pohlman, who was her agriculture teacher for three years at Crestview, recalled her pride when she would don her blue corduroy jacket with the gold FFA badge on the left pocket and show her cows and hogs at the Van Wert County Fair. At the end of her junior year, she was elected to the position of sentinel with the FFA, quite an accomplishment for someone who as a freshman was one of only two girls in FFA with a dozen boys.

Her farm roots guided her education, and at the age of fourteen she chose two periods of agriculture and two of biology among her other subjects, and the next year followed up with even more biology and vocational agriculture. According to friends, the only time she got upset with the farm was when chores prevented her from making plans for a weekend night.

For Michelle did indeed have a social life. Although shy around strangers, she warmed to them quickly and "once you got to know her, she was fun," a friend remarked. She would team up with her pals and go to the roller-skating rink, munch down some fast food, or just cruise the larger towns in the area, Fort Wayne across the state line, or Van Wert, where the local teens gathered on weekend nights. She liked her rock music soft, not punk.

It was not unusual for girls and boys to go stag to even the most social occasions, and at the end of her junior year, Michelle bought a floor-length emerald green gown and attended the junior-senior prom in the company of her best friend, Lori Foster. Afterward, at a smaller party, she met a young man who was attending the Vantage Vocational School near Van Wert, a school she would attend that summer to make up a chemistry class. Before long, she and Jeff Feasby began to date.

She sometimes wore glasses, and anyone looking back

now at those deep, brown eyes can see an almost haunted expression in the face of the pretty teenager with cascading brown hair. The fact that she harbored a terrible secret during her high school years, when her uncle would sneak up on her while she slept, drag her out of her home, and rape her repeatedly, would only become known in later years. During school, teachers only glimpsed that something was amiss when they examined her test papers. The handwriting was a tight little scrawl, as if the writer were almost afraid to express herself clearly, and the answers to a quiz might all be jammed into a corner of a single page.

Michelle did not give up her secret, even to her closest friends, during those two important, formative years of her life that were ruined by John Rogers. To speak out would have been to bring arguments and controversy into the family. In such cases, most incest survivors believe it is they, and not their attacker, who has done something wrong and therefore mask their true feelings at all costs.

As her junior year came to a close in 1989 and her hideous secret was exposed and her uncle went to prison, Michelle's handwriting opened up remarkably. She was not the pariah that she had feared. Most friends and family stood solidly beside her and Michelle slowly began to realize that what had befallen her *was not her fault*. Suddenly, her test answers filled entire pages, as if she couldn't say enough, whereas before she had been secretive. The grades improved and Michelle started talking to friends about attending college to study agriculture or becoming a veterinarian. She wanted to take care of animals that were sick or hurt and unable to speak, a condition that was not unlike her own ordeal. A sunny smile began to peek from the pretty face, and she could pay attention to how many earrings to wear, to what kind of new necklace to buy, and to her new boyfriend, Jeff.

* * *

Michelle was a bit jealous of her kid sister, who was growing up fast right behind her, refusing to stay in her shadow. If Jo had recaptured some of her youth by living vicariously through Michelle, they were both merely passengers on the Christe Express.

Christe was a firecracker of a kid. Pretty and blessed with a sassy personality, from her earliest years Christe lived life as if she was worried that something might escape before she could try it. She had enough personality for her whole family. As Jo was the opposite of Hal, Christe was the opposite of Michelle.

Where the older sister loved the farm, the younger yearned for whatever was just over the horizon. The little scooter was more than a gasoline engine to her; it represented freedom, and she would tuck one of her many animals on the seat in front of her and putt-putt around the farm. As she grew, she became adept at driving anything. By the age of twelve, she could back a pickup into a narrow barn door, leaving six inches of space on each side, and when Hal bought a huge Gold Wing motorcycle in 1985, Christe made herself at home on the rumbling machine.

Animals were a passion, dating from her babyhood when her favorite toy was a six-inch-high stuffed brown bear that was her best playmate. Every birthday cake was decorated with an animal, such as a green and white pig, and she would take kittens to bed and wrestle dogs on the floor. Her favorite television cartoon character was a tiny dinosaur named Littlefoot. A dimple on her left cheek was the leftover mark of a dog bite from when she was a child.

If her father wanted a son, that's what she would be. "Christe thought for a long time that she was a boy," Hal remembered. Never mindful of her diminutive size, she began playing softball with the Wren teams early, carrying a Rawlings leather glove that was almost half her size. They let the little squirt be the team catcher, and when she would bat, her best friend would run the bases for her. Charlie Hustle, they called her, because of her unflagging energy. Her adventurous spirit was shown in the full-tilt way she would ride a dirt bike, something that seemed as natural to her as eating. It was noisy, it was fun, and it would get her somewhere fast.

By the time she was wrapping up the eighth grade in 1989, Christe was a bubbly kid who moussed her hair, which she lightened from its normal brown. On some days, she stylishly sported as much jewelry as her mother and sister combined, and was considered everybody's best pal. Her nervous energy made her chew her nails, but that was a small price for an extrovert who considered time spent before a mirror to be a wise investment for a teenage girl.

Christe, too, was in 4-H, but she wanted a social life that extended beyond a cow. She joined the Crestview marching band flag corps in junior high school and won the red, white, and blue uniform of a cheerleader. She began dating while still in junior high, the braces on her teeth just seeming to add attractiveness to the gleaming smile, pug nose, and wild hairdo. Pink was her favorite color, Guns n' Roses her favorite band.

Where her sister Michelle had hidden in anonymity, Christe pushed to break free. She was going to be a freshman in high school in 1990, and by golly, people would really know who she was. She was an average student, but a really good friend, one of those people who lit up a room simply by walking through the door. "It wasn't a party until Christe showed up," recalled Ed Glossett.

When teachers remembered Christe, they would recall that if you wanted to say "good morning" to her, you had to be quick, because she would always sing it out first. When one asked how she made her bangs stand up like a crop of feathers, Christe leaned over and giggled the secret: "Lots of spray."

As sisters, Michelle and Christe were close, although there were the normal sibling rivalries. Michelle got tired of Christe always getting the attention, and Christe didn't like Michelle acting like some sort of superior being just because she was older. They would argue on the school bus ride to and from Convoy and things were not helped much when Christe started meeting all of the senior boys at the combined school. The year that Michelle went to the prom with a girl, her little sister went as the date of a senior boy.

But despite their differences, Michelle and Christe were always ready to stick up for each other if one got into trouble.

The strain under which Michelle lived in her last few years of high school erupted one day when she had taken more than she could endure, and she exploded in anger at her father. Hal, surprised, argued back and warned her not to continue to "lip off and give me a bunch of crap." He had never struck a woman in his life, and never would again, but on that day, he slapped his eldest daughter hard, not once, but several times. The fight was over immediately, Michelle cowering on the floor and her father standing above her, ashamed of what he had done.

"It was an attitude adjustment for both of us," he said later in ruefully recalling the conflict. "We had more respect for each other after that." As years went by, he would vividly remember the fight and blame himself for being opinionated and losing his temper. Hal said the problem actually was that he was so stubborn, and Michelle was so much like him. The two of them settled into an uneasy truce.

As a result of having two teenage girls, the Rogers household was a maelstrom of activity, as kids would gather to watch television, talk, and just hang out. Hal's only rule was that they stay out of his orange rocking chair, and Jo was the model of a patient mom. "She was a good mother and could have had a half dozen kids. Nothing bothered her," said Hal.

As Hal concentrated on making the farm work, Jo was able to relive her single girlhood days vicariously through her pair of young daughters. Indeed, to many she seemed intent on being more of a sister to them than a mother as they grew older. She may have missed out on some fun things, but the prom dates, the county fairs, and the church socials that Michelle and Christe attended had a beneficial effect on their mother. She preferred talking about the girls' boyfriends and social lives to being cast as a stern parent.

The girls learned early what farm life was all about, no matter how much they might gossip with their mom or watch shows on television about flashy teenagers who lived in swank locales like Beverly Hills, Miami, and New York. That was clearly the stuff of fantasy, for reality was working at least thirty hours a week on the farm, getting up at or before dawn and doing chores before heading off to school. After classes, they would return to the dairy for more outside work, feeding and milking the cows, at times joining their efforts so seamlessly that Hal could actually sit down for a rest while the girls finished things. Since they were bright enough to understand the importance of what they were doing, he was comfortable to let them handle things on their own.

"He told them the cows were their ticket to whatever they wanted," one friend said. Money the girls made from the farm went into sensible capital growth mutual funds.

"I expected a lot out of them," Hal admitted. Their

young bodies may have been female, but they were anything but fragile. Heaving hay and lifting milk cans provided their exercise and, while they remained petite and
feminine, both were very strong.

Their work was no more than the program followed
by both of their parents. Hal was on the farm full-time,
but in order to bring in needed cash, Jo took outside jobs.
She worked for three years at Borden's, until it closed,
and about 1984, she began working for the food ware-
houser Peyton Northern, just across the border in Bluffton, Indiana.

In 1987, Jo began the grueling midnight shift. She
would leave the farm, head south to Willshire, and get
on the straight and narrow U.S. 124 for the twenty-mile
dash into Indiana. Just past the sprawl of the Elm Grove
and Fairview cemeteries, the road dead-ended at the
Dutch Mill Restaurant, which advertises ''One Dozen
Dining Rooms on the Wabash,'' and she would turn left
on Highway 1 and make her way to the long, tan cinder
block and aluminum warehouse that is as flat as the Indiana farmland that surrounds it.

Throughout the night, she worked as a forklift operator, moving around heavy equipment and pallets of
goods. In the morning, she would reverse her trip and
arrive at the farm in time to help Hal and the girls with
the early work. Finally, she would go inside for a bite of
breakfast and head for bed and welcome sleep. She did
not complain.

The harsh life took a toll on her beauty and, while Jo
remained attractive, her face also reflected a lifetime of
toil. Still, she made time to have fun through her daughters, accompanying them to county fairs and 4-H events
and church gatherings, and teaching them how to shop.
Unlike her husband, she never showed favoritism to one
girl or the other.

* * *

In the early summer of 1989, Jo was thirty-six years old, Michelle, seventeen and Christe, fourteen. It was green and cool on the dairy farm, as Crestview began its summer recess. The girls had worked hard, made good grades, and the family unit had survived the John Rogers episode. They needed a break from the strain of it all, a fresh start, and together they planned a vacation from Zip Code 45898.

7

All thoughts turned to vacation. They planned for weeks, considering destinations such as Gatlinburg, Tennessee, but the lure of Mickey Mouse finally won out. All three of them had grown up viewing Disney World in Florida as a fantasy, and now they had the opportunity to see it in person. Michelle, with her nightmare finally behind her, confided her excitement to friends and actually made up a ''countdown'' calendar that ended with the date they would leave—Friday, May 26.

Hal encouraged them, although it was plain that he would have to remain behind. The spring had been unseasonably wet, with steady rains flooding the fields and delaying the planting. With some three hundred acres under cultivation for corn, wheat, and soybeans, and about 140 head of cattle, Hal would be almost overwhelmed by work while his family was on holiday. A teenaged boy had answered a newspaper advertisement for a farm helper, and it would be just he and Hal holding down the fort until Jo, Michelle, and Christe returned.

In addition, the dissolution of the farm partnership with John was still on Hal's mind. His brother Lewis was helping with the touchy situation in which John's legal fees were deducted from the value of the property as it headed toward a ten-thousand dollar buyout. Because of what John had done to Michelle, Hal no longer wanted any contact at all, personal or professional, with John and certainly wasn't about to let him keep half the partnership when John wasn't doing any of the work.

If there was a single plus to that entire morbid affair, it was that Hal and Jo had purchased John's 1986 Oldsmobile Calais by picking up the payments when John needed money. No cash exchanged hands and the deal added to the bitterness felt by John and Hal's mother, Irene. So a good set of wheels were available for the Florida trip, and Hal urged the girls to go. His only advice was, "Whatever you want to see, go see it."

Vacations didn't come along that often for farmers and their families, and every minute should be cherished. The only vacations Hal and Jo had ever taken were a trip to Pennsylvania before Christe was born and a brief ride on the Gold Wing down to the Florida panhandle. It had rained on them throughout the motorcycle expedition, but they enjoyed it nonetheless. Vacations meant memories.

Michelle, head over heels in puppy love, saw her new boyfriend, Jeff, the night before she was to depart, and she had left him with the usual mixed signals of a teenaged lover. She told him she was going to miss him and that she really didn't want to go to Florida, and he replied that he didn't particularly want her to leave, either. But in a telephone call the following morning, Michelle had seemed thrilled and excited, said the car was all packed and they were all raring to hit the road.

The would be gone for a week, since Jo had to return the following Monday for a midnight shift at Peyton Northern and Michelle was due to start summer school on June 5 to make up a chemistry class. In addition, the fortieth wedding anniversary of Jo's parents was approaching in October and their gift was to be a family portrait, which still had to be arranged.

Even with careful advance packing, the ebullient mother and young daughters had a lot of last minute preparations. After helping with the farm's morning chores, they spent some time cleaning up and it was about 1:30 P.M., some ninety minutes behind schedule, that Jo hurried over to her husband. Hal was about ten feet from the milking barn, unloading corn gluton feed, when she ran up and gave him a big goodbye hug and kiss. As she slid behind the steering wheel, the fellows working with Hal teased him about the midday smooch.

The Oldsmobile nosed out of Van Wert County, cut east to Interstate 75 at Lima, then headed due south along that wide ribbon of concrete that would eventually lead to the heart of Florida. At the wheel, Jo didn't have to bother with a map, but just followed the red, white, and blue I-75 signs. The trip started out as ordinary as a holiday jaunt could be. After all, this was not some complex agenda. It was to be fun and sun, down to Florida and back, over the same familiar, busy roads and highways that were almost worn into grooves from the vehicles that fifteen million Northern tourists drove to Florida each year. There should be no surprises.

With about five hundred dollars cash in Jo's purse, the girls with some hundred dollars in spending money apiece, and a single credit card with a five-hundred-dollar limit, they would be budget conscious on the trip, but that was not a worry. Van Wert County was in the rearview mirror, the cows fading in the distance. Mickey Mouse was up ahead.

They made Friday a travel day, putting the miles behind them in order to be closer to Florida for an early start the next day. Five hundred miles away from Willshire, just on the southern side of Chattanooga, Tennessee, they pulled in at the friendly gold sign of the Best Western motel on the outskirts of Dalton, Georgia, where big signs proclaimed the town to be "The Carpet Capital of the World."

They shared a room there, took in the usual attractions of an interstate crossroads area, filled up with gas, and prepared to get on about their business. A motel, a gas station, a barbecue joint and a Waffle House was all they required after about ten hours on the road. They probably thought it all looked exotic and just fine. Strange people, strange place.

The adventure had finally begun and on Saturday morning, May 27, for the first time in their lives, Michelle and Christe woke up somewhere other than Ohio.

It would have been early afternoon by the time they reached the Sunshine State, driving the length of Georgia. A few miles south of Valdosta, Georgia, they crossed into Florida and couldn't wait to make their first stop, a rest and welcome area the state of Florida ran at the town of Jennings. They gathered informational pamphlets on the various attractions and piled back into the car, hurrying now to the I-75 bridge across the Suwanee River and then branching east on Interstate 10 into Jacksonville.

Veteran travelers by now, they welcomed the sight of the metropolis of Jacksonville, a city so different from the ones they knew in Ohio. Everything back home was landlocked. Jacksonville almost seemed to float on the St. John's River and the Atlantic Ocean just beyond the city limits. They checked into a Days Inn for the night and the next morning, they visited the famed Jacksonville Zoo.

"Lori, hi!" Michelle wrote in a postcard to her friend Lori Jenkins, who lived ten minutes away from Willshire. The printing was swirled and incomprehensible in some places as Michelle tried to crowd her enthusiasm into the card's small space. "It's nice down here," she lied about the scalding heat, although she mentioned the thermometer had hit ninety eight degrees. She said they had just gone to the zoo, which was really neat because "I got to see all my long lost relatives" and had also spotted one monkey that reminded her of Jeff. "Mom and Chris say hi," she cheerfully wrote in the note she would mail two days later with a Barberville postmark.

Sunday, May 28, was another long day, as they left Jacksonville and drove south-southwest into central Florida until they reached Ocala. There they boarded one of the famous glass-bottom boats for a ride through the sparkling clear waters of Silver Springs, with a rainbow abundance of fish beneath their feet. This sure wasn't Ohio.

Then, back in the car, they headed east once again, this time aiming for the Cape Canaveral area, home of the American rocket program. They took a room on Sunday at the Quality Inn at Titusville, just across the Banana River from the launching pads of the Kennedy Space Center. Their clothes became lightweight and minimal as the temperature soared into the high nineties.

On Monday, May 29, they finally reached their goal. Zoo monkeys, Silver Springs fish, and Cape rockets were fine, but they weren't The Mouse. Orlando, the home of Disney World, bloomed in the front windshield.

With a discount card that gave them a half-off rate, Jo, while still in Ohio planning the trip, had telephoned the Gateway Inn in Orlando and made a reservation for their first night's stay, renting a sixty-dollar room at the two-story motel that featured a miniature golf course. Once there, Jo wrote Hal's postcard, confirming for him that the "kids were having a great time, dragging me everywhere." It was almost as if she were reluctant about telling Hal, still locked to the farm work, that she was also having a good time, perhaps feeling it was unfair.

Michelle jotted a postcard to Jeff and mailed it to his

home in Convoy, wishing him a happy birthday, pledging that she loved him, and signing with her nickname, "Chelle."

Jo also placed a telephone call to Hal and asked him to pay some money toward the outstanding balance on the credit card because she was having problems using it. She had already reached the limit and the trip still had several expensive days to go. Before he could do so, he discovered that Jo had managed to contact a friend at the Willshire branch of their bank, who had already adjusted the credit limit.

The girls decided to spend three days in Orlando, splitting the time between Sea World on Monday, the magic of Walt Disney World on Tuesday, and Epcot Center on Wednesday.

South Florida's major city of Miami might have been struggling with a dreadful surge of violent crime against tourists, but that was far away from Orlando, which was doing a booming business with visitors during the long Memorial Day weekend. Sore feet were the order of the day as Jo, Michelle, and Christe probably forgot about the dairy business all together during Disney-made interludes that transported them from dream to dream. It was primary, A-Number-One escapism from real life, exactly what the vacation was designed to accomplish.

On Thursday morning, June 1, they saddled up once again and headed the Olds west across Interstate 4 toward Tampa, with the plan of visiting Busch Gardens, spending two nights, then once again pulling back onto Interstate 75 and driving straight north toward home. Before leaving Orlando, Jo telephoned ahead and made, but did not pay for in advance, a reservation at the Days Inn at Rocky Point, giving them an exact target for the end of their vacation. The room was waiting when Jo walked into the spacious lobby about noon and checked in.

Thirty minutes later, Michelle dialed the number of the Union 76 station back home so she could once again wish Jeff Feasby a happy birthday. She was anxious to know how he enjoyed the birthday balloons that she ordered delivered to him, then added that they planned to leave Florida on Saturday morning and drive straight back to Ohio, arriving no later than Sunday night. Michelle, who had Jeff's class ring, also told him they were at the motel, and that, "We want to go to the beach, but Mom won't let us go in the ocean." Jeff would say later that it was little more than a "hi-bye conversation" because he was at work.

Jeff was a bit embarrassed, but happy, about all of the attention from his new girlfriend. A postcard, a telephone call, and balloons. She was far away, and maybe thought some monkey looked like him, but she cared enough to remember his birthday. Typical 'Chelle, he thought.

Jo's reluctance to let the girls go into deep water was understandable, since none of them had done more than dog paddle in some shallow Ohio lakes, and the little pond behind their home was better for fishing than swimming. Hal would recall later that water was among their greatest fears, because they could not swim.

One other telephone call was made from the room about that same time, checking with Busch Gardens, probably to obtain either hours of operations or directions.

And that was where police lost track of them.

Somewhere along the way, Jo, Michelle, and Christe Rogers had placed themselves in harm's way and an exciting vacation had ended in death.

Now that the authorities knew who the victims were,

police could get on with the job of trying to find the unknown killer.

The image of the Rogers girls and their mother had been one of overwhelming normalcy. The family had only just emerged into the sunshine from a terrible court ordeal when the new tragedy struck. It was almost too much for one person, almost too much for a whole town, to bear.

The three deaths shook the faith of everyone in Van Wert County, and children who knew Michelle and Christe would never forget how they were violently snatched away just at the prime of life. Everyone would wonder why it happened, and there would be no answer.

Hal Rogers was a wreck, as most men would be whose wife and two daughters were killed after having survived a painful, nasty case in which his brother, having raped one of the girls, ended up in a prison cell. The quiet, slender Hal, protected by a ring of close friends, refused to talk to anyone but police officers.

Neighbors and friends rallied around to help Hal through his torment, keeping strangers at bay, particularly the pathetic, intrusive camera teams from the tabloid television shows who wanted to turn his pain into entertainment beneath the guise of news.

At the funeral services, tears did not stop flowing as teenagers viewing the closed caskets realized their friends were gone forever. At the grave sites, Hal Rogers plucked flowers from a few bouquets and gave them to the weeping girls as mementos. To the heartbroken Ed Glossett, Christe's first boyfriend, he gave the little stuffed teddy bear that had been his favorite daughter's favorite toy.

Not all eyes were on the caskets nor the crying girls nor the preacher that day. Detectives from Florida and Ohio were among the mourners, carefully watching the people at the funeral, remembering that the reason Jo and Michelle and Christe Rogers were being buried was that they had been murdered.

The murderer was still free.

8

There was precious little with which to work, but the police attacked the case with an entire task force of detectives and patrol officers. Not only was it multiple homicide, but the manner of death had been unusually cruel, a family had been almost wiped out, and the horrible crime had been committed against tourists who had only been out to have an enjoyable time.

The only hard evidence available was what had been found on the bodies, what was left behind in the motel room, and what had been found in the Oldsmobile at the boat ramp, including the hand-scrawled directions to the boat ramp that had been discovered in the car.

One of the first steps was to obtain a list of everyone who had stayed at the Days Inn for the past two weeks and determine if any of them had anything to add. A team of detectives was also dispatched to earlier stops the victims had made in Orlando and Titusville. The Days Inn room was swept for fingerprints, but only those of the family or the service personnel were found. The heavy blocks of concrete and the rope tied to two of the victims were sent to the FBI for detailed analysis. And photographs of all three—putting faces to the names that had already become well known throughout the Tampa Bay metropolis—were distributed on fliers in hopes that someone may have seen them.

Police distributed the photographs to area businesses and went back to the ramp on a Thursday, in hopes of finding someone who came there every week at the same time, to show the pictures. All results were negative.

The note found in the car, with what appeared to be the handwriting of one of the victims on it showing directions from the motel to the boat ramp, received a cursory examination and was placed in the growing file of documentation. It was on stationery from the Days Inn.

Like so much else in the case, even the medical examiner's decision on the official cause of the deaths was inconclusive. "Homicidal violence—asphyxia" only meant that the victims died from a lack of oxygen, not that strangulation or drowning or choking was responsible.

By June 11, the *St. Petersburg Times* ran a story that accurately depicted the hurdles facing the investigators. "Police at a loss without witness in bay murders," the headline declared, and Detective Sergeant Bill Sanders echoed that. "So far we have nobody other than some employee at the motel that has seen them."

The intense publicity that followed the case might have been an ally had it produced anything other than dozens of telephone tips that required valuable hours to check out. Few provided any help at all.

The most valuable tip came from a woman who told police that she and her husband had been at the boat ramp on the afternoon of the Rogers' disappearance and that her husband had seen the parked Oldsmobile's out-of-state license tags and commented, "There's a car from Ohio." She said that happened at 2 P.M. on June 1.

From that, police had a ninety-minute window in which the women might have been seen. Michelle had called Jeff at 12:30 P.M., according to motel telephone records, and the car was at the ramp at 2 P.M.

They also looked at the possible money motive, a natural line of inquiry in any homicide investigation. Christe and Michelle each had five-thousand-dollar life insurance policies, which would be doubled if the death was accidental, and Jo carried a pair of policies that totaled about seventy thousand dollars on her life. But they determined that Hal Rogers was not a man who was desperate for money, and anyway, he was solvent, a man able to withdraw several thousand dollars from the bank on only his signature, and the owner of a small but prosperous farm. No, the cops decided early on, this wasn't about insurance.

Detective Ralph Pflieger spent two days in Ohio and came up dry, despite the shocking disclosure of John Rogers's crime. By June 15, officials in St. Petersburg were saying, "As far as we're concerned, it's a closed case up there."

A man who prowled the boat ramp urging women to go for rides was found and cleared. A wild tip from a woman who claimed she received a vision about the crime when she hugged her television set was discarded. So many tips had come flooding in that four detectives were assigned just to the job of ranking the hundreds of calls in importance, so other cops could check them out.

A special computer program was set up to cross-check the people listed on the guest lists of the motels with boat registrations in Florida and Ohio. Thousands of names were checked by the computer. No matches of significance were found.

Time, so important to solving a crime, began slipping away as the triple murder remained unsolved and its news worthiness to the television channels and newspapers faded. The cops were losing their media ally as the trail grew cold.

"We're running out of things to do," police spokesman Bill Sanders said on June 16. Telephone tips were down to a trickle and the task force began being stripped of its members, on both sides of the bay, who had to return to other duties.

St. Petersburg seemed to be caught in the middle of some kind of homicidal crime wave. A total of forty-nine people would be murdered in that placid city in 1989, which meant that as dreadful as the Rogers' killings might be, other murders demanded police attention too, and there were only a certain number of police officers who could handle them.

Three weeks after the bodies were discovered, the blood tests came back on the victims. No trace of narcotics had been found in their systems, eliminating the possibility that a trace could be made to some drug source.

In hopes of rejuvenating interest and getting a true witness to pick up the telephone, St. Petersburg police posted a reward offer of five thousand dollars and two days later, another fifteen-hundred-dollar reward was offered by friends of the Rogers in Ohio. The news was received by the public with a slight surge in telephone leads, but they led nowhere and by the time August rolled around, only four detectives were still working the case, and even they were not on it full-time.

In mid-August, WTSP Channel 10 sent reporter Kathi Belich and a photographer to Ohio and she not only returned with an interview from Hal Rogers, but she brought him back to the Bay Area. Police did not know he was coming, and it did not really matter to them, for he had already been cleared of any suspicion. Rogers, who stayed with a friend during his brief Florida visit, told Belich the entire tragic incident still seemed "like a dream now to me. It seems like they're on vacation and I'm waiting for them to get home.''

The mystery dark vehicle pulling the boat on a trailer with out-of-state tags through the Days Inn parking lot had not been found.

In early September, the investigation had literally ground to a halt, for there was simply nothing more that could be done. The special task force was formally disbanded, its total efforts outlined in three black looseleaf binders gathering dust on a shelf at the St. Petersburg Police Department headquarters.

Four months after Jo, Michelle, and Christe Rogers had been lured from their motel and murdered, police had no idea at all who might be responsible, and there was nothing they could do to change that situation.

And unless something unexpected came up, it looked as if the files were slowly closing on the Rogers' murders.

Not all crimes are solved. So in an effort to share information about unique crimes still on the books around the state, the Florida Department of Law Enforcement prints a bulletin each month that highlights some of the more interesting cases that local law enforcement units have been unable to crack.

In October, the current FDLE issue finally worked its way to the desks of St. Petersburg detectives familiar with the Rogers' killings. Since the paper chase had died down in the intervening weeks, there was actually some time for them to do something other than follow useless leads.

One case featured in the FDLE bulletin set alarm bells ringing for several St. Petersburg detectives and a Tampa crime analyst.

It was the summary of the violent rape of a Canadian tourist in nearby Madeira Beach back in May, a few weeks before the Rogers' women were attacked. The similarities were striking—a blue and white boat was involved, a tourist was the victim and she had been stripped nude from the waist down. The Rogers' handwritten note the police had found led them to believe that a blue and white boat was involved; they were tourists from Ohio; the bodies were found naked below the waist. This was the best lead since the identifications had been made, and it had been waiting right next door in Madeira Beach.

In time to come, there would be a flap over whether the Madeira Beach police had informed their St. Pete counterparts of the situation, but the real answer would probably be that, when the Rogers women died, any recall of a single rape in a beach community weeks earlier would have been difficult to link to the murders because the crimes seemed to be so different.

However, the ball was now in play again, and a pair of St. Petersburg police flew to Canada to interview Gayle Arquette and Linda Lyle about their experience. With their help, a composite sketch was drawn of Gayle's attacker, and soon police were distributing fliers with the picture and description of both the suspect and his boat.

The gray sketch depicted a white man in his middle-to-late thirties with a high forehead, short reddish blond hair and a light mustache and deep-set eyes. He was estimated to be about five foot eight and have a chunky 190-to-200 pound build, with leathery, tanned skin and ruddy cheeks. The police flier described the boat as an older model, seventeen-foot fiberglass inboard-outboard powerboat with a faded blue hull, white interior with a pair of dark blue captain's seats, and a navy blue top that was folded back on the stern. The flier also stated that the suspect drove a dark-colored Isuzu Trooper with tinted windows, the same sort of sport utility vehicle that witnesses had placed at the Days Inn when the Rogers disappeared.

When newspapers learned of the private distribution of

the flier among police agencies, police decided to make it available to the public. "We would rank this toward the top of all the leads we have received, and Lord knows we've gotten many of them," stated Bill Doniel, the manager of public information for the St. Petersburg police. "Hopefully, someone is going to see this composite either in print or on television and recognize who that individual is and call us."

As Sherlock Holmes would have said, the game was, once again, afoot.

9

Public reaction to the sketch of the rape-murder suspect was immediate and overwhelming, just like the call for potential witnesses back when the Rogers' bodies were discovered five months earlier. It was to become a familiar aspect of the long investigation. Every time a story would appear in print or on television, it would spur citizens to come forward with information. Unfortunately, almost all of it would prove to be useless to police.

But they weren't making much headway just circulating the man's sketch among police agencies around Florida, either. So when the *Times* revealed the existence of the artwork, police and prosecuting attorneys held a meeting and decided to run it publicly. Perhaps someone, somewhere might recognize it.

The response this time was even more than back in June, with more than one hundred calls coming into the St. Petersburg police in the first hours of the weekend. Detective James Kappel, who was heading the little team of investigators, was given additional personnel to help answer the telephones. The newspaper said the size of the force tripled to meet the need, which meant it went from only two detectives to six for the duration of the

crush situation. Tampa police announced a special telephone line for tipsters, but it didn't work and callers were
encouraged instead to leave their names and numbers on
an answering machine. "We'll get back to you." Tips
that surfaced through the 911 emergency number were
checked out by patrol officers.

A police spokesman pledged that every lead would be
followed up. They included one from a citizen who saw
a guy whose name he didn't know walking on a beach
with a frisbee three years ago, and a driver who thought
the suspect might be another motorist a year earlier who
had cut him off at an intersection. Snapshots were delivered to headquarters of men who had made someone angry in the past.

The sketch ran each day of the weekend, and the tips
exploded on Monday morning after people had seen the
Sunday papers. At St. Petersburg police headquarters, the
telephone rang all day long, pressuring detectives to keep
up with the job of answering calls. Investigating the leads
would take longer, and officers were assigned to shuffle
them into some order of importance.

If nothing else had happened, at least people were talking about the Rogers case again. As if it were a bouncing
ball, the case had peaked in June, fallen flat until October,
and in November, it was again on the ascent. Maybe, just
maybe, there might be a nugget of truth in the avalanche
of information.

Major Cliff Fouts, head of the SPPD Criminal Investigation Section, said the unit received more calls in the
first three days after the picture and boat description were
published than were taken in the two weeks that followed
the murders.

When the phones quit ringing, about five hundred tips
had been catalogued. Of those, maybe a dozen contained
anything of substance. Police checked them carefully and
came up with nothing.

Two weeks after the sketch went public, the exhausted investigators had come up against that familiar stone wall again. The Rogers case was back where it started—at a standstill.

Police had been pleased with the response, although it brought to light the fact that somewhere along the line, the Madeira Beach police and the St. Petersburg police had dropped the communications ball. The similarities that were striking enough to be recognized in October should have jumped out as significant much earlier in the investigation. Officials of both departments downplayed the difference to avoid an embarrassing public conflict between the agencies.

It was concluded, once more, that when the case broke, it would probably be because of hard, determined, relentless police work and not because Joe or Jane Citizen decided to drop a quarter in a pay telephone and gave up the perpetrator. After all, wasn't it through the FDLE bulletin that the potential links between the rape case and the murder case had bubbled to the surface? Police knew that most of the time, it is best to play the evidence close to the vest, which was why the picture of the suspect had not gone public immediately, and when it did, nothing came of it.

Lieutenant Matthew McShane of the Madeira Beach police said the choice could be difficult. Release the picture, and a lot of new tips would flood in. But by doing so, police also ran the risk of having the suspect see the sketch and take off.

Although the the outlook was bleak for the investigators at the end of the first six months, things were beginning to stir. As with a simmering stew, some ingredients just took longer than others to become part of the whole.

A number of things were happening, none of them

connected at the time, but all of them important. It would take months, even years, to complete, but pieces of the puzzle were beginning to shift into a recognizable picture.

One person who would eventually play a major role in the case was being moved into a new job within police headquarters in St. Petersburg, while a second major player was putting in another day at work in the Pinellas County administrative office headquarters in Clearwater, a third was toiling away as a burglary detective, a fourth was planning a new billboard campaign, the fifth person was attending college in Tampa, a sixth was helping run a family-owned glass company and a seventh was in Cincinnati, Ohio, about to get a surprise visit from her father.

Glen Moore was born in Savannah, Georgia, but at the age of fifteen wound up in St. Petersburg when his family moved there. He began civic service with the parks department when he was just out of high school, then studied police administration in junior college and, at nineteen, became a police cadet, joining the force as a patrol officer two years later. As a rookie, the husky Moore was picked for the departmental wrestling squad and a comic cop announcer gave him the rowdy ring nickname of Boom-Boom Moore. The kid turned out to be a good athlete and dropped his first sparring partner on his head, knocking him silly. The second partner was Moore's superior officer, but rank made no difference in the wrestling arena. He got dropped on his noggin, too, and when the boss could think straight again, he slightly reworked Moore's nickname. Ever since, Moore was known as Boomer.

The tough moniker is a misnomer, however, because Moore is primarily a gentle person, who, rare in his profession, does not even curse. Despite the pistol on his hip and the steely eyes, he gives the impression of being a thoughtful professor because he peppers the traditional, methodical approach to crime solving with a constant stream of new ideas on how things can be accomplished.

In November, when the Rogers case was six months old and the tips were trailing off to nothing, a special investigative squad for violent crime was formed within the police department. Boomer Moore was named to replace the retiring Sergeant Bill Sanders, who had been with the troubling case from the beginning. Moore had been aware of some parts of the investigation, but not all, because of his other duties.

Now, however, every time he walked into his new office, he glanced up at those three four-inch ring binders that contained the information on Jo, Michelle, and Christe Rogers and wondered how the secrets in them could be shaken loose. For the moment, however, that had to wait, because the violent crimes team was up to its ears in work as murder swept the sunny streets of St. Petersburg.

In the 1950s and 1960s, when housing developers capitalized on the desire of homeowners to have waterfront property, it soon became obvious that there was a limited amount of housing sites that could be situated in such locations in attractive areas. There simply was not enough dirt beside the water to fill the projected needs of everyone moving away from the cold Northern winters and into the warm Florida sunshine. So they began to build more.

Through the careful use of dredge, bulldozer, and dump truck, developers were able to sculpt soggy land that was once questionable into building sites. Many such areas were fingers of land stretching out into a bay or harbor. A road would run down the middle of the finger and houses could be built on both sides, with small piers for boats in back yards that sloped directly to the little manmade canals.

One such development grew on the upper edge of Tampa Bay just off busy Hillsborough Avenue on the Tampa side, and was christened Tampa Shores. A succession of ''D'' streets—Donbrese, Dalton, Dowry, and Drummond—march away from the main road, and each home has water just beyond its doors. Many have docks or slips to berth their pleasure boats, usually fitted with overhead pulleys, known as davits, that can be used to pull the boats out of the water.

Lines of tightly-packed, low, neat, ranch-style bungalows are arranged on the desirable properties, with mature shrubs, lawns, and trees signifying that the neighborhood has been there a while. One can step out the back door, jump into a boat, maneuver through the narrow canal into Dick Creek, head southwest in the Bay, and within ten or fifteen minutes be at the boat ramp on the Courtney Campbell Parkway.

Many of the residents have lived there for years, but a sprinkling of newcomers and people who sell keep a bit of transience about the area. There are few rentals. As a result, neighbors get to know each other. They take walks, ride bikes, or just stand around in the evening in their driveways and chitchat about the developments of the day.

Jo Ann Steffey lived at 10713 Dalton Avenue with Herb Hart, next door to their friends Mozelle and Herb Smith at 10715. Jo Ann had retreated from the Washington, D.C., political zone after a full career to return to school and start another job. An active woman, she was not the kind of person just to sit around and do her nails. Her neighbors, Mo and Smitty, had founded a glass company and still worked there, although they had turned over the daily operations to their son-in-law. A driveway separated Steffey's and the Smith's homes and they regularly emerged to enjoy the late afternoon coolness and talk.

A short distance down the street, the house at 10709 Dalton Way always seemed out of place. In Florida, particularly in the tightly-packed neighborhoods, the exterior emphasis was on an openness that seemed to increase the space in which one lived. But at 10709, things seemed almost forbidding. Instead of an open front, there was a buff-colored stucco wall topped with decorative wrought iron fencing. Seen from the road, a large double-door wooden gate gave access for a boat trailer to the dock in the rear. The six-foot wall spread across the front to an arched gate with an iron grille in front of the main entrance. Atop each of the five squat columns spaced along the wall were small concrete decorations of pineapples, an old Colonial-era sign of welcome and health. Only the top half of the windows in the house peered over the wall, except for a slender window of opaque glass between the front door and single roll-up door of the adjacent garage. A small lawn eased gently away from the house to Dalton Avenue, and a waist-high palm bush was the lone plant on the neglected lawn.

The house carried an air of secrecy that was totally uncharacteristic of the man who lived there. Debra, his wife, and their little daughter, Whitney, were seldom seen, but Oba Chandler was more than visible.

He was friendly and could chatter like exactly what he was, an aluminum salesman. People walking on Dalton would be instantly engaged in conversation as they passed the driveway where Oba was washing his boat. A group of neighbors chatting in a driveway would suddenly be joined by the gregarious, smiling Chandler, who would step right into any conversation with a joke or an observation. He was always on the lookout for work, trying to sell neighbors on the need to install or improve the aluminum screen porches on their homes.

The Chandlers had moved into the house in December 1988, and Oba's friendliness quickly made him a familiar sight around Dalton Avenue. He preferred casual attire and his offhand manner matched his clothes. Oba seemed to enjoy life, to enjoy being around people, to enjoy living in Florida. He knew so much about the area, including many items from the distant past, that most people assumed he had grown up in Florida.

He liked to introduce himself to strangers by his nickname. "Call me Obi," he would say with a smile and firm handshake. "Like in Obi wan Kenobi," the cinematic *Star Wars* guru of the Jedi Knights. Everyone thought Obi was a pretty neat guy.

Not Jo Ann Steffey, however. She had lived around the Washington Beltway too long to be taken in by a superficial come on. Obi had not bothered her in any way whatsoever, and to her knowledge, he had never bothered anyone else, either. But she was innately suspicious whenever he would barge into a private conversation. Just like the house in which he lived, Jo Ann thought there was something a little off-center about Obi wan Kenobi, something a little spooky behind that engaging smile and line of banter. "I just thought he was weird," she would say later. "I didn't want to have anything to do with him."

She was busy. Trying to cram four years of school into as short a period as possible, Steffey scheduled courses whenever she could and burrowed down in continuous study. So when the composite drawing was published in the newspapers and broadcast on television, during the weekend of November 4, her attention was elsewhere.

But then she took time out to read the Tampa edition of the *St. Petersburg Times* and her eyes were drawn to the sketch and the description of the man the police were looking for in connection with those murders earlier in the year when the three tourists from Ohio were killed.

Steffey finished dressing, gathered her books, climbed into her car, and backed out onto Dalton Avenue. As she drove away, heading for a ten o'clock class, she happened to glance over at the home with the secretive air behind the little wall at 10709.

"As I drove by his house, it hit me," she said. "I looked at the house and said, 'Damn! It's him!' "

But by then, Obi wan Kenobi, who had spotted the sketch on the evening television news shows the previous night, was gone.

10

In Cincinnati, Ohio, Oba Chandler's daughter Kristal Sue Mays was also attending school on an evening in early November 1989. After class she dropped off a girlfriend on the way home to Harrison Avenue. She telephoned from her friend's house to make sure everything was all right at home, where her grandmother was babysitting the boys. She was told that her father was in town and that he wanted to see Kristal and her husband Rick right away.

That alone was unusual after what had happened during the last visit by Oba Chandler to his daughter, which had ended in disaster. Nevertheless, Kristal and Rick followed the instructions and drove over to a motel to see him. Winter was coming early to the Ohio Valley that year, and a bitterly cold wind slapped at their car.

Searching the parking lot, they finally found his black Jeep Cherokee backed into a space behind the last building in the rear of the motel complex. Rick noticed the odd way the vehicle was parked in the dark lot, backed into the space with the Florida tag and trailer hitch hidden against the wall.

As they parked, a door opened in the building opposite the Jeep, and her father stood there, watching them approach. She noticed that he was wearing lightweight clothes, appropriate for Florida but not for Ohio at this time of year. He glanced around the parking lot, as if searching for a spy.

Kristal and Rick were taken aback by the condition of both Oba Chandler and the room when they entered. Stained and empty coffee cups were strewn everywhere and ashtrays held small hills of cigarette butts, the telltale signs of someone who was riding a caffeine and nicotine high. Obviously, he had been waiting for them for some time. The room reeked of tobacco smoke.

As soon as the door was closed and locked, Chandler began mumbling, almost incoherently rambling as words spilled out of him. His eyes darted about the room, not stopping long enough to focus on any one thing for very long.

He was on the run, he said. The police were looking for him in Florida. Something about a rape, something about murdered women. Kristal was shocked, for despite everything she felt about her father, he was never at a loss of control. She had never seen him in such a state before. Instead of being in control of himself, he seemed to be teetering on the verge of a nervous breakdown. He wasn't making any sense at all.

Oba claimed that a buddy had telephoned him down in Florida, to warn him that the police were on their way to his house to pick him up. He had left before they arrived, moving so quickly that he had left Florida without any money. But he had some gold rings, including one of his wife's wedding rings, and was ready to sell them for cash. Did Kristal and Rick want to buy one?

Kristal became so upset that the couple left the motel. When they got home, the telephone was ringing. It was her father, profusely apologizing for the way he acted, but still rambling in his conversation. Kristal decided there was nothing to be done that night and she would consider her options in the morning.

Kristal returned to school the following day and Rick went back to work, both of them disturbed by this sudden appearance of Oba on their doorstep again, apparently trailing trouble in his wake. Rick had agreed to buy one of the rings, and stopped at the bank for some cash.

When Kristal got home, Oba had called again, and they returned to the motel. They did not want to stay in his cramped, smelly room that seemed like a smoky cave, and talked Oba into coming to dinner with them.

When they stepped outside, the winter wind sliced through Oba's thin windbreaker and clothing, so Rick and Kristal went shopping and bought him a coat and some shoes.

At a White Castle diner, he broke down and began to cry. Again the disjointed phrases began to spill out. Debbie wasn't a good mother to Whitney. Some nonsense about picking up women at a pier. Copious tears.

They returned home, taking Oba with them. While her father and husband settled into the living room, Kristal went through the large connecting doorway into the kitchen, where she could make some coffee and take part in the conversation at the same time.

Oba was still talking fast, mentioning raping three women, mentioning murdered women in Florida. Kristal was frustrated as she tried to make sense of her father's babbling.

He said he had a plan. He had stashed money away in El Salvador, Oba said, and he could go get it, but first he had to get a key from a friend. He asked Rick to accompany him up to Dayton, Ohio, so Oba could get a duplicate birth certificate for identification. He had come to Cincinnati because he didn't have anywhere else to go until he got his getaway plans together, he said.

The entire scene was beyond bizarre. Kristal and Rick believed something was dreadfully wrong and Rick had a good idea what it might be. On an earlier visit to Florida, Oba had claimed to him as they passed a dock at John's Pass that he had forced women to have sex with him there. Now, in Cincinnati, he mentioned to Rick that police "were looking for him for the murders" of three women. Rick had written the earlier claim off to Oba's braggadocio. Now he took it more seriously.

Meanwhile, Debra, Oba's wife of only eighteen months, was still back in Florida and had heard nothing from him. He had not told her he was leaving and she had no idea where he was, fearing that he had abandoned her for an old girlfriend.

But another fear had also surfaced. Lula Harris, one of Oba's sisters who lived nearby and frequently acted as a babysitter for them, had discussed with Debra the artist's sketch of the possible rapist and murderer that appeared in the newspaper. The two women agreed that it looked like Oba. Why had he vanished just when it came out?

Kristal knew that Oba had retreated to the home of an old girlfriend and contacted him to have him call his wife Debbie in Florida.

What was said in that conversation is unknown. However, a husband who picks up and runs away from home would have had a lot of explaining to do to the wife left stranded hundreds of miles away—particularly when the wife was curious about a police sketch of a wanted criminal, a sketch that looked a lot like her husband. Oba Chandler, however, had a singular talent. He could talk himself out of trouble.

To Kristal and Rick, it all smacked of secret agent stuff, as if someone was trying very hard to hide.

Meanwhile, Jo Ann Steffey returned from her classes the day she thought she recognized the sketch, determined to figure out what was happening. "I wasn't scared, not then. I just wanted to find out," she recalled.

Chandler's car was gone, but she knew that the police were looking for a blue and white boat, the same colors that were on Chandler's big Bayliner. The boat was no-where in sight, but Steffey knew it might very well be at the dock.

Arriving home, she walked directly through her house and out the back door, all the way down to the canal. There were several fences that ran to the water on the intervening properties, but she got her balance and a handhold and leaned out to look toward the Chandler dock. Indeed, a boat was hanging on the davits, a tidy little speedboat.

Thoroughly puzzled, she walked back into her house, thinking that detective work might be harder than it seemed.

The color scheme of the boat hanging over the pier at Chandler's place was white and red.

11

The fact that Oba Chandler had chosen to turn up on the Cincinnati doorstep of Kristal and Rick Mays, when put in context later, was strange. But then, Obi was a strange guy. Perhaps no more odd than any other criminal who had gone through numerous wives and girlfriends whom he abandoned, sired a string of children whom he also abandoned, used at least nineteen false identities, deserted from the military, and had three dozen arrests and a major escape from prison, but strange nonetheless.

He was the son of parents who fled the hardscrabble life of Appalachia for the bright lights and promise of the big city of Cincinnati only to find themselves consigned to the dark edges of metropolis, too.

His father, Oba W. Chandler, Senior, was a Native American, Cherokee or Sioux, no one is certain, who was born in the isolation of Manifee County, Kentucky, and had grown up around the coal fields, where life was both cheap and hard. Oba, Senior, had four sons by a first marriage, and raised none of them.

Oba, Senior, left Kentucky with his second wife, Margaret Johnson, and moved north to Cincinnati, where he installed his second, growing family in a little apartment on Clay Street, ten blocks north of the downtown area that, to a family from the coal country, glittered like a beacon of success.

Success always seemed to elude Oba, Senior, who managed only to obtain laborer's work for the National Distillers and Chemical Company.

Margaret gave birth to the fourth of her five children, a boy named Oba after his father, on October 11, 1946, at Cincinnati General Hospital. The only boy would have three older sisters—Alma, Helen, and Lula—and one younger sister, Rose Lee. The father ruled his tiny home and big family with a strong hand, brooking no opposition. One can only imagine the visage of those dark eyes set deep in a hard face, as the strong father advanced, leather razor strop in hand, to administer justice on his children if they broke his cardinal rules—they must not lie, they must not steal, they must not cheat—or any of a number of other commandments. The four girls were forcefully reminded to dress properly, which meant non-provocatively, with loose sweaters buttoned all the way to the top as a standard uniform. One daughter would recall many years later that she did not believe her father understood how to raise children.

Oba, Junior, grew up hard, and by the time he was ten years old, only Helen, Rose Lee, and he still lived at home. The eldest daughters, Alma and Lula, had departed—the first to an early marriage and the second to a reform school. Apparently, that year would be the defining moment of young Oba's life.

On May 30, 1957, Helen Chandler, only twelve years old, descended to the dark basement of the Cincinnati apartment house in which the family resided. There she discovered her strong father dead, swinging from a hangman's noose made of half-inch-thick rope that had been secured over a sturdy beam in the cellar.

Family members still disagree on how Junior behaved at the funeral of his father two days later. Oba, Senior, had been laid out in an open coffin propped against a couple of chairs in the living room of a relative in Jackson, Kentucky, and mourners viewed the worn, chiseled face through a thick veil placed over the corpse to keep away insects. The man who had never worn a suit a day in his life was buried clad in a dark, pin-striped coat and trousers.

Later, up at the cemetery on a small hill, after a preacher said the appropriate words for the departed, the grave diggers began to fill the resting place of still another hard luck story from Appalachia. According to one cousin, young Oba began to say, softly, "He didn't have to do that," and then jumped into the grave even as it was being filled to stomp down the dirt on his father's coffin. Other family members deny such an outrageous thing ever took place.

After the death of his father, Oba, Junior, in the words of a Johnny Cash song, "grew up fast and he grew up mean."

With his father's death, those solid restraints on his behavior seemed removed. The boy quickly slipped into paths that offered much more enjoyment than sitting in a classroom. Petty thefts of bicycles and toys and shooting his BB gun at passing automobiles contrasted with his mother's demand that Junior regularly attend church, where he learned enough about religion to parrot the appropriate words years later when they might help him con a judge.

When he was fourteen years old, things took an even more serious turn. Needing a set of wheels to expand his lifestyle, young Oba took a car for a joyride and was arrested. It would not be the last time he and the police

would collide and he would later admit to having been
arrested twenty times as a juvenile.

Before long, he stopped going to school with any sort
of regularity, dropping out of the eighth grade at Cutter
Junior High in Cincinnati. However, Oba had street
smarts and a sharp instinct for survival and an IQ that
would be measured one day at 120, considerably above
normal. He discovered that, although he might come up
short in the book-learning department, he knew how to
use words.

His sister Helen had married by 1960 and was living
in Tampa, so her younger brother was sent to live with
her, beginning his Florida odyssey. It did no good, for
Oba continued to skip school in favor of hanging out with
the guys, chasing girls, and playing pinball.

Before the year was over, he was shifted over to Pinellas Park to live with his sister Alma and her husband,
dodging classes at Pinellas Park Junior High School
enough to be packed up and sent back to Cincinnati after
only a few months. Florida obviously didn't make a dent
in the rebellious teenager. He was returned to Cincinnati
in March 1961, then moved with his mother to her home-
town of Newport, Kentucky, where his father was buried
and Oba soon would be arrested for auto theft.

By the age of fifteen, in 1962, he had discovered a
singular talent—an ability to convince girls to have sex
with him. That year he began a relationship with a teenaged girl and before they separated, he was the father of
two little girls, Kristal and Valerie. He did not stay with
the young mother, beginning a pattern that would mark
his life, attracting women and then coldly dismissing
them. A relative would say later that he treated women
like garbage.

At the time, of course, Oba Chandler, Junior, was still
just a kid himself, and he bounced back to Florida to live

for a while with his mother, who had remarried and also lived in Pinellas Park. Police would later speculate that it was about this time in his life that Chandler started not only conning his way into having sex with various women, but probably forcing them to participate, although the only time he was charged in such a case, in Cincinnati, the charges were dropped. During those years, he was picked up numerous times by police on a multitude of charges, including the theft of two shotguns. He also fathered a son, Jeffrey Scott Chandler, in Florida on November 15, 1964.

At the age of nineteen, two days after Christmas in 1965, when the Vietnam War was dragging America's manpower into its maw, Chandler did something entirely out of character. Although, as the father of three children he could easily have dodged the draft, he went to Jacksonville, Florida, and enlisted in the United States Marine Corps. Only one week after arriving at Parris Island, South Carolina, for basic training, Private Chandler was up on charges for disobeying orders and using disrespectful language.

Naturally his relationship with the Corps did not last long. The motto of the Marines is *Semper Fidelis*, Always Faithful, and Oba was never big on being faithful to anybody but himself. By the time he reached Camp Lejeune in North Carolina for advanced infantry training in March of 1966, he decided the Corps was not for him. He didn't particularly want any part of Vietnam anyway, and while still in the United States, he deserted.

He was caught in St. Paul, Minnesota, 107 days later and sent to the Camp Lejeune brig to serve six months at hard labor and was kicked out of the Marines on January 11, 1967, with a general discharge. Oba bounced back to Minnesota for a while, moved in with a girlfriend, and had another child, a third daughter, while holding a job briefly with the Ford Motor Company. He also lived in Ohio and Wisconsin for brief spells as his pattern of crime escalated swiftly from petty larceny to outright robbery.

On January 28, 1969, at the age of twenty-two, it is believed that Oba committed his first big league crime. Rita's Beauty Room in Cincinnati was robbed of twenty-one wigs worth an estimated thirteen hundred dollars. Police found the wigs in Chandler's home and he was indicted for receiving and concealing stolen property.

While the courts worked on his case, he remarried, again, on February 19, 1969. Two months after the wedding, he became the father of another daughter, but not by his current wife. It wasn't until the end of the year that the newlyweds gave birth to a child of their own, still another girl.

As punishment for the stolen property charges, Oba received his second taste of hard time, serving ten months of a one-to-seven-year sentence at the Ohio Reformatory and the Lebanon (Ohio) Penitentiary. In December, Oba received an unusual Christmas present. On Christmas Eve, his latest wife gave birth to another son.

He was paroled on April 23, 1970, and quickly demonstrated that the prison experience had minimal effect. Chandler would be arrested six times within the next five years, several times for crimes that had a touch of the bizarre, such as masturbating while peeking into a woman's window. For a while he worked on his grandparents' farm in Ohio, but in 1971, he moved in with a girlfriend in Cincinnati three months before she bore him another daughter.

Until then the known crimes of Oba Chandler had not included violence, a factor that was about to change dramatically. Many friends and relatives considered him a small-time crook, not a big-time thug. They were wrong.

He, his current girlfriend, and latest daughter moved to Florida where Oba began his long-lasting career as an aluminum contractor. Police later said that he was a suspect in several burglaries during that period of his life.

As usual, a divorce at the end of 1972 was followed immediately by another romantic relationship which produced still another child, and then still another marriage in August 1974, which lasted one whole month. The bride had it annulled when Chandler stole her new truck.

The active criminal life included an arrest by U.S. Marshals for unlawful flight to avoid prosecution for burglary and larceny, and an Ohio arrest for not having a valid driver's license.

The stakes went up sharply in February 1976. While attending a boat show in Volusia County on the east coast of Florida, the twenty-nine-year-old Chandler spotted a couple carrying a wad of cash. With an accomplice, Oba approached the Daytona Beach apartment where his targets lived, and told a sob story about how their car had run out of gas. When the husband started to unlatch the door, the thieves kicked it in, revolvers in hand. Police said the man was knocked senseless and his hands and feet were tied with stereo speaker wire. When he came to, Chandler and his accomplice began yelling at him to tell them where the guns and money were. While the accomplice kept a gun to the victim's head, Chandler forced the wife into the bedroom and made her strip from the waist down before tying her, too. Records indicate that as she lay helpless on the bed, he stroked the cold steel pistol barrel over the terrified woman's stomach.

When the bandits left, they took $1,200 in stolen cash, a pair of shotguns, and a Doberman Pinscher puppy that Chandler eventually gave away. Chandler was arrested two weeks later and charged with kidnapping, armed robbery, and possession of marijuana and drug paraphernalia. As a result of a plea bargain with prosecutors, Chandler was given a sentence of ten years in prison in January 1977. During prison interviews, he told authorities that the reason he committed the crime was to feed his cocaine habit. Within five months, keeping clean in his personal appearance and kowtowing to authority, he was deemed a safe enough convict in the Doctor's Inlet Road Prison near Palatka to join a crew made up of medium-security inmates doing road work. He liked prison even less than he liked the Marines. Once outside, he simply walked away.

Since he was now an escaped prisoner with a couple of heavy beefs on his record that indicated he was slowly racheting up the severity of his crimes, Chandler realized he could not get far by continuing to use his own, unique name. Therefore, he assumed the alias of James Thomas Wright when he became an apartment manager in Sanford, Florida, and set up housekeeping with a new girlfriend. Even family members that he contacted were told to refer to him only by his new name. He also had a pocketful of identification, driver's licenses, and Social Security cards bearing other names, if needed.

He clung to his new identity like glue, with good reason. On April 26, 1978, in Altamonte Springs, Florida he was arrested on charges of loitering and prowling. Police grabbed him in October 1979 on a similar charge; then in July 1981, he was arrested for tampering with a coin machine. Police had nothing major against James Thomas Wright, and each time he was released after paying light fines for his minimal trespassing of the law. They had no idea they really had been holding Oba Chandler, an escaped felon. Long since divorced, he had taken up with several other women during that time.

Incredibly, while he was still wanted for the escape,

he became Confidential Informant Number 122 for the
Orlando Metropolitan Bureau of Investigations, using his
fictitious name! He would later brag to a judge, when
seeking clemency, that his undercover work helped police
in that central Florida city bust a ring of pornographic
book stores and peep shows in which he had worked
while known as Jim Wright. To the chagrin of police, it
would not be the last time that Chandler would fool them
into letting him help as a crimestopper.

Chandler's strange run of luck came to a halt the very
next year, 1982, when he collided with agents of the
United States Secret Service.

He was living in Maitland, Florida, with a girlfriend
and a pair of large dogs he called Adam and Eve while
he operated a small aluminum-siding business.

Far away in Tennessee, two young men on a spending
spree at the World's Fair were nailed with a packet of
phoney twenty-dollar bills. They immediately agreed to
squeal on their source and pointed the Secret Service,
which handles counterfeiting crimes, toward a man in
Maitland that they knew only as "Jim." The Secret Service investigated the case for three months and on September 27, 1982, while driving through an intersection,
Jim Wright's car was suddenly blockaded by Secret Service agents who jumped out of their vehicles with guns
pointed at him. Popping the trunk of the car, the agents
found $8,340 in counterfeit twenties.

This time they discovered Oba's true identity. He entered a guilty plea and, in March 1983, was sentenced to
seven years in federal prison in Texas with another five
years on parole. While there, he tried to con the judge
who sentenced him with a teary, heartfelt letter of remorse.

"I was going to turn myself in as soon as my girlfriend
completed school to finish my time in Fla.," he wrote

Judge John Reed. "I never had a moments [sic] peace of mind since I escaped from a road Gang [sic] in Jacksonville. Judge Reed, I need this chance in my life to keep the things I've worked for these last five years." Naturally, he promised the jurist he would never again get in trouble, if only the judge would reduce the sentence. Reed refused.

Still the system saw fit to cough Chandler out early again. He had used his federal time in Texas to get a high school equivalency diploma and start some college work, and apparently was minding orders well enough to win parole on May 25, 1984, after about a year in the federal slammer.

Chandler was not set free, however, only escorted back to Florida to resume his interrupted sentence for the Daytona Beach armed robbery.

At that time, his first child, Kristal Sue, had no relationship with her father, and she wanted to know more. He had not helped raised her, and her mother was rather silent when she asked questions about him. No wonder. Her mother said that Oba Chandler had promised to marry her, and on the Big Day, as she was getting into her wedding dress and preparing to go to the church, Oba drove up to the house with another woman and a child. He yelled up that the other woman was his new wife, but he wanted Kristal's mother to come downstairs and show his new wife his latest baby—Kristal. It was not an auspicious start for the relationship between father and daughter. Her mother simply said Oba Chandler was not to be trusted.

However, afternoon television in the mid-1980s was featuring a constant string of shows that pictured happy children being reunited with parents that they had never seen. It piqued her curiosity about her father and, in 1986, she decided to hire a private investigator to locate him.

According to her husband Rick, the P.I. needed "about three minutes" to accomplish the job. Chandler was sitting in prison down in Zephyrhills, Florida.

Kristal rounded up her sister Valerie Troxell and they went down to visit their incarcerated father and meet some of the members of their far-flung family in Florida. One meeting during the two-week trip did not go well at all, and would emerge later as an embarrassing episode for all involved.

Chandler was thrilled that two of his many children had located him. He was cheerful and told them that he had tried to find them a number of times, but was blocked by their mother. He planned to move up to Ohio again when he was released, he said, to be near his real family. When they left, Oba launched a campaign of friendly telephone calls and letters to stay in touch with the daughters he had abandoned so long ago, and get to know his grandchildren.

On December 12, 1986, Oba Chandler was finally released from prison. The slate was clean. He was free to start a new life, and for a while, it seemed as if he might be going straight after all.

He fell in love, again, and got married, again. This time the bride was the soft-voiced Debra Ann Whiteman of Tarpon Spring, Florida, who joined him at the altar on May 14, 1988, only ten days after she divorced her first husband. Although some of his grown children attended the ceremony, Chandler had told the registrar who issued the license that this was to be his first marriage, and told Debra it was only his second. The string of divorces and an annulment were not mentioned.

He actually helped pay the way down from Cincinnati to Florida for Kristal and Valerie to attend the ceremonies. Kristal had been upset at first because she had liked Barbara, the woman that her father had been dating before Debbie came on the scene. Oba, however, told her he was dumping Barb because Debbie was younger and prettier. "That to me was really dirty," she observed.

If that was upsetting to her, Rick was upset about something entirely different. At first, Kristal and Valerie had kept the incident a secret, but flying down from Ohio, Kris decided to tell Rick the truth about something to avoid a potential confrontation. She claimed that during her trip to Florida to find Oba and meet the family, Oba's grown son Jeff had made a pass at her, his own half sister. Suddenly, Rick was not thrilled about coming down for the wedding.

They arrived on Friday and were met by Oba, who had rented a Cadillac for their use. Of course, they had to pay back everything he had laid out, but the car was beautiful. Oba met them at the airport, took them to their motel in Clearwater, and joined them for lunch on Saturday before the wedding.

Rick and Kristal drove up to the Tarpon Springs apartment for the afternoon wedding, but left immediately after the ceremony because Jeff had also arrived. Rick refused to shake his hand, and upset, he and Kristal skipped the reception and returned to the motel. Rick later apologized to Oba, whom he considered a "great guy," and said the animosity did not involve him, just Jeff.

The following year, Oba and Debbie bought the house in Tampa Shores, with a pier out back where he could tie up his powerboat, a blue-and-white, twenty-one-foot Bayliner he had purchased for a hundred dollars from the German man who had previously owned the house. In German, the craft was called "Zigeuner," which translated into English as "Gypsy," and Oba added the Roman numeral I to the name. Debra gave birth to their first child, Whitney, born on February 6, 1989.

Three months later, on April 24, 1989, Chandler

bought a 1985 Jeep Cherokee, using funds from the sale of a 1987 red Toyota pickup that he had co-owned with Barbara. She had taken the vehicle when Oba left and he reported it stolen. The matter was settled when it was sold.

Outwardly, life seemed to be settling into almost a normal routine for Oba Chandler, so much so that Rick and Kristal drove their new Chevrolet station wagon down to Florida again for a holiday in 1989. Things seemed pleasant enough, with the grandchildren playing in the pool and Oba taking them out for boat rides on Tampa Bay and on fishing jaunts.

It was only when Oba and Rick were alone, and the conversation lapsed into ''man talk,'' that Rick Mays realized that his father-in-law wasn't as squeaky clean as he appeared. He would recall later an incident when he went out with Chandler on an aluminum installation job. As Oba drove his big black Jeep Cherokee over the John's Pass bridge into the coastal village of Madeira Beach, he pointed to the boat dock and boasted how he had picked up a couple of women over there and taken them out in the boat and forced them to have sex with him. Rick wrote it off to Oba being a braggart, always crowing about how much sex he was getting, how all you had to do in Florida for sex was to just point your finger at a woman.

Rick and Kristal soon returned home to Cincinnati, but they had not heard the last from their strange relative. The visit in November 1989 wasn't the first time Oba surprised them. And it certainly wouldn't be the last.

12

Nothing happened to Oba Chandler as he hid out in Ohio, As the weeks passed, he began to breathe easier. Despite the picture in the newspaper and on television, no cops had come knocking on the door to arrest him. As November came to an end, feeling safe, he cautiously returned to his home in Tampa Shores and started making plans to move away.

He may have been somewhat nervous, but not as nervous as his neighbor, Jo Ann Steffey. She had all but discounted her earlier theory that Chandler was the man police sought because the boat she had seen on the davits was the wrong color. But in an afternoon conversation with a neighbor, she brought up the subject and they reminded her that he had sold the blue and white boat a few months ago. "Bang. I remembered," she recalled later. She had seen Chandler washing his Bayliner in the front yard the day it was sold. The craft was, indeed, *blue* and white, just like the one being sought in the crime. Still, she was reluctant to go to authorities, and although she had told her suspicions to several friends and relatives, she felt they would keep her secret.

Then, when the dark-colored Jeep Cherokee showed up again, she noticed two things—that it had a trailer hitch and that Chandler had started keeping the vehicle out of sight, in the garage. Debra's car, a taupe sedan, was parked in front. Another piece of the puzzle seemed to fit and she began to be frightened. What if word of her suspicions got back to him?

December came and went and, bloody 1989 came to an end for the Tampa Bay area. Forty-nine murders in St. Petersburg that year, a record, had swamped the police department and even succeeded in surpassing the importance of the Rogers' triple murder. That case was going nowhere fast.

In an attempt to get something moving on the case, the police decided to turn to television. At the urging of the FBI, the St. Petersburg police agreed to assist the producers of a show titled *Unsolved Mysteries* prepare a reenactment of the crime. The show, law enforcement people felt, had a good track record of helping authorities. It was an unusual tactic, but nothing else had worked.

Of the hundreds of tips that flooded in during the seven months since the crime, none had panned out as a firm lead. Several possible suspects were investigated and cleared. The police were no closer to solving the crime on December 31 than they had been when the bodies were discovered in early June.

Hal Rogers came down to Tampa Bay once again, alone, for the Christmas holidays. He was still shaken by the loss of his family and but was beginning to deal with the situation, getting new support through people who had also lost loved ones to violence. Only they, he felt, were really able to understand the ordeal he was enduring. He told reporters that was not bitter about the lack of progress in the case, explaining that the water destroyed all evidence and that the police had gone into the matter with the odds stacked against them. Rogers also speculated that the killer of his wife and daughters had help and warned the unknown murderer, "You have to be looking over your shoulder."

In January 1990, Jo Ann Steffey began the winter quarter of her college studies. Late on a Saturday night, she was at home alone and, walking into the kitchen, once again glanced at the composite sketch of the wanted man that she had attached with a magnet to her big Kenmore refrigerator. It was curling, growing a bit yellow with the passage of time. Then she glanced out the window and was stabbed by fear.

Standing beside her driveway, beneath a streetlight, was Oba Chandler, staring toward her house. "He's just standing there," she said. "It scared the holy bejesus out of me!" Steffey snapped off all the lights in her kitchen, then backed into the darkness, her eyes never leaving the man standing only thirty-five feet away from her door.

They remained like that for about five minutes, two motionless human statues. Finally, Chandler broke the spell and called out to his dog. A little fuzzy white dog trotted up to him and he turned around and walked back to his own house.

Steffey turned on the lights again, now wanting the safety of brightness, where moments before she had wanted to hide in the dark. She closed the blinds on the windows, slumped into a chair and thought about what she had just endured. She concluded that she could no longer keep silent about her suspicion. What should she do?

The answer, she thought, lay in the schoolroom. One of the students in her Tuesday accounting class was a deputy sheriff who drove to school in his cruiser, usually in uniform. When they arrived for class that evening, she found the deputy sitting in the lunchroom and sat down at the table with him.

There she told her story to the deputy, who nodded with solemn understanding. Steffey asked the officer not to bring her name into his report of their meeting. "Now I know they are going to check him out. I don't want anyone to know I've done this because I don't want to listen to them harp on it if I'm wrong and they make a mess of this thing. So I didn't say anything to anybody else. I figured the police would check him out."

In the following weeks, Steffey kept a close eye on the neighborhood. No police cars came. No detectives came. Nothing happened at all. She mentally kicked herself for telling the deputy about her neighbor. Obviously, she thought, the police had followed up her report with thoroughness and the reason Chandler was still walking around was that the investigators had cleared him of suspicion. She was happy that her name had been left out of it.

At police headquarters, Sergeant Glen Moore was unaware of the tip given to a deputy sheriff in Hillsborough County about the Rogers case. In fact, the fate of Steffey's confidential information to the deputy was never discovered.

Moore still had his hands full, helping the homicide unit clear away that forest of 1989 murders. But he began to think more frequently about the unsolved Rogers case, and knew that the results thus far had been pitiful. "I kept having the feeling that there was a lot more that needed to be examined," he said of the department's position on the triple murder at the time. The cops who were assigned to investigate the murders had simply been overwhelmed and unable to concentrate for an extended period on the Rogers case. "It was forgotten," said Moore.

* * *

When the task force approach had been abandoned, one of the detectives sent back to her regular duties was a serious, sharp-eyed investigator named Cindra Cummings, who had been on the police force for fifteen years. She had originally seen the news of the Rogers deaths while on her day off and was horrified that a mother and two daughters had been so brutally wiped out. "They weren't doing anything wrong. They were just tourists," she said.

Cummings, who had a reputation as a meticulous and obsessive investigator, had been pulled off the burglary detail to help sift through the mountain of early tips and clues on the case. She had tracked down clothing similar to that worn by the victims, helped trying to track down all hotel guests in the Tampa Bay area who had boats, the names dredged up in a computer comparison with boat registrations, and ran down other fruitless leads. But as time passed and nothing panned out, law enforcement agencies had begun to pare down the extra staff assigned to the case, and after two months, she went back to her burglaries.

When Glen Moore shifted jobs in the batch of promotions and transfers during November 1989, he didn't forget Cummings, who had worked for him in burglaries. She was impossible to forget anyway, not because she was a woman, but because of her tenacious approach to her job. "Cindy never gets frustrated, never gets overwhelmed," said one cop. "She just gets the job done."

Like Moore, her behavior was a bit different from that of her colleagues. The only time another cop had heard her curse was when, as a patrol officer, she was writing a ticket for a man she found driving under the influence, and he slapped the notebook from her hand and took off running. Cummings was suddenly angry and said something very appropriate but not in the language she normally would have used. She then caught the guy and put the cuffs on, angrier at him for forcing her to forget her composure than for trying to escape. Trying to escape from Cindy Cummings was neither smart nor easy. A strong woman for her tiny size, she runs long distances for exercise each day and in a police combat shooting course, she took the first-place gold medal among both men and women officers in the expert class. Only two men, both of whom were ranked as "masters," outshot her, and she ended up third overall among the two hundred shooters in the competition.

Moore knew that with her record, Cummings was within easy reach for promotion to sergeant herself for a department that liked to advance minorities. "What do you want to be?" he asked her when he was transferred.

"A homicide detective," she replied. Becoming a sergeant was something she only wanted when her name hit the top of the list, not to be selected while qualified males were rated ahead of her.

"Now's the time," Moore replied, happy to have the low-key detective join the team. Cindy Cummings went over to homicide as the first female investigator that department had seen in years.

When she entered the corner office of the homicide unit, she saw the three original black notebooks on the Rogers file, and two more that had been added. They contained an estimated seven to eight hundred open leads. Despite what had been said for public consumption, every lead in the case had not been followed to a conclusion at that point because the department had been so swamped with other crimes.

13

Once he realized the heat was off, Oba Chandler's life fell back into a more normal rhythm in the first half of 1990. Indeed, things were looking up a little bit, although he was feeling a cash crunch, as any self-employed person does from time to time. However, all of the time he had spent cozying up to the people who lived near him was finally paying off. He had installed a screen porch on the home of one neighbor down on the corner and was pleasantly surprised when another neighbor made a deal with him to screen in their vacation home at Double Branches.

Mozelle Smith, a stylish lady nearing retirement age, had been enjoying an afternoon scotch and soda outside one day when Jo Ann Steffey walked across the driveway with a beer and whispered, "Our new neighbor's probably a murderer." Mo knew the friendly Chandler had a dark car and a blue and white boat, but had brushed off Steffey's comment as alarmist. There were thousands of such boats in the Tampa Bay area. As far as Mo and her husband, Smitty, were concerned, Chandler had been an interesting, polite fellow. "Sure, Jo Ann," she had replied, and promptly forgotten about the comment.

On a bicycle ride around the subdivision one day in

early 1990, Smitty said, he had stopped by to see the porch Chandler had installed down the block. Smitty liked the work. He told Mo that he had verbally agreed with Chandler to enclose the open porch on their second home at Double Branches.

"I don't know why you did that," Mo responded to her husband, who believed a man's word and handshake were his bond. Mo was more suspicious in her business dealings. "You know you have to go through me first to get it okayed," she told Smitty. Mo decided to drive out and check the job when Chandler began work.

She did not like what she found and promptly let him know of her displeasure. There was no insulation being installed, which meant the aluminum roof would transform the sun porch into a baking oven in the summer.

When she spoke to Chandler he was not taken aback. If anything, it seemed as if he enjoyed bargaining. "Smitty and I didn't figure insulation," he told Mo.

"Well, you and Smitty just done the wrong type. I won't have it if it doesn't have insulation," she said. "Guess you might as well pick up and go." She had no intention of letting the building go any further with substandard work.

Chandler flashed his famous smile. "There's no problem," he said. "Let's just go inside and write up a contract and figure out what you want." He was always ready to make a deal.

While Chandler's crew continued their work outside, Mo and the contractor went into the house, where a single large room was divided into living and dining areas and the kitchen. They sat at the bar and made their adjustments. The porch would have to be one foot higher than the originally planned eight feet, to provide an additional flow of air and allow room for a thick belt of insulation. Two fans would stir the air.

"This is beautiful," Mo Smith said, satisfied with the specifications. She asked Obi for the money numbers.

He took out an order form that carried a letterhead of his name and stated that he was licensed-bonded-insured and that his contractor's license number, obtained in April, was RX0060328. In his distinctive handwriting, Chandler wrote that he agreed "To build one Screen Room" with a pitch roof, and outlining the details of the construction. He signed his name with a curling swirl, Oba Chandler. The date was June 5 and the agreed upon price was $2,776.

Mo was happy. Smitty was happy. Oba Chandler was very happy. He had made his original deal with Smitty for about eighteen hundred dollars, and the renegotiation with Mo had boosted the price an additional thousand, guaranteeing him a tidy profit for a minimal change in plans.

He did not realize that, by signing for the perfectly legitimate deal, he had just made the worst error of his entire crime-filled life.

In Ohio, memories were vivid at the Crestview Junior Senior High School graduation ceremonies as the summer of 1990 rolled around.

June 1 marked the first anniversary of the mysterious and tragic deaths of Jo, Michelle, and Christe Rogers, and they had not been forgotten in their home county, no matter how stagnant the investigation in Florida had become. The Crestview High School yearbook was dedicated to Michelle and Christe.

At 6 P.M. on the Saturday on which the anniversary fell, the bells of a half dozen churches slowly began to toll in their memory, the languorous pealing reaching out sadly over the rich farmland. Jim and Colleen Etzler and Jo's parents, Wilhelm and Virginia Etzler, tied colored ribbons to every telephone pole for thirteen miles between the school, the family homes, and the cemetery. The trail of light-blue ribbons for Jo, lavender for Michelle, and peach for Christe—their favorite colors—traced the paths of their lives.

Each time the high school cheerleaders had donned their red, white, and blue uniforms for a sporting event that year, they had worn a stripe of black around their arms to commemorate the missing energy of Christe, who would have become one of them.

Michelle would have been a member of the 1990 graduating class, and while the ceremonies went on as scheduled for the fifty-eight seniors, a single chair was left empty for her. On the vacant seat was a single red satin rose of the type given to each graduating girl. Dan Norris, the principal at Crestview, predicted that this would not be a one-time thing. "Twenty years from now when the kids get together for their reunion, they'll be talking about Michelle."

A newspaper reporter from Florida telephoned Hal Rogers on the anniversary and, out of character, the mild-mannered farmer snapped at her when asked if he was observing the anniversary.

"What do I want to observe it for?" Rogers shot back. "What day is it? The day I last saw them? The day I last talked to them? The day they were murdered? The day they were found? The day they were buried?

"It took me a long time to realize that I didn't have any good days. Just some weren't as bad as others."

Money was still tight for Oba Chandler as the summer of 1990 arrived. The jobs he was picking up in his aluminum business just weren't making enough to keep three crews running. The Internal Revenue Service was after him for back taxes, some $2,618 he owed from 1988. He had not been paying the utility bills on the three-bedroom, two-bath home on Dalton Avenue and a lien was about to be filed. On June 1, the first anniversary of the Rogers' deaths, Chandler missed making his mortgage payment, but took his wife Debra out for dinner.

He was disturbed by an article that appeared May 29, when the *St. Petersburg Times*, in a one-year anniversary story on the Rogers case, stated that police were working on the best lead they had come across in recent months. Then he read another report that a national television show was being planned for one of those programs which encouraged people to call in with tips. Obviously, the troubling sketch would again be telecast.

In July, Debbie Chandler resigned her job as a salesperson for Alumco Industries. She had been working there when she met her future husband, and had even processed some business deals for him through the company, something she would rue in years to come. One of the deals involved the theft of seven thousand dollars-worth of aluminum, which had provided enough cash for Oba and Debra to take a six-week West Coast vacation, where they visited California, Oregon, and Washington.

"You'll never guess what," a neighbor told Jo Ann Steffey in June of 1990. "Chandler's leaving! He's moving!" The neighbor was angry, because the aluminum and screen porch Oba had installed had started to crack and leak.

Steffey, who had obtained her license to sell real estate, checked out the Chandler place. He had just put in a new lawn and planted roses around the mailbox, the kind of thing someone would do who was planning to keep the house, not get rid of it. No "For Sale" sign was in sight. But the very next day, a huge U-Haul rental truck pulled up in front of the walled home and he was gone. He and Debra would relocate temporarily in the Fort Lauderdale area, on the other side of the state.

Steffey was not saddened by the view of the rental truck trundling down Dalton Avenue and out of Tampa Shores forever. For months, Steffey had lived in dread of the gregarious Oba Chandler. "I had come home every night, knowing that I had squealed on him. But I figured I had done what I had to do and that if he was the bad guy, they would have gotten him."

Then her problem loaded up his furniture and drove away. Her troubles might be easing, but the situation with Rick and Kristal Mays in Cincinnati was about to seriously deteriorate.

The police had not been idle during the intervening months. As the 1989 case load eased, Boomer Moore returned to a classic bit of police work in his new job with the homicide unit. In burglary, he had regularly had his troops review every major case in a no-holds-barred brainstorming session that could stir up new ideas and potential leads. The practice had been uncommonly successful in closing cases, and he brought the same practice to the homicide team.

Every murder case still unresolved had been examined since April 1990 with a pair of detectives assigned to follow up each case. It had been obvious from the start that the Rogers case was going to require the most intense effort, so it was saved to be the last one reviewed, to maximize the effort and minimize the chance that, once again, it would be pushed aside.

A veteran homicide detective, Jim Kappel, at one time named officer of the year in St. Petersburg, had been the lead investigator on the case from the beginning. He alone was most aware of the complexity of the case and the frustration of running into dead ends with it. As the review progressed, his fellow detectives came to appreciate the long and frustrating road that Kappel had travelled with the case. "I really thought Jimmy had done

everything he could do," Cindy Cummings would recall.
"There is only so much that one detective could do."

Kappel was about to retire and Boomer needed to as-
sign a two-person team to pick up the case. When he
asked Kappel to recommend names of those who could
do the best job, the older cop instantly gave his two
choices—big, tough J. J. Geohagen and slight, determined Cindy Cummings. "We jumped at the chance,"
Cummings said.

Boomer Moore had been successful at finally getting
the Rogers case off the shelf, but as his entire squad of
homicide detectives gathered in the yellow-walled office
every day for two weeks to brainstorm the Rogers murders, one thing soon became frighteningly clear. "It
dawned on us that we had a guy running around loose
who was going to kill again," Moore said.

Time became a commodity that could not be wasted.
Organization became paramount as J. J. and Cindy began
to work the telephones constantly and go through the case
file step by step. Moore moved into the backup role, running the administrative side of things, while his detectives tracked down whatever was available. He wrote a
ten-page report to summarize the case and assembled a
list of things that needed to be done. But towering behind
all of the police who touched the case was the very real
thought that the paperwork on this one, although it was
only a year old, had the potential of becoming a gigantic,
unwieldy monster as detectives began, once again, to
document every single item and lead of the past year.
The daunting task would have to be faced, they all decided, because every detective in homicide had been living with the itchy, uncomfortable feeling that they had
personally let the public down by not solving the murders
of Jo, Michelle, and Christe Rogers.

After work every day, when Cindy Cummings would

go jogging beside the water, and when she would see a blue and white boat, it would send her head spinning. "We didn't have a face," she said. "I wanted to turn to the last chapter and find out who did it."

14

The house at 10709 Dalton Avenue was a mess. A month after Chandler had left, a "For Sale" sign finally went up, but the place was already ragged. Except for someone in a little red sports car who periodically picked up the mail for a few weeks, no one came around. The roses around the mailbox died and the new lawn withered to a crisp brown in the bright Florida sun. The pool went stagnant. Rumors began to circulate around the neighborhood that Chandler had skipped town owing a pile of debts and that the IRS was after him for back taxes.

Jo Ann Steffey, who by this time had collected a small folder filled with newspaper clippings about Chandler, had finally removed the sketch from the refrigerator. The newspapers had gone quiet on the Rogers case as the months had passed, except for the anniversary piece in 1990, and she was able to push her worries about Chandler from her mind. The rumors, however, made her consider the situation again, as if it were lingering over the area like a bad smell.

The mystery deepened when a neighbor who knew someone that wanted to buy a waterfront house suggested the old Chandler place, which was standing empty. The realtor handling the house responded that there could be no deal. It was a dead listing because they could not find the owner.

Steffey wondered about the earlier transaction when Chandler had purchased the house. He paid $109,800 for it and floated a hundred-thousand-dollar mortgage. How in the world, she wondered, did someone like that qualify for such a high mortgage? Now it was clear the place was heading into eventual foreclosure.

It all made for some lively gossip around the Tampa Shores neighborhood. Steffey confided to family members that she felt that something was definitely wrong. She thought things were finally beginning to move when a deputy sheriff's cruiser pulled up in front of the empty house and the officer, finding no one home, began asking questions of some of the neighbors. He had an arrest warrant, he told them. For Debra Chandler, on a charge of stealing seven thousand dollars' worth of aluminum from her former employer.

Oba Chandler had driven all the way to California to search for a new place to live, and had again bounced back to Florida, and in September moved his family into an apartment at 11600 NW 33rd Street in Sunrise, near Fort Lauderdale. He was tired of being broke, particularly after the State Street Bank & Trust Company completed foreclosure proceedings on the Dalton Avenue house and repossessed his black 1985 Jeep Cherokee. He dreamed up an idea on how he could make some money.

It had been almost a year since he had fled to Cincinnati in panic, and nothing had happened in the interim that might indicate the police were on his trail, his creditors back in Tampa were the least of his worries.

So he piled into the brown pickup truck he had obtained to replace the Cherokee, and set off again for Cincinnati. It was a business trip, he told his wife, and he would call her soon. Maybe they could ease back a bit when he was done, take a well-deserved vacation.

Without calling ahead, he arrived at the home of his daughter Kristal and son-in-law Rick and their three boys in the first week of September. This time, he was in full control of himself, showing no signs of the state of panic that had gripped him so tightly the previous November.

Oba had a quiet talk with Rick, talking money. He had stolen some drugs he wanted to sell. All Rick had to do was make the original contact to set up a deal, then sit back and count the money. Partners. Rick would walk away with about six thousand dollars of easy money.

Rick Mays fell for the line. Obi, the "great guy," waited at the house while Rick contacted someone he thought might be a potential buyer and set up a meet with his father-in-law.

Obi was offering to supply a large quantity of marijuana in exchange for $29,000 in cash. A few days later, when the drug deal was set, Chandler stayed behind, waiting in his truck while Rick walked down to the house and told the guy that Chandler was ready to meet him. A pal of the buyer, carrying the money in a bag, accompanied Rick back to his house.

The friend walked around to the passenger side of Chandler's little truck and tossed the bag of cash through the window. It landed on the seat just as Chandler pulled out a pistol and pointed it right between the eyes of his startled son-in-law.

He had displayed the pistol when he first arrived, and Rick had taken it from him and hidden the weapon in his basement, because he didn't want the firearm around his children. Obviously Obi had found it, for now the hole in the barrel looked about four feet wide to Rick Mays. "I'll shoot," Oba said, rather calmly.

Mays was dumbfounded. "What about your daughter?'' he pleaded. ''You know these guys are going to come back and get your daughter!''

Oba Chandler stared at him as if he were looking at a fool.

''Family,'' said Oba, ''don't mean shit to me.''

Rick dove into the cab of the truck, trying to grab the ignition key. If he could keep Oba from driving away with the money, he could thwart the whole deal and keep his family out of danger from an angered group of drug buyers. His father-in-law proceeded to beat him about the head and hands with the pistol. ''At that point, I didn't care. I was going to die anyway,'' Mays later told lawyers. He was unable to get to the key before Chandler pushed him away from the truck and roared off down the road, richer by $29,000.

The shaken Rick Mays and the potential drug buyer's bag man looked at each other, then went back to the potential customer's house to explain how the deal had suddenly gone sour. Not surprisingly, the customer was not amused. Mays soon found himself in the middle of a hell provided by his father-in-law.

Soon, he became the object of beatings and torture by a biker gang that roared up on their motorcycles, intent on getting their money back and convinced that Mays was part of a conspiracy to rob them. ''I thought they were going to believe the story that they got ripped off because their buddy was with me and saw it happen,'' he said later. Wrong.

For the next few hours, they brutally toyed with him. He was handcuffed, beaten mercilessly, and had several guns pressed against his head by cursing, angry men. He was told they were going to take him to a farm in Kentucky and set their pit bulldogs loose to tear him apart. They were going to bury his car, with him inside. A shotgun was thrust into his mouth and a knife was stuck against his throat. One finger twitch by his tormenters, and it would all be over. Of course, by killing him, they would erase their main link to the man who had actually stolen their money. For kicks, the tormentors started ramming Rick's new truck.

What apparently saved Mays was a telephone call that interrupted the infuriated drug dealers who were busy terrorizing him. It was Oba Chandler, calling to say they had probably realized two things by now—that they had been ripped off and that he didn't care too much about his family. The bikers did, indeed, realize Rick Mays was now useless in any attempt to find Chandler.

Let's make a deal, the brazen Oba Chandler told the men he had robbed once already that day. Bikers might act tough, but Oba *was* tough. There was no doubt who was in control of the situation. You want to get your money back and I want to buy cocaine. I'll trade. The proposed deal was the height of charlatanism. One crook was telling a bunch of other crooks that they could get back the money he had stolen from them only by selling him cocaine. He was offering them the unique opportunity of buying their own drugs with their own money and letting Chandler walk away with $29,000 of coke. The bikers declined his offer.

Rick Mays was released and drove his now-battered truck home only to find two Cincinnati policemen waiting for him. One of the bikers had tipped the cops that Rick and Oba had stolen jewelry from him. When the police saw the cuts and bruises all over Rick's face, they called a paramedic to patch him up while they questioned him.

Kristal, in school at the time, was then contacted by the police, who were concerned that the man on the run, Oba Chandler, might come back after his grandchildren. Rick and Kris took the kids to the home of her sister and readily agreed to the police warning not to return to their home for a while. Rick refused to bring charges against anybody. All he wanted was to forget the whole mess. There was more than a little wisdom in that decision. That night, someone with a gun blew out the window of his truck.

Sherlock Holmes, the greatest sleuth in literary history, arrived in St. Petersburg in late 1990 to help out on the Rogers triple murder.

By some quirk of bidding, the computer system that had been installed years before in the St. Petersburg Police Department had been the property, not of IBM or another big dog in the commercial computing world, but of Martin-Marietta, a company more known for its military hardware production than friendly computers that had application in the civilian world. With the downsizing of the military, however, the company desperately wanted to improve its competitiveness.

One of the best targets of its software and hardware might be police departments, where data processing was an important element in fighting crime. Martin-Marietta needed an edge, however, and found it in the relatively new British investigative computer system that had first been used in helping solve the terrorist bombing of a Pan American 747 that blew up over Lockerbie, Scotland, in December 1988, killing 259 passengers and crew in the plane and another eleven on the ground.

With typical British understatement, the system was given the official, unwieldy name of Home Office Large Major Enquiry System, the rather redundant title designed to yield the acronym of H.O.L.M.E.S. Martin-Marietta and the program's British designers saw the Rogers case as a way H.O.L.M.E.S. could penetrate the American police marketplace for mainframe computers, and the company used its contacts within the St. Pete PD to draw the interest of Sergeant Glen Moore, who was always looking for better ways to fight criminals.

The Rogers case would be the first use of H.O.L.M.E.S. in America, and the company and the British helped pay the costs of sending Boomer Moore to England for a week of training. Boomer wanted something that could simplify the complex method they'd been using to handle the Rogers case, where a witness might be interviewed several times by different officers in different agencies, and then detectives would not be able to find the various reports. H.O.L.M.E.S. promised to be able to sort out this kind of information as well as compare various statements and items of evidence.

When Moore returned from England, he was sold on the methodology. He thought the SPPD should have H.O.L.M.E.S., which promised a way to break through the blizzard of paper that enshrouded the case and seemed to keep investigators bogged down at their desks. H.O.L.M.E.S. could shift the investigation back into an aggressive mode, rather than keeping police in the defensive posture of reacting to tips and filing papers.

Boomer was also smiling to himself. He realized that Martin-Marietta and the British designers would spare no expense to make damned certain H.O.L.M.E.S. performed as well as Sir Arthur Conan Doyle's fictional detective in its American debut. Suddenly put into a marketing showcase, the system would not be allowed by its designers to fail. "We got the Cadillac," he said.

During November, almost everyone connected with the Rogers case sat in a small room for three weeks, glued to the keyboards and computer screens, learning how to use H.O.L.M.E.S. beneath the watchful eyes of four British trainers. It was not an easy process, for a police officer is not necessarily computer literate by training.

"I welcomed the machine, but I was just not very smart when it came to computers. I had a headache every day," Cindy Cummings would recall later. "But the investigation had come to a standstill. We had to learn it (H.O.L.M.E.S.) or we couldn't go on."

Once the training period was over, the hard part began. Throughout December 1990, the police officers and administrative staff went through the tedious process of logging every scrap of information they had on the Rogers killings into the H.O.L.M.E.S. database. They had only just finished their training when they were plunged into actually running the system, giving H.O.L.M.E.S. the details on the crime itself and on each of the 1,270 leads received to date. "Entering the data was a tremendous chore," Moore said, apparently having picked up the British ability to understate catastrophe.

Oba Chandler, meanwhile, wasn't working quite as hard as the St. Petersburg police. On October 29, the very day that he had robbed the bikers of their money, he telephoned Debra at the apartment in Sunrise. She told him she had just been called by a Clearwater detective concerning the theft of the aluminum and that she was worried. No problem, said Obi.

He arranged for her to meet him in Tallahassee, Florida, and they once again headed west. Oba had money that was burning a hole in his pocket. The casinos of Las Vegas were calling his name. In Nevada, he gambled to his heart's content and made the gracious gesture of spending more than three thousand dollars to buy Debbie a ring. The man who only a few weeks earlier had been unable to pay his light bill was now throwing money around like a high roller. They drove around California, then climbed north along the coast to see Oregon, and Washington State, snapping photographs as they went. Finishing their third trip west in five months, they headed back to Florida again, Debra flying out of Salt Lake City to visit her parents in Massachusetts while Obi went to Sunrise to pack their belongings for still another move.

* * *

The cops were working on their new computer system, the bank was taking the house and car, the Dalton Street neighbors were hoping he would never return, Rick and Kristal Mays were praying they had seen the last of her father, and Chandler was having a merry holiday season as 1990 came to a close. He drove up to Massachusetts to retrieve his family and took them home to their newest Florida address, 992 Shockney Drive in Ormond Beach.

Prosecutors in Florida's Sixth Judicial Circuit, reviewing their record for 1990, might have muttered a little bit when they remembered the case of Mark Edgar Hartzell. He had murdered a woman named Bonnie Straughan with a single rifle shot to the face, killing the Tarpon Springs woman in front of her husband and children shortly after the family had ordered Hartzell out of their home.

The defense lawyer in the case was Fred Zinober, a Clearwater attorney who had worked as a prosecutor for four years before going into private practice. Zinober convinced a jury in Clearwater that Hartzell was innocent by reason of insanity, a disturbed man who believed he had acted on a command given to him by God during a radio broadcast. "In his mind, she was damned," the lawyer claimed, and Hartzell believed Bonnie Straughan had to die in order to be cleansed and resurrected. The prosecutors insisted that Hartzell knew he was killing a person, not shooting a grapefruit. The jurors bought Zinober's defense, deciding that Hartzell did not shoot the woman out of a sense of revenge, and found him innocent of the charge of first-degree murder. Hartzell was sent away to a mental institution.

Prosecutors could only shake their heads in wonder. They could not remember the last time an insanity defense had worked in Pinellas County. A slam-dunk murder case had ended with the killer getting a hospital bed instead of the electric chair. The feeling among lawyers was that Zinober, the former prosecutor, had become a formidable opponent in court, a defense attorney who could make a jury jump.

15

The dirty fingernail work of reexamining the Rogers murders accelerated in January 1991. Boomer Moore steered the case through the administrative and bureaucratic shoals at headquarters, keeping the needed officials interested in the fresh approach to the stale case through a constant sales job. Cindy Cummings and J. J. Geoghegan switched from being computer novices back to being detectives.

The entire atmosphere surrounding the case was undergoing a subtle change. Instead of being passive participants, the police were clearly on the offensive again. They had a renewed faith that, sooner or later, something would give and they would get the break needed to nail the killer.

In the meantime, the case was still being looked at from start to finish, which meant that a trip back to Ohio was in order. This was not a reflection on anyone's previous work or conclusions that Ohio had nothing to do with the murders, but new eyes were on the case now and with the passage of so much time since the crime occurred, maybe somebody or something new might pop up.

Accompanied by FBI agent Phil Ramey, Geoghegan

and Cummings returned to the Van Wert area in the cold of late January with a list of twenty-nine people they wanted to interview. They split up the names and started talking, and each time one of the interviewees would mention another name, that person would also be put on the list to be interviewed. Before it was done, seventy people would talk to the two detectives and one FBI man.

Friends, relatives, schoolmates of Michelle and Christe, Jo's coworkers, even people who barely knew them were interviewed. Rumors had to be eliminated. Pictures were gathered. Mental health counselors were consulted. Videotape of the funerals was examined. Personal data was gathered on the girls and their mother. "They (the victims) became real people to us," Cummings said. "I knew more about them than I did members of my own family." From the dairy farm to the church to the 4-H club, the investigators gathered information. Nothing was considered insignificant during the intense questioning that went on from January 27 until February 5, for it was all more fodder for H.O.L.M.E.S. "We worked from 6 A.M. until midnight for ten days. We felt closer to the family than ever, and we were driven to help solve this case," said Cummings.

The team that went to Ohio had escaped some of the tedious duty of December, when almost everyone else was filling up the H.O.L.M.E.S. database. Not only did they have to conduct the Van Wert interviews, but the second stop on their trip would be even more important and required monumental preparation.

Directly from Ohio, they flew to Washington, D.C., and were driven to Quantico, Virginia, for a series of meetings with the experts of the FBI's Behavioral Investigations Support Unit. The work of that special team had remained beyond the public realm during its formative years, but had become popularized by the Thomas Harris novel, *The Silence of the Lambs*. It was made into a thrilling movie that won Anthony Hopkins an Academy Award for his portrayal of an evil genius prisoner named Hannibal Lecter and Jodie Foster an Oscar for playing the part of the FBI agent who solves the case. Part of the plot that held movie audience enthralled was the way a psychological profile of the serial killer had been accurately pieced together by the Behavioral Investigations experts.

The FBI will not use that valuable resource on just any crime, but the St. Petersburg police and FBI agents in Florida had persuaded the wizards of Quantico to agree to take a whack at the Rogers case. Once that was possible, it was up to Cummings, Geoghegan, and Ramey—now joined by Boomer Moore—to provide the data from which the experts could craft their scientific guess as to just what kind of person had committed the terrible triple murder. A more general profile had been offered early in the case, but now the St. Pete cops wanted the full workup. This was the real world, not Hollywood. There was a flesh-and-blood multiple murderer walking around free.

It was a grueling business, but Cummings, whose main assignment was to prepare for the FBI meeting, came ready to work. In what later would be called a model for how police should present such cases, she coolly led Behavioral Investigations through as much data as possible. She, Geoghegan, Moore, and Ramey took them step-by-step from the crime scene of June 1989 through the most recent interviews in Ohio. The FBI probed deeply, wanting to know as much as possible about the victims in order to help sketch the profile of the person who killed them. They questioned the Florida officers almost as if they were grilling a suspect. They wanted everything, and the Floridians laid it all out in sessions that stretched over four days.

While the FBI team took the reams of material and went to work cobbling together what would be a rather terrifying profile, the four exhausted Florida cops finally took a few days off, put aside their badges, and played tourist among the historic sights of the nation's capital, snapping pictures of each other like schoolkids on a summer outing. Once they had caught their breath, they got on a plane and went back to work, anxious to exchange the frigid northern temperatures once again for the Florida sunshine. They were also eager to learn what the behavioral types had found amid the thousands of pieces of material. "We were just hoping that somewhere in all that mess, there would be something to help us out," said Moore.

When the FBI report came in, it was dreadful reading for the St. Petersburg police, for it confirmed what they most feared. They were dealing, the FBI experts said, with "a Serial"—a person who probably had killed before and would probably kill again—and all of his victims probably would be women. They concluded that a first-time killer wasn't likely to wipe out three people for his first murder. And once he thought he had walked safely away from the multiple, he probably would do it again, and next time, the bodies might not be found because he had learned something from the Rogers slayings.

The chilling psychological portrait of a killer came back from the FBI in May 1991, almost two years after the deaths of Jo, Michelle, and Christe Rogers. Along with the profile, the FBI sent the local police a tip—use the media! The print and broadcast people could reach a lot more people, faster, than individual cops knocking on doors. Publicity could be a useful tool in either flushing the killer out of hiding or jogging the memory of a witness. That would be represent a 180-degree turn from the normal stonewalling of the press that was police procedure.

Moore called a news conference to discuss the FBI profile, and as the experts in Quantico predicted, the police received substantial media play in publicizing a case that was already two years old. From then on, the police would consider massaging the media whenever they wanted to keep the case going, even if nothing was really happening. The Bay Area media happily walked into the relationship, almost hungry to be used by the investigators.

"This is a very heinous crime, particularly when you have family members probably seeing each other being violated sexually and then seeing the mother, sister, or daughter thrown into the water to die a horrible death," Moore told a Monday news conference. "I would say the honeymoon is over for this killer. We're going to hunt him down until we find him."

The killer, the detectives believed, would turn out to be a respectable man who lived in the area and exhibited no outward sign of being a monster. Instead, said Moore, "This will be a normal person who goes to work everyday. I think you will be surprised."

The FBI predicted the murderer was a white man with above-average intelligence, a neat and meticulous man with considerable social skills. He would have a compulsive nature and acquaintances would view him as controlled, rigid, and confident. His age range was pegged in the early thirties.

The man would be a smooth talker, able to present a nonthreatening manner to his victims when he was soliciting them.

He charmed Joan Rogers and her daughters into making the sunset cruise, finding the three independent and friendly females easy prey for his deadly scheme.

Based on what had been discovered in the Ohio interviews, the FBI concluded Jo, Michelle, and Christe would not have worried about going on a nighttime boat cruise if the right opportunity arose.

Moore then dropped a bit of information that had been missing from the previous public knowledge of the case. There actually had probably been two trips on the boat, not one. They had gone out on the bay during the early afternoon, then the Rogers family members returned to the Day's Inn for a while, and were last seen having dinner at the motel restaurant between 5:30 and 7:30 P.M.

Previously, police had insisted the ninety-minute window between the time of Michelle's telephone call to Jeff Feasby and the sighting of their car at the boat ramp was the critical point of reference. This new fact, that they had been in the restaurant, meant they had met Chandler twice, obviously going back the second time because they did not feel threatened after the initial boat ride.

Then the FBI profile raised the curtain on the dark side of the killer and created a probable scenario of what happened that horrible night. The key was that the murderer had an active fantasy life and was interested in bondage and total control, possibly tying up his partner during sex.

"The offender receives his gratification from the control of and domination over the victims," said Moore. "He derives pleasure and satisfaction from their suffering."

He had coldly planned the murders from the very start, when the three innocent victims happened to cross his evil path. "This was probably one of his fantasies," said Moore.

He did it for the pure thrill of satisfying his fantasy desires, raping and drowning the women simply because he enjoyed terrorizing his victims and watching them suffer. As an example, according to Detective Cummings, the killer taped the mouths of the victims so they could not scream, but did not blindfold them. "He wanted to see their terror," she said.

The worst conclusion possible was made. The three were probably still alive when they were dumped overboard, tied and taped and bound to forty-pound cement blocks.

Then the killer, quite capable of navigating around Tampa Bay after dark, chugged away in his blue and white boat. There was some supposition that, because no bruises or defense wounds were visible on the water-damaged bodies of the victims, perhaps the killer had help in his crime.

The killer was probably surprised when the bodies were recovered because he thought the weights would conceal his murders. He probably became tense and withdrawn while he weighed the possibility that he would be discovered. He also would take an avid interest in reading about the case.

Moore said this information was being shared now to persuade anyone with fresh leads to come forward. "There are people out there who know something about this case. It just hasn't rung any bells yet."

He said police had already invested some twenty-thousand hours of investigation in the case, and had examined some fifteen hundred leads. Dozens of law enforcement people had participated.

And, he added, from a dozen possible suspects that had emerged from the pack, two had not yet been cleared and did not know they were being investigated. One of those, he said, was the rapist who attacked a Canadian tourist off Madeira Beach, a short time before the Rogers were killed.

Unknown to the investigators, most of the various indicators in the psychological profile were pointing right at Oba Chandler.

And the FBI was right about tuning in the media. Be-

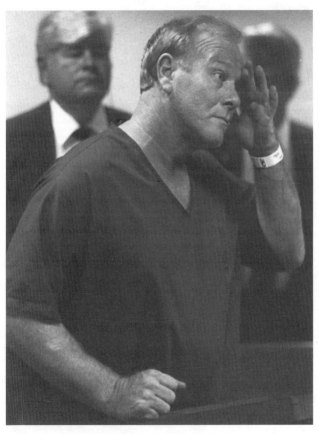

Oba Chandler appears in court after his arrest.
(*Courtesy of the* Tampa Tribune)

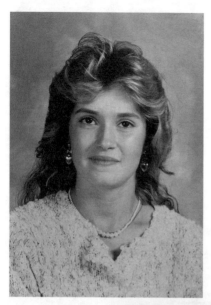

Michelle Rogers, age 16 (above), and Christe Rogers, age 14 (right). (*Courtesy of Hal Rogers*)

Joan Rogers on Mother's Day, 1989. (*Courtesy of Hal Rogers*)

The gravesites in Schumm, Ohio. (*Author's Collection*)

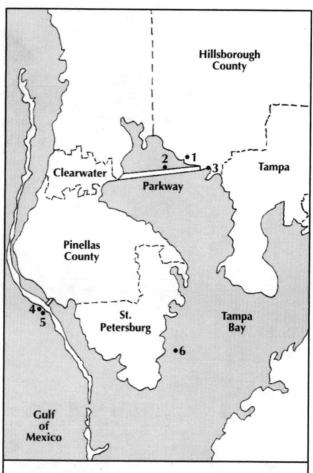

Hillsborough County

•1

2•
Clearwater

•3 Tampa

Parkway

Pinellas County

4••

5•

St. Petersburg

Tampa Bay

•6

Gulf of Mexico

1. Oba Chandler's House 4. Madeira Beach
2. Boat Landing 5. John's Pass
3. Day's Inn – Rocky Pt. 6. Bodies found

Michelle Rogers at her church confirmation. (*Courtesy of Hal Rogers*)

Christe Rogers playing softball. (*Courtesy of Hal Rogers*)

John's Pass, where Chandler picked up his Canadian rape victim. (*Author's Collection*)

Detective Cindy Cummings smiles after the verdict at "The Wall" of documents. (*Courtesy of Cindy Cummings*)

Police composite sketch. (*Courtesy of St. Petersburg Police Department*)

Police mug shot of Oba Chandler. (*Courtesy of St. Petersburg Police Department*)

Billboard asking for information on the deaths of the Rogers family. (*Courtesy of Patrick Media Group, Inc.*)

Chandler's blue-and-white Bayliner boat. (*Courtesy of St. Petersburg Police Department*)

cause of the sudden burst of publicity, the case was alive again.

One other thing was cooking in the investigation about that time. The filming crew from *Unsolved Mysteries* arrived in St. Petersburg for three days of taping a reenactment of the crime. Once again, the police were using the media—this time, a national television show—in hopes of shaking loose a vital lead.

The St. Petersburg and Tampa police, the FBI, and even the usually unhelpful U.S. Coast Guard public information people pitched in to assist in the taping.

An added bonus was the arrival in St. Petersburg of Hal Rogers for the show. While in Florida, he agreed to undergo a polygraph—lie detector—test. When he passed without incident, the police finally put to rest the possibility that the murders had any link whatsoever with Ohio.

Oba and Debra Chandler retrieved their furniture from storage near Ft. Lauderdale and moved up the Florida coast. In October, they took over a house at 438 DeLeon Drive in the middle-class subdivision known as The Woods in Port Orange, just a bit south of Daytona Beach, the fabled playground of Florida's east coast. Since a credit check may have proved somewhat awkward, the lease and the utilities were placed in the name of Whitney Chandler, who was three years old.

At the time, Chandler was using his real name and the fictional name of James Wright almost interchangeably. Neighbors got to know the gentle, friendly man as Obi. They considered him a nice guy nearing middle age who enjoyed boating. He frequently offered to take neighborhood kids fishing and drove a 1976 Eldorado motor home that his wife had purchased.

The Chandlers kept to themselves and never caused

trouble for anyone in the area. Local police would later say there wasn't so much as a barking dog complaint against the new arrivals. Outside of his neighborhood, however, it was quite a different story.

Later, when police pieced together Chandler's movements during that time they would suspect him of involvment in an armed robbery and in the abduction of a fifteen-year-old girl, who had been hauled into a van, bound and gagged with duct tape and sexually molested before she managed to escape. In addition, he began making numerous trips to the Tampa area, checking in at various La Quinta Inns under the name of Juan Kenobi.

Chandler was constantly on the lookout for ways to make a buck. Just because he was back in Florida did not mean the money troubles were over. After all, $29,000 can't last forever.

The robbery in which he eventually became a suspect, and for which he would eventually be acquitted over a question of freckles on his hands, occurred on March 31, 1991—Debra Chandler's birthday—in Daytona Shores. He was alleged to have pulled a .38 caliber pistol on a man and a woman, robbed them of $140,000 worth of jewelry, fifty dollars in cash, and their Dodge van. During the robbery, the woman was tied hand and foot with duct tape, and her mouth was taped closed.

Robbery or not, Obi Juan Kenobi wasn't particularly concerned about his cash flow situation. He knew that he could always depend on his family for money.

16

Newspapers took due note when June 1991 arrived, marking the second anniversary of the still unsolved triple-murder case. The people of Van Wert County were again interviewed by reporters, who found that little had changed in the long and empty period since the deaths. "You can't imagine what it's done to the people who knew the girls. My daughter . . . still cries about it," said Convoy resident John Reynolds, one of those quoted in an Associated Press story. A neighbor, asked about the state of Hal Rogers, replied, "He's never gotten over it."

The major exception to the universally sympathetic picture of the Rogers family came a month before the second anniversary, when the *Tampa Tribune* published an in-depth article that claimed the soft-spoken Hal Rogers was actually far removed from the gentle farmer image that had been portrayed for the past two years. Reporter Tim Collie described Rogers as "a hot-tempered, distant man who hid his eyes behind dark glasses."

Collie examined the dark family secret with a different slant. A source said, "You had the girl (Michelle) repeatedly raped right under her father's nose for two years.

When we told the parents, they didn't even flinch. It was like it was no big deal.''

Hal Rogers was said to have vented his anger on farm animals, terminated the psychological sessions Michelle was having with therapists after the rapes, flirted with the friends of his dead daughters, and ordered his pastor never to touch him again. The story stunned the Rogers family, angered their friends, and caused a sensation among those who had worked on the case. Hal Rogers said he did not grant an interview for the story. Police began to question this idea of cooperating with the press.

The *Tribune* came back about a month after publishing the critical piece with a much different story on the actual anniversary. Reporter Vickie Chachere's overview of the investigation did not once mention the Hal Rogers who had been painted as being so thoroughly ''weird'' in the earlier piece. Family members, friends, police, and attorneys would still remember the Collie story, and none too fondly. ''It just devastated Hal at a time when he most needed support,'' said one.

However, there was no doubt that the publicity generated by the news conference on the FBI psychological profile was a success. Twenty-four hours after the conference was concluded, between one-hundred-fifty and two-hundred new leads had been given to investigators, flooding in so fast that the nine detectives and support staff members had a hard time keeping up.

That had been the pattern since the case began. A news report would generate new leads ranging from useful information to the ridiculous, like a report about a neighbor who had kicked a cat and, therefore, seemed like someone who might be able to kill three people in cold blood.

Out of the new batch, two anonymous callers apparently rang some bells in police headquarters, and even the cautious Boomer Moore said those unknown tipsters knew what they were talking about. So, using the media megaphone once again, he told reporters that police had matched up some very good information from those callers and wanted to hear from those two people again. "This is by far the best thing we've had yet," he said.

One of the callers had named two men and the second described the same two men without giving their names. The two names were placed at the top of a short list of suspects. By September, the police had tracked down the men . . . and cleared them.

In a more concrete move on the second anniversary of the crime, Moore announced that the five-thousand-dollar reward being offered in the Rogers case was being increased to twenty-five thousand dollars, certainly enough to interest anyone with hard information. It was believed to be the largest reward the St. Petersburg Police Department had ever offered in any crime.

The bottom line, however, was not good. Two years after the murders, police had spent a lot of money and a lot of time and still had very little to show for their efforts. All they could do was continue to plug away.

Oba Chandler had resumed his part-time job as a paid police informant, a "concerned citizen" staking out relationships with the Tampa Police Department and the United States Customs Service. Although he now lived on the other side of the state, his contacts on the western side of Florida had remained intact. And if Chandler could sell aluminum porches and siding to people, he felt he could certainly peddle information to the cops, because he had done it before.

In July, he gave detectives in Tampa and customs agents a piece of interesting news—a couple of guys he knew were in the market to buy some drugs and he was willing to act as a middleman to have them arrested. The law enforcement officers were aware that their snitch had a record, but he had paid his debt to society, hadn't he? Confidential informants normally are not people who have never seen the dark side of the law, and other than for skipping out on creditors in the Tampa Bay area, Chandler was not wanted by police.

A meeting was set up with the potential drug customers and police hauled a thirty-two-pound bale of marijuana to a motel parking lot to exhibit as bait. One of the men named by Chandler showed up, did some bargaining, and departed with a two-pound sample of government grass.

A few weeks later, concerned citizen Chandler notified the detectives that the customers from Pinellas County were ready to buy five pounds of marijuana at a price of six thousand five hundred dollars. The meeting was to be in Chandler's gold and white Eldorado recreational vehicle, parked in the big paved lot of the West Shore Plaza shopping center.

The police, posing as drug dealers, moved just a bit too soon, however, marring the chance of a clean arrest when they struck before the actual exchange of money for marijuana. Steve Segura was caught carrying two handguns and his friend, John Mark Martin, had a scale. Police found more than six thousand dollars in cash on them.

Segura protested in court that he and Martin did not go looking for the drugs, that Chandler had approached *them* with an offer of cocaine. When they turned it down, he said Chandler pushed the marijuana. Segura said he and Martin wanted only enough marijuana for their personal use. Martin said he smoked the weed only because he suffered from glaucoma, an eye condition that is eased by using marijuana.

Segura, charged with the purchase of a controlled substance and carrying a concealed weapon, was sentenced to five years on probation, a one-thousand-dollar fine and five hundred hours of community service.

Martin faced a pair of misdemeanor charges—attempting to purchase marijuana and possession of drug paraphernalia. He was not formally convicted, but given a year on probation and ordered to pay a fine of eighty-five dollars and serve twenty hours of community service.

Part of the reason Martin got off with a lighter sentence may have been that Chandler had asked the cops to go easy on the man. After all, the confidential informant explained, Martin was his nephew-in-law, the husband of a daughter of Chandler's sister Alma.

"Family don't mean shit to me," an arrogant Chandler once told Rick Mays in Ohio. He meant it then and he meant it now.

In retrospect, one can see that time was beginning to move faster in the deadly case, and almost every month from the beginning of the summer of 1991 would see another development. Slowly but inexorably, police investigating the Rogers murders were being drawn closer to the mercurial Oba Chandler.

In August, the little house on Dalton Avenue in Tampa Shores finally was returned to the bank through foreclosure. The eventual new owner would have to have two large truckloads of accumulated debris hauled away from the house before he could move his family in.

And in late October, the investigators decided to play still another evidence card in hopes of shaking things loose. Among the items found in the search of the Rogers' automobile seven days after the bodies were found had been a brochure on which someone had scribbled directions to the Days Inn on the Courtney Campbell Causeway.

The pamphlet had been kept under wraps for more than

two years, but police now circulated a picture of it again obtaining a flash of media coverage, which had grown rare in the aftermath of the psychological profile.

Handwriting experts, explained Sergeant Moore, had determined that the directions scrawled on the brochure were not made by Jo, Michelle, or Christe Rogers. The police had traced the origin of the informational sheet and determined the family had picked it up at a Florida welcome station on Interstate 75 at Jennings, just south of the Georgia line. It was entitled, "Clearwater Beach, Your Destination Island," and included a rough map of the Clearwater-St. Petersburg-Tampa area. Police had also interviewed a number of people originally thought to be connected with the brochure and all were cleared.

In both pen and pencil beneath an advertising paragraph extolling some of the highlights of the area are lettered the words COURTNEY CAMBELL (sic) CAUSEWAY, RT 60, and DAYS INN, each with a single wavy line underneath them. Moore pointed out distinctive points of the writing, including the way specific letters were made, such as the almost nonexistent lowercase *r* and the distinctive little hook on the *y*.

Elsewhere on the brochure, it had been determined that Jo Rogers wrote BOYSCOUST (sic) and COLUMBUS. Moore handed out photographs of the directions on the brochure, adding that a palm print of an unknown person had been discovered on the paper. Obviously, the writing was a direct link with someone who had crossed the path of the Rogers family, and police were not shy about saying that person had been promoted high on the list of people they wanted to talk to. "We are saying this is the suspect, folks," Moore said. "Find the guy."

He speculated that the women had gotten lost between the time they arrived in Tampa around 11 A.M., when they would have run into the interstate maze that laces the town, and stopped to ask directions to the motel, which were scribbled on the brochure.

As usual, the telephones at police headquarters started ringing off their hooks. More than a hundred people responded, including one man who claimed to a radio talk show on WYNF-FM that it was he who gave the women directions. "I've seen the lady and I'm the one who gave her directions," the caller said. Police examined his story and, in effect, told him to crawl back into the woodwork. His recitation of the times involved did not match the facts.

As usual, the Rogers story faded from public view again as quickly as it had surfaced.

November came and the bogged-down Rogers case went national. *Unsolved Mysteries* was normally broadcast on Wednesday night, but the Rogers event would be part of a Sunday night sweeps-week special on November 3, entitled "Diabolical Minds: Case Studies." NBC tabbed the show for prime time, 8 P.M.

John McLaughlin, a researcher for the show, argued that by using the re-creation of the case in a valued entertainment slot, the television production team was helping police move toward a solution by putting the facts before twenty-five million viewers. "We hit more people in one night than they could ever hope to in ten years," he said. He added, however, that "we are not investigators."

Indeed, such police dramas have critics who claim the shows are merely a scam to make money off of misery. There is no real answer to whether such a show frightens the criminal involved or simply feeds his fantasy by letting him relive his crime while simultaneously getting a dose of fame on national television. Occasionally one of the current cop dramas results in an arrest. More often it provides a vicarious experience for voyeurs who like to see violence at a distance.

Hal Rogers, who agreed to be interviewed for the show, later commented to the *St. Petersburg Times* that, "I figure the person who did it is sitting back there and laughing." He also predicted that the killer would eventually, someday, be caught.

In addition to Rogers, there were interviews with policemen, a sociologist, an FBI agent, and others, plus the reenactment of the women at the boat ramp prior to the fatal trip and the discovery of their bodies. That gruesome scene had been held privately for several years among the few people involved. Now it became a flashy bit of Sunday night television entertainment.

Detective J. J. Geoghegan headed the telephone team waiting for tips in St. Petersburg. Cindy Cummings, flying out to visit her sisters in Sacramento, stopped over in Los Angeles to be ready when the calls began rolling in over the show's toll-free number, 1-800-876-5353, that was displayed on the screen. "We were hoping the murderer might call," she said.

In reality, the investigators refused to get their hopes too high. They all had been through this publicity routine too many times and did not want to experience more disappointment, if the plan to use a national television show failed to turn up anything worthwhile.

Sure enough, the calls came, some 160 in all during the next few days. Each one was entered into the ever expanding H.O.L.M.E.S. database. The result was as expected; a lot of tips but no leads.

When she returned from California, a somewhat embarrassed Cummings had to show up at a St. Petersburg Rotary Club luncheon. She was one of two police officers to be awarded the 1991 Ned March Award and a check for three hundred fifty dollars to recognize their exceptional service during the year.

She wanted to share the credit with the other members of the team, but Boomer Moore had selected her personally for recognition. "She has put her heart and soul into this case. Her dedication to solving these brutal murders has been an inspiration to the rest of the investigative team. I have never seen her give up on any aspect of the investigation, no matter how hard, frustrating or discouraging it gets at times," Moore wrote in his nomination. In addition to the countless hours of routine investigation, answering telephones and conducting interviews, Moore said Cummings had spent months preparing the presentation that allowed the FBI Behavioral Sciences experts to put together the profile of the killer.

December and 1991 ended in the same way as 1990 and 1989. There had been hundreds of leads but no breakthroughs. No one was in custody for the Rogers' murders.

As if to mock the efforts of the investigation, on December 15, the body of Kathleen Guy, who had recently moved to Florida from South Carolina, was found in Hillsborough Bay. She had been tied up and attached to a heavy concrete block before being thrown into the water. The case, which bore so many similarities to the Rogers case, eventually proved to be just another false trail.

On the bulletin board of the task force office in the St. Petersburg Police Department was pinned a color photograph of two little girls staring into a camera with deep, dark eyes as they stood before a Christmas tree that loomed green above a pile of presents. Michelle, age eight, is dressed in a blue velvet pinafore over a white sweater, while Christe, age six, stood at her left side in a rose dress and white sweater. The arm of Hal's orange rocking chair is visible to one side, a reminder of the hominess of the scene taken on Christmas Day 1980. The children are unsmiling, and their expressions seemed to reflect the sadness of this tangled investigation in which so much was at stake, but was going nowhere fast. Every day the cops would look at the picture of those innocent faces and think, Cummings said, "That's what it's all about." Then they would redouble their efforts.

17

Things were moving below the surface, as if a sudden undercurrent had grabbed the murder case and was dragging it toward a conclusion at some place and time yet unknown.

In January 1992, Jo Ann Steffey graduated from college to begin her second career, packing four years of work into two and a half years of study and coming out with a magna cum laude ranking. Like many of her fellow college graduates who were younger, she learned that her hard-won success in the classroom, even with her years of work experience in Washington, did not guarantee a job upon graduation.

She had hours on her hands and, except for part-time work at the college, there was nothing to do but sit around her home at 10713 Dalton Avenue, writing resumes and going on job interviews. "I started thinking about it again," she said. "It" meant the suspicions she harbored that her former neighbor Oba Chandler might be a killer. She talked to her family about it but took no other action, still thinking the police already had cleared Chandler of her earlier suspicions.

* * *

As Cindy Cummings was the first to acknowledge, the rest of the department had not been just sitting around during the last half of 1991. As 1992 began, the investigators could count some eight hundred men who had been checked out for possible involvement in the slayings since the case started. They had winnowed that roster down to a dozen solid potential suspects and dug up everything they could about those, down to what kind of underwear the men wore. That meant there had been literally hundreds of dead ends, and the hours involved to run down false leads counted just as much as those that proved useful.

The intensity had not let up, even within the department itself, where the Rogers investigators usually kept their doors locked. It wasn't that they didn't trust their fellow officers, but it would have been pure folly, after so much work, to take the chance that unauthorized information might leak out and spook a suspect. The number of notebooks on the shelf had grown substantially, and would continue to do so. If fact, the huge amount of paper on the case would eventually occupy floor-to-ceiling rows of shelves filled with black notebooks, and the area they occupied came to be referred to simply as "the Wall."

Glen Moore had found his responsibilities were shifting considerably from investigator to salesman, keeping the case alive while bureaucrats and budget bean counters growled about the work hours and cumulative costs being run up by the Rogers homicide team. If no results were forthcoming, they argued, let's cut it back. Two and a half years had gone by and nothing seemed to be shaking, despite expensive trips to England, computer programs, FBI profiles, thousands of hours of investigations that could have been used to solve other cases.

Boomer Moore really didn't care about the bean counters. He pledged total support to the Cummings-

Geoghegan squad and every time a new boss came into an important slot that touched on the investigation, Moore went into his smile-and-a-shoeshine routine and sold, sold, sold. He had postponed his retirement in order to lead this case and he wasn't about to give up.

Some of his victories were short-lived indeed. When one superior showed up in the chief's chair in February 1992, Moore spent a whole day reviewing the department's most famous and perplexing unsolved murder case, rolling out his portfolio of slides, books, and reports. At the end of the day, the new chief asked, "How many people do you want?"

Boomer gulped. Here was an unexpected opportunity to build up the team even more. "How about four?"

"How about six," responded the new chief. He went several steps beyond that, handpicking officers from a list of the best people in the department. Then he gave the beefed-up unit the freedom to spend six more months to operate solely on the Rogers murders.

Wow! Moore walked out of the chief's office with a big grin. He had gotten everything he wanted, and more, in the way of support and the chief even promised steak and lobster dinners for the team when they solved the case.

He had known of bosses who had shown determination in supporting their people against all odds, but this was going even beyond that! With total backing like that, what could go wrong?

The chief left his job. Boomer Moore had still more selling to do.

It was retreading old ground, but what the hell. Nothing else seemed to be working very well. So late in March, when *Unsolved Mysteries* scheduled a rebroadcast of the show featuring the Rogers murders, the detectives once again set up the telephone banks.

The show went on the air on Channel 8 promptly at
8 P.M. on March 25 and, as usual, the buttons on the
telephones in Florida and California immediately began
to blink. There were tips from the East Coast. There were
tips from the Midwest. There were tips from Florida.
Thirty came in during the first hour after the show.
Within a few days, there were hundreds, most of them
commenting on the subject of the dark Bronco or Blazer
and the blue and white boat, neither of which had been
located. If nothing else, it provided the detectives with a
long list of things to do and people to call.

Naturally, Cindy Cummings was working the telephones on the night of the broadcast, and one of the calls
she picked up was from a St. Petersburg woman, and she
wrote down the name: Connie Dickson.

Dickson said that although she lived in St. Pete, she
had a sister over in Tampa who lived only a few doors
away from a man whom she had long considered to be
suspicious. The helpful Dickson gave Cummings the telephone number of her sister, and the detective called.
Dickson's sister, Kay Swilley, answered. It was a call
from the police! No, Swilley told Detective Cummings,
she did not know the man's name and he had moved out
long ago. Cummings asked her to walk down the street
and get the address of the house in question. She did.
Cummings wrote it down.

"There was nothing different about this lead," Cummings recalled later of that busy night. "Now we had an
address." They also had dozens of other new leads,
swiftly growing to hundreds from across the nation. It
was all more data on which H.O.L.M.E.S could chew,
whenever the information could be sifted, prioritized, and
finally entered into the computer. With the new load of
leads, no one could guess when that might be.

Sometimes what people say and what they think they

say can be as different as what people hear and what they think they hear.

What was missing from the Dickson-Swilley-Cummings exchange that night of the broadcast was a proper line of identification of who was who. Swilley did not live at the house from which she had spoken to Cummings. She had been there visiting their third sister, who wasn't home when the detective called, and therefore did not speak directly to the inquiring officer.

The house in question was on Dalton Avenue. That was where the third sister lived—Jo Ann Steffey.

Also answering the telephones that night was Eileen Przybysz, who had worked her way up through the civilian ranks of the police department over almost twenty years. One of only six civilians employed in the department to perform such vital tasks as dispatcher, Przybysz eventually won the unusual position of civilian investigator and was then assigned to the Rogers task force.

Barbara Sheen Todd had been bothered by the Rogers murders from the very first day the news broke in 1989. A smallish, black-haired dynamo, she had daughters about the same age as Michelle and Christe and was horrified by the deaths. There was no doubt where her sympathies lay. One of her daughters dated a deputy sheriff and a stepson worked for the state attorney general. There was something else, too. Barbara Sheen Todd had been a Pinellas County Commissioner since 1980 and a champion of children's rights who was never satisfied to sit idly by when she could help her county move forward. As months passed, she kept up with the Rogers case with a great and growing sense of personal dismay. "It didn't fade in my memory," she would say several years later. "It was one that wouldn't go away. It almost felt as if those girls were my girls." As she went about her job as one of the highest ranking officers in the county, she would tap her fingernails on her desk during her rare idle moments, wondering what she could do to help.

May 14, 1992, would turn out to be the most critical day of the long investigation.

Jo Ann Steffey read the morning newspapers of both St. Petersburg and Tampa that day, and looked at the graphic of the odd handwriting that illustrated the stories. Sitting on her couch, she read on and learned the police were saying that identifying the writing was their last, best chance of solving the case. She put down the newspapers with the thought, "Well, this is it. I still think it's him. I don't care what anybody else thinks, I think it's him."

The articles also said the police believed the killer might have had an office along busy Dale Mabry, a major traffic artery in Tampa. Steffey did not know the location of Chandler's old office, so she picked up the newspapers and went to see her neighbors, Mo and Smitty.

Smitty said they thought Chandler actually had worked out of his home, right down the street, and that swerved Mo's thoughts to the screened room that Chandler had put on their second house. "I've got some of his handwriting," she said. "The contract! I made him sign a contract for the porch!"

"We're out in the driveway by the truck," Steffey recalled, when Mo went inside her home and hunted for the document containing Chandler's handwritten specifications for the porch job. For about two hours, Mo Smith ransacked her home, rooting through old checkbooks and papers, but could not lay her hands on the agreement she had forced Oba Chandler to sign.

Steffey decided to call the cops anyway. Surely, they would be able to get a copy of Chandler's signature, if it was so important to their case. Around noon, she went back home and dialed the number in the paper. "I want to talk to somebody about the Rogers murders. Are you the right person?" she asked.

"Yes," replied civilian investigator Eileen Przybysz.

Steffey recalled later that she gave the investigator her name, told the police that she lived on a canal that fed into Upper Tampa Bay, then identified Oba Chandler as the person she suspected of being the killer, and again gave police the exact address. In fact, she said, she gave the police everything she knew about Chandler, why she had been suspect of him for almost three years, and the fact that he had moved away. Before she hung up, she honestly told the investigator, "I'm very nervous."

Later that afternoon, Mo's long expedition to find the pieces of paper she wanted finally paid off. They had been at the second home, where the porch work had been done. She called Steffey and told her to bring out her newspaper clipping.

On the tailgate of Smitty's truck, they smoothed out the newspaper illustration of the handwriting, and beside it put down the contract and check signed by Oba Chandler. "It was a perfect match," Steffey said. "My knees went to water." To give it a closer look, they took the documents inside to Mo's kitchen table. The results were the same, and the neighbors knew that the friendly man who had inhabited the little house behind the wall down the block was the man being sought by the police.

Mo Smith, however, was reluctant to get involved. The slightly built woman was under the care of a doctor and the excitement generated by discovering a potential murderer was hardly the kind of thing that would be recommended by a physician who wanted his patient to avoid stress.

Steffey returned home about 4 P.M. and called the task force number again. Eileen Przybysz answered.

"I called her, said I had it (the contract) and that it was a match, a perfect match. Her response was, and I remember it, 'Well, you said he was gone.' "

Przybysz asked if Steffey could fax the material to the police, but Steffey did not have a fax machine. Steffey was as nervous as if the documents in her hand were made of hot metal. Too jittery to think of just getting in her car and driving to the police headquarters to hand it over, she promised instead to mail it. Hanging up, she returned to see Smitty and Mo and got their permission to send in copies of their material. Smitty realized that their knowledge could be a dangerous thing. "Jo Ann," he said, "if it is him, by God I hope they can find him."

The following morning, Steffey, growing more terrified about what she knew, typed out an envelope to the task force and gave the packet to Mo Smith, who promised to drop it at the post office. But Mo called from work a short time later and told Steffey they had a fax machine at the Professional Glass office and could send the documents immediately.

Steffey dialed the task force number again and a man answered. She asked for the fax number and told the policeman that he could confirm her identity by telling the civilian investigator that "Jo Ann from Tampa" was calling. "She was in the background and I could hear her yell out that it was okay to give out the fax number." Steffey relayed that number to Mo Smith.

By that time, the documents had become an item of great interest at Professional Glass, with almost everyone giving their opinions of whether or not the writing matched. The unanimous decision was that there was no question—the same person wrote both.

Mo's daughter, Dale Curtis, was one of the front office

employees at the family owned and operated business, and made arrangements to fax the documents. Knowing that her mother was in no condition to take the lead on such a course, she also called the Task Force and the civilian investigator repeated her request that the information be faxed, adding that the police had received thousands of leads in the case.

Therefore, both to keep Mo's name out of it, and since Steffey previously had talked at length with Przybysz, Curtis put Steffey's name in the informational box that identified the sender of the fax that replicated the documents and canceled check. She signed her own name at the bottom of the fax transmission.

Having turned over the information, Steffey, who was living alone at the time, grew even more nervous about pointing a finger at such a dangerous man. Like Mo Smith, she worried that Chandler might discover their involvement and seek retribution. "I'm really scared. I won't go out of the house after dark. I mean, I bolt that house down when it gets dark." Mo Smith had similar concerns. "He knows me, I know him," she said. "If he's in a lineup, I'd know him. If I was in a lineup, he'd know me."

The two women who pointed their fingers directly at Oba Chandler would spend several sleepless nights after their disclosure. Their only consolation was the belief that the police would take care of it from there.

They were wrong. More sleepless nights lay ahead.

Oba Chandler spent much of the first part of 1992 working up a close business relationship with a series of pawnshops, coin dealers, and jewelry merchants. Although he would later be cleared of the Daytona Shores robbery which had netted the thief $140,000 in gold and jewelry, Chandler had suddenly come into the possession of a great deal of such items.

Beginning in January, he started selling scrap gold to Diversified Numismatics, Inc., in Orlando, with a teasingly small amount worth $275. He pawned a three-quarter-carat diamond ring at Goldsmith's in Tampa, then increased his visits to Diversified Numismatics, which began to buy more scrap gold from him in larger amounts, once for $583 and twice for $275. In March, Diversified Numismatics paid $583, $621, and $540 for scrap gold to their now regular customer. In April, a ring and bracelet went to Dyers Jewelry for a hundred dollars, and the firm paid him forty-seven dollars for a pawned ring. Then it was back to Diversified Numismatics to unload gold coins, rings, and scrap gold for $1,903.

Chandler scooted up to Ohio briefly and traded his pistol, a .38 Smith & Wesson for a .38 Bryco, then came back to Florida to continue spinning cash out of his secret horde of gold and jewels. In addition to the coin dealer, he added Prestige Pawn in South Daytona to his short list of favored buyers, although he would occasionally drop an item for cash on some other shop. During 1992, Chandler, claiming he worked for Bay Jewelers, sold Diversified Numismatics more than $13,600 worth of jewels and coins.

18

From May 14 on, Jo Ann Steffey and Dale Curtis repeatedly made telephone calls to police, giving more information and asking what was happening. Dale went on vacation for a week in late May just after sending the original fax, and called Przybysz when she returned. Nothing had changed. Steffey, frightened and on the verge of becoming a nervous wreck, called any time she remembered additional details.

The entire Dalton Avenue neighborhood had become handwriting experts as word spread door to door, friend to friend among the people who had lived around Chandler. But the neighbors saw no movement from the police department.

June 1, 1992, marked the third anniversary of the Rogers killings, and the Task Force detectives were stretched to the limits of their patience. Hundreds of leads had come in during the three years and, although they had some strong suspects from time to time, they did not feel they had enough to make a move. H.O.L.M.E.S. was almost choking on the reams of data being entered by hand in no particular order, the Wall was growing page by useless page, and the telephones continued to ring, the dark eyes of the little girls in the picture on the wall staring at the detectives accusingly.

The case dominated the lives of the investigators. They could think of little else and they knew time was probably turning against them. The trail was cold and they were under administrative pressures to solve the crime or scale back the expensive task force that was draining so much time and dollars away from other cases—cases that *might* have a chance of solution. "We were bogged down and we knew the dollars could not go on forever," said Cummings.

Boomer Moore, at a loss for what more he could do, spent off-hours riding around Tampa with his wife, trying to solve the puzzle of exactly where and how Jo Rogers got lost on the interstate and where she may have made the fatal connection with the killer. He knew the media was starting to lose interest again because the third anniversary passed with minimum attention from the press.

At the end of June, Jo Ann Steffey decided to escape the pressure and took a two-week vacation to Virginia, hoping everything would be better when she returned to Florida. About the same time, Dale Curtis telephoned the task force to ask if the handwriting on the documents she had sent in had matched, as everyone thought it would. A month after sending the urgent fax, she was told there had not yet been time for a comparison. A month later, she called again and received the same answer, that the backlog of things to do was so huge they just had not gotten around to it yet. When she hung up the telephone, learning that nothing had been done, she had no explanation for her mother when she asked why the police were dawdling.

Willing to try almost anything to shake free some useful information, Moore agreed to another form of mass media. The newspapers and television had played a major role in keeping the story alive, but their interest was clearly on the wane as newer, fresher stories competed for space and time. The national crime show had churned out hundreds of leads, most of them questionable. The new idea at the task force was to put the message onto a media favorite of the mass market advertisers—roadside billboards. With Florida's population constantly on the roads, thousands of people would pass the billboards, reading the messages. Someone might know something. The Florida Department of Law Enforcement had occasionally tagged an outdoor advertising company for help in publicizing the pictures of a most-wanted criminal, and the St. Petersburg police decided to give that practice a try.

There was a friendly and sympathetic ally sitting behind a nice desk in a spacious corner office at Patrick Outdoor Advertising. S. Wayne Mock's company was widely known for its policy of helping the community. Periodically, when an advertising campaign expired, there would be what Mock describes as a window of opportunity, which he would normally fill with public service advertisements to help out charities, like the United Way, rather than leaving the boards idle.

Like almost everyone else in Pinellas County, Mock had been following the crime and the investigation for years. A quiet man with a strong sense of family, Mock felt the triple murders had been particularly vulgar. This was not a gang-style shooting or a knifing in a tavern parking lot. "Those are not as shocking as three women on vacation being tossed into the bay," he said. He had friends in the police department, and an arrangement was soon worked out.

Mock's company donated everything except the cost of having the billboard printed. Soon, ten billboards went up around the county. What would have cost an adver-

tiser some six hundred dollars per month per billboard
was being provided for free. The old boy network even
figured out how to pay for the printing costs. Jim Culverson, a detective involved in the case, talked to his
father about the problem. Culverson's dad is a doctor
who, some twenty years earlier, was the personal physician for Wayne Mock's wife. The doctor, matching
Mock's generosity, wrote out a check for the needed
thousand dollars.

The large billboards planted by the roadside were a
stark request for public assistance. WHO KILLED THE RO-
GERS FAMILY? was emblazoned in large red type across
the top, with ON THURSDAY, JUNE 1, 1989 in a smaller
black banner line just below it. In the middle of the billboard, spread out like playing cards lying face up on a
table, were head-and-shoulders photographs of the three
victims—a drawn, stern-looking Jo on the left, the haunt-
ing look of Michelle in the middle and the happy, smiling
face of Christe on the right. Below, in red and black,
were the words: $25,000 REWARD FOR ARREST AND CON-
VICTION. It gave the St. Petersburg Police Department
number of 893-7104, the direct line to the task force, and
in the lower right corner was a replica of the patch of the
St. Pete police.

One of the people who saw the new billboard was County
Commissioner Barbara Sheen Todd, and a light clicked
on in her head. Of course that would not be news to
anyone who knew her, for Todd is nothing if not an idea
factory. And once she gets onto an issue, she clings like
a bulldog until something is done.

Many men, some of whom outranked her, had felt
those steely light blue eyes drill into them, and they
winced when she barked. Todd had spent a lifetime in
public service activism, overcoming the hurdles placed
before aggressive females. She did not go over or around

such obstacles. She went through them. Her tenacity was such that within a few years, she would be drafted to run for the office of lieutenant governor of Florida. She lost in the 1994 Republican primary and vowed never to seek office again as number two on any sort of ticket.

That she was a leader, not a follower, was demonstrated in the way she became involved with the seemingly insoluble Rogers case. It had been needling her like a toothache. Three women tourists had been in her area for what should have been a happy vacation and some maniac had murdered them. That just would not do. The woman who had once organized the Child Safety Task Force of Tampa Bay, after a man exposed himself to one of her daughters at a bus stop, had a reputation for quick action. She was born in Pennsylvania but grew up in Florida, and was outraged that the Rogers family had been slaughtered on her home turf.

When the travel brochure with the curious handwriting was printed in the St. Petersburg newspaper and the billboards featuring the photographs went up, a concept crystallized for her. "Tom," she said to her husband, "I think they should take this paper and blow it up on a billboard. See if anybody would recognize it." She handed him the newspaper photo of the handwriting.

Her husband knew a hurricane was brewing. "If you feel that strongly, you should call the detectives," he said.

"I don't want them to think I'm weird," she said.

"Barbara," he replied softly, "you're a county commissioner, not somebody off the street. They'll listen."

She picked up her home telephone and dialed the Major Crime Squad. Instead of a routine lead that would be handled by a detective or an administrative assistant, County Commissioner Todd soon had Sergeant Glen Moore on the horn and was explaining her idea.

Boomer listened. Any police sergeant would listen

when a county commissioner decided to get involved in one of their cases. At first, he was realistic about her scheme to plaster the crucial handwriting sample on huge signs, because the department still had no funding for such a thing. He doubted that Dr. Culverson was ready to spring for another thousand dollars. "We don't have the money," Moore said.

Todd thought for a minute and the face of Wayne Mock floated to her consciousness. "Don't worry. I'll find sponsors. How many boards do you need?"

"Six?" ventured Moore. He heard a quick affirmation and then the commissioner hung up.

She next dialed Patrick Advertising and, playing her county commissioner card again, soon had Wayne Mock on the phone. "Wayne, I've got a little challenge for you," she teased the general manager, tweaking his interest but also making him wary. He knew that when Barbara Sheen Todd had a little challenge, you had better reach for your wallet.

She carefully explained the situation, and Mock was intrigued. Who knows? It just might work. But it would cost money. Todd had a terrific idea, she said. You can donate it. Mock knew when he was beaten. "We can work it out," he pledged.

Todd called Moore again. We got a deal. Have your people work it out with Wayne over at Patrick. What had been a troublesome and special effort for the first set of billboards had been railroaded through for the second important billboards in a matter of minutes by the aggressive county commissioner.

Moore knew a good thing when he saw it, and arranged for both Todd and Mock to join him at a news conference to announce the new boards. The media might be tired of routine stories saying the police still had not arrested anyone, but the angle that a county commissioner had decided to weigh in with her novel idea would surely generate a new round of interest.

On June 30, Moore called the unusual news conference to announce that the police were going to do something that had never been done before, display evidence on a billboard for the general public. Barbara Todd and Wayne Mock were at his side and he saluted them for having the idea and donating the work and space.

"Normally, our policy is not to discuss evidence or have the public view evidence in unsolved homicide cases. However, the Rogers case is so unique, and the necessity to capture the killer so compelling, the need to display this evidence overrides normal procedures," he told the reporters.

"We need to locate the writer of this printing. . . . He will be the killer."

Moore encouraged area residents, particularly those around Tampa, to get involved, because "the person who knows the killer is in a unique position; possibly in danger. We believe this killer has killed before and will probably kill again, if he hasn't already."

These were not the sort of words that the Steffey and Smith households wanted to hear. Dale Curtis called the cops again and wanted to know, if the handwriting was so important, what was happening with the documents that had been in the hands of police for many weeks? Sorry, she was told, the backlog, you know. A detective had done some initial work on tracking down who had owned the house in question, but the results were still tentative. The Smiths and their relatives at Professional Glass started to consider hiring their own handwriting expert.

Steffey's reaction was stronger. When she read the story in the newspaper about the press conference concerning the new billboards, she simply screamed out loud in the solitude of her home, *"What are they doing?"*

That evening, Mo Smith walked to the side of her house on Dalton Avenue and Steffey, sitting on her patio next door, wearily asked, "Mo, what do you suppose they're doing over in St. Petersburg?"

There was no good answer to that one.

She called civilian investigator Przybysz at 8 A.M., and bluntly said, "I can't believe you people are putting up those signs."

"I was just thinking about you," the civilian investigator replied, according to Steffey. "I've got your information right here on my desk."

However, life soon returned to normal and Steffey, Smith, and Curtis tried to put the worrisome, unsolved case out of their minds.

Before the new billboards could be designed, a decision had to be made on how the material on the brochure should be depicted. The usual method of having an artist produce the desired copy would not work, because of the importance of showing the unique writing style, such as the so-called felon's hook on the *Y*. An actual reproduction, however, blowing up the small writing on the pamphlet to something that could be used on a huge billboard ran the risk of losing clarity and quality. But that was the only way to ensure the accuracy of the writing, and so that was the technique chosen.

The new boards were even more spare in layout and jarring in content than the earlier version with the pictures of the victims. On a plain white background, the scrawled directions from the brochure were displayed large on the entire left-hand side. In scarlet, the right half of the billboard asked:

**WHO WROTE THESE
DIRECTIONS?**

YOU MAY KNOW WHO
KILLED THE ROGERS FAMILY
$25,000 REWARD
ST. PETE POLICE 893-7104

The main success of the billboards was not to awaken
a passing motorist but to bump up the campaign to identify the handwriting high enough in the awareness of the
police investigators to link their seemingly separate effort
for identification with the avalanche of telephone calls
and faxes from the families of Jo Ann Steffey and Mo
Smith.

On July 31, a frustrated Dale Curtis called again, reminded the police of the earlier faxes, and was told that
any such transmission could not be found. Two and a
half months after sending in the first fax, she was asked
to retransmit the material.

Once again she fed five sheets of paper into the Professional Glass fax machine, pushing the START button
at 1:09 P.M. The machine hummed away for three
minutes and twenty-eight seconds, and again dumped the
samples of Oba Chandler's peculiar handwriting onto the
desks of the task force.

Curtis's cover letter to Investigator Przybysz expressed
the Smith family's perplexity:

Irene,
    Here is another copy of Oba Chandler's hand-
writing and on the back of his check is his driver's
license number. Although I'm sure you received
numerous samples of handwriting, many of us are
convinced that this handwriting is the same as the
one published in the papers. We feel so strongly
that they are one in (sic) the same that due to your

lack of response we were tempted to pursue this with a handwriting expert of our own.

However, due to Commissioner Todd's new personal interest we have recontacted you. We expect a response to this information as soon as possible.

Thank you for your assistance.

Within thirty minutes, Dale received a telephone call from Przybysz. "She called back and asked for the original documents," Curtis recalled. "We said that Oba had the originals, we only had the yellow copy."

The Smith family members were not the only people at the end of their tether. Herb Hart, who had returned as Steffey's housemate, was so tired of waiting for the St. Pete police to move that he wanted to take the information directly to the FBI.

Finally, the investigators were pulling together the loose ends.

A few days later, on August 3, Detective J. J. Geoghegan was out at Professional Glass asking questions and requesting the original documents that had been faxed. Mo Smith was reluctant and gave the cop a third-degree questioning.

Helping law enforcement was important, she knew, but that probably wouldn't win any favors from the Internal Revenue Service if she had to produce the Chandler contract in a tax audit. Before she handed the incriminating document to the police officer, she made Geoghegan sign an itemized receipt of what he was being given and present his identification to Diana S. McCoy, a notary public, who stamped the document to make it legal.

19

When J. J. Geoghegan took a look at the documents containing Chandler's handwriting, he immediately took notice. Because of the fine details involved, the fax versions had been somewhat blurred, but the originals were clear, unmistakable. "You didn't have to be a handwriting expert to see it," he told a reporter. "I knew at that point, we had a fifty-fifty chance. He either killed them or gave them directions."

The police investigation that had floundered for so long suddenly took on a bright, new focus. Geoghegan had a temporary new partner when he went to Dalton Avenue because his buddy throughout the investigation, Cindy Cummings, had finally given in to exhaustion and taken a two-week vacation. When the St. Petersburg detectives drove up to Tampa Shores, Cummings was in Vermont, out of contact on a bicycling holiday.

By the time she returned to work, Geoghegan and the task force had already accumulated two full notebooks of information on Oba Chandler. Boomer Moore called her over to his desk when she arrived back at the office, and slid two pictures over to her—the artist's sketch of the alleged Madeira Beach rapist and a mug shot of Oba Chandler obtained from probation documents. Then he

lay down a picture of the actual boat to compare against
the police sketch of the one used in the assault on the
Canadian woman. Each depicted a middle-aged man with
a high forehead, short hair, the seagull-shape of a light
mustache, thin lips, and dull, lifeless eyes in an oval face.
"It was unbelievable. They were identical," she said. "It
was so eerie that it gave me a chill. There was no doubt
from then on."

Arresting a suspect in the case was not as simple as a
television viewer of police shows might believe. Although they finally had a name, the laborious process of
nailing Oba Chandler was far from the point at which
police could pounce. The detail of the law had to be
carefully observed as the investigators began opening up
Chandler's past history in order to spin a web of evidence
from which he could not escape.

The task force now had a new supervisor to guide the
investigation, Executive Assistant State's Attorney Doug
Crow, the diminutive prosecutor who, horrified, had
stood by three years earlier when the Rogers' bodies were
pulled from Tampa Bay. He had been haunted by the
case since that day and was determined that there be no
mistakes in bringing the suspect to court. Once behind
bars, Crow never wanted to see Oba Chandler on the
street again.

For weeks, the detectives piled stone upon stone to
figure out who this Oba Chandler guy was, tracked him
to his current home in Port Orange, dug up every shred
of his history that they could without alerting him, and,
finally, figured out the best way to arrest him. Cindy
Cummings was given a tight deadline of five days to
prepare an in-depth presentation on the case as it neared
its important final phase—an arrest.

Chandler, however, moved ahead with plans of his own.
Only two weeks after the investigation swung into high

gear, and with almost every cop in Florida looking for him, he drove to the familiar environs of Pinellas County for some more mischief.

In early September, he spent the day carefully watching the movements of people at a jewelry convention at the Countryside Mall in Clearwater, just north of Pinellas Park. Then he went back to Port Orange.

On September 11, the same day that St. Petersburg police sent a sample of his handwriting off to an expert for comparison with the scribbles found on the brochure, Chandler was back in Pinellas, this time with wife Debra and three-year-old daughter Whitney in tow, and carrying a semiautomatic pistol.

After dark, they drove to Ulmerton Road and parked briefly at the side of the Residence Inn motel, where Chandler got out of the car. While he was removing some items from the trunk of the car, Debra shifted her little daughter into the front seat. Chandler walked away and his wife drove around to the rear of the building, found a splash of light, and picked up a children's book. She began to read a story to her child.

George Eash and Peggy Harrington, representatives of Van-Lightner, Inc., a wholesale jewelry manufacturing company based in Van Nuys, California, were heading for a rest after a long day at the convention and jewelry show. At 9:45 P.M., they parked their rented automobile in the lot of the Pinellas Park Residence Inn. As they opened the doors and got out, they noticed a stranger weaving toward them. When he first emerged from the bushes, they thought he was a vagrant, a harmless street person.

Their impression changed quickly when the man began waving a large handgun in their faces and yelling. "Leave your purse and wallet! Don't look at me! Keep your face down!" yelled the man. Harrington tossed her purse and Eash pitched his wallet onto the front seat, ready to obey the gunman.

The man jumped into the automobile, slammed the doors, started the car, and took off, leaving the two jewelry company workers thankful to be alive. They were shocked, however, at what they had lost. The purse and wallet were negligible, when compared to the cases in the trunk of the car. Those satchels contained about $750,000 worth of jewelry. That car thief didn't know what he had just stolen, they thought, as they yelled for motel workers to telephone the police.

Debra Chandler had hardly begun the story for Whitney when Oba sped into view. "All I had time to do was park the car under the light, pick up the book, and start reading her the story, and he came around the corner in a different car," she would later tell police.

Following her husband, they drove in a two-car convoy to a second motel on Ulmerton Road, where they parked and Chandler hurried to the trunks and shifted three cases into their car. They immediately hit the highway for home, back across Florida to Port Orange in Volusia County.

In one of the many ironic twists in the case, the Residence Inn at 5050 Ulmerton Road is only a few blocks away from Patrick Outdoor Advertising at 5555 Ulmerton, where just outside the front gate was a large billboard that featured Oba Chandler's handwriting.

Detectives flew to Ontario, Canada, and met with Gayle Arquette, the victim of the 1989 assault off Madeira Beach, and her friend Linda Lyle. When they showed the women a photopack that contained the color photograph of Oba Chandler among the pictures of several other men, recognition came instantly for both of them. As questioning continued, Gayle asked that the picture be turned face down on the table, because the staring eyes of Oba Chandler bothered her.

With their identification, police finally had a reason to arrest Chandler. It would not be for murder, but for sexual battery, a serious felony charge that could put him behind bars while the murder case came together.

The Chandler home at 438 DeLeon Drive in Port Orange was under constant surveillance, and every time Oba Chandler drove away, he was tailed. To keep him from becoming suspicious, the automobiles that trailed him would periodically give way to a police spotter aircraft that kept him in sight as he curled through the streets, oblivious to the fact that his every move was being tracked.

Since the police had been investigating the case for more than three years, it wasn't like starting from scratch. With a name and an address, things came together in a hurry. As Cummings recalled, "Until we had Oba, nothing fit. . . . Now everything did."

The task force drew in representatives at the beginning from a number of law enforcement agencies to avoid unexpected turf battles since the supposed crimes of Oba Chandler spread not only across the state of Florida, but into several states and even beyond American borders. The last thing any of the police wanted was a tussle between the people wearing the badges over who was in charge of what. Not surprisingly, however, they were all so united in their dislike for the suspect that cooperation came swiftly and often.

September 17, only six days after Chandler had robbed the jewelry salespeople, was set as the tentative date for the arrest. The strands of the legal net were tight, the people were ready, the timing was right. Police who had followed thousands of fruitless leads, waited years for the right break, and suffered through an unending trail of disappointments, were now ready to pull the trigger on the bad guy. Cummings was ebullient and had to bite her tongue when a friend asked her about the slow progress on the case. "When are you going to quit beating a dead horse?" the friend queried. Cummings was evasive and said not a word, although she knew the end was in sight. But the next day, with a forecast of bad weather on the eastern horizon, she drove over to Volusia County to be in on the arrest. She had lived and breathed the case for so long she had an overpowering urge to confront the villain in person, to see what he was like.

The arrest warrant was in place and it was almost time to move. As he rode over to the east coast to participate in the arrest, Boomer Moore had one last reason to dislike Oba Chandler. Moore's youngest son was the hotshot quarterback for East Lake High School, playing arch rival Tarpon Springs én route to winning a college football scholarship. While his father was miles away closing in on the vicious criminal who had made his life a nightmare for the past few years, the young quarterback scored the winning touchdown in the last two minutes of the big game.

Chandler was being tailed by the aircraft when he pulled his car into Sounds Unique in Lake City, Florida, to have a car alarm and radar detector installed. He was carrying around so much jewelry that he didn't want to take a chance of being robbed himself. While the alarm was being installed, the weather turned ugly in a hurry and the little police plane bouncing around in the turbulent skies could no longer hold its station. It peeled off for home, radioing the land units to take up the surveillance.

By the time the cars showed up at the auto alarm store, the employees had finished their installation and the customer had driven away, into the rain.

Oba Chandler, totally unaware that police were tailing him, had vanished.

20

Oba Chandler, with a carload of hot jewelry, headed back to his familiar roots in Kentucky and Ohio. He had managed to melt down some of the gold in Florida to Diversified Numismatics in a pair of transactions for almost eight thousand dollars, but was wary of placing the stolen goods on the market there.

Debra was pregnant with their second child, so he headed north alone, having given her several pieces of jewelry as a gift. Debra, remembering how Oba had once vanished without a word, stashed the jewels in a safe-deposit box as a potential source of cash. She insisted later that she did not know the merchandise had been stolen.

Chandler spent the night of September 18 in a Holiday Inn, and the next night at a Super 8 motel in Hazard, Kentucky, working the area during the Black Gold Festival that celebrates the area's economic link with coal. Relatives whom he approached with the story that he was working for a jewelry company and offering to sell them some of his cache became suspicious and wary immediately. Chandler had been out of the clannish area too long to be automatically accepted as a trusted insider, even when he sprinkled a few gold rings among them as bait.

Moving on to Cincinnati for three nights and using the name of Ron Howard, Chandler visited an automobile dealership near Cincinnati in hopes of trading jewelry for a car, but couldn't find one in the showroom that he liked. So he offered the salesman the opportunity to buy some of the expensive ornaments for cash. The salesman took a look and realized the jewelry was worth far more than Ron Howard was asking for it, and set about coming up with the cash. He paid $350 down, borrowed more from his mother and even more from a bank, and made the deal.

After Ron Howard left, the salesman tried to capitalize on his profit, taking gold jewelry later assessed to be worth as much as fifty thousand dollars to a jewelry store, where the owners passed on the purchase opportunity, saying it was too rich for their blood. They recommended a second dealer, who examined the jewelry and became suspicious of a deal that seemed too good to be true. When the dealer ran the information by police, they identified it as originating from a recent jewel robbery in Pinellas Park, Florida. The automobile dealer who was stung eventually looked at a package of police pictures and identified the photo of Oba Chandler as the man who represented himself as Ron Howard.

Chandler had left Florida with one car and a bunch of jewelry. On September 23, he paid cash for a 1987 Nissan Pulsar and headed home to Florida. He paid a Hazard resident, Willie Rooten, one hundred dollars to drive the second vehicle to Florida for him.

Police had not given up on finding Chandler, betting that he was still unaware that he was being pursued and thinking that he would return to his home eventually. They were right.

They had discovered information that placed him in both Hazard and Cincinnati, then tracked him back through Tennessee, heading south. A telephone "trap and trace" pinpointed a call to his house about 2:30 P.M. as being made from around Valdosta, Georgia, not far from the Florida line, on Thursday, September 24. Oba was on his way. Sixty-three miles from Valdosta to Lake City on Interstate 75, then sixty-five miles east to Jacksonville on I-10, around the I-295 loop to avoid that metropolis and onto I-95 for the final 108 miles to the Daytona area.

Within three hours, the arrest team left a rented office and once again moved into place. They had been staking out the southwest Port Orange neighborhood with all-day, all-night shifts for so long that a number of residents had reported the strange goings-on to local police, who soothed their worries. Actually the locals preferred to stay out of this one, and let the task force now led by the FBI and the FDLE take charge.

As the two cars neared the crowded Daytona Beach area, Chandler led Willie Rooten straight down I-95, past the exits to the beaches and the Daytona International Speedway and the I-4 turnoff toward Orlando. At the Dunlawton Avenue exit, which would lead east into Port Orange, he pulled his blue Toyota Corolla into a corner gas station for fuel at about 6 P.M., and Rooten drove the Nissan into the carwash to get rid of the road grime.

Police pounced.

John Halliday of the Florida Department of Law Enforcement pulled his car into the station and immediately recognized Chandler from the photograph. The agent moved to the back of the car the suspect was filling with gasoline and told him he was under arrest. Chandler was surprised, but offered no resistance. Con men usually roll over pretty easily once the cops show up, but police knew Chandler not as a fast-talker, but as their prime suspect in a terrible triple murder. Taking no chances, they had pistols out and pointed at the startled Willie Rooten when he eased out of the carwash.

Chandler was told he was under arrest for a sexual battery charge. Wearing a blue and green pullover shirt and blue jeans, weary from the long drive, Chandler did not look to Detective Cindy Cummings much like the deadly charmer whom the FBI had profiled as able to take the lives of innocent people. In fact, she was disappointed at the suspect who had driven the St. Pete cops nuts for three years. This pudgy guy, who made her lose five pounds because of worry during the past few weeks, was no Superman. "He looked like just another dirtbag," she said.

Rooten was taken away and interrogated, put up at a motel overnight, then given bus money back to Kentucky.

The police loaded Chandler in the back of an unmarked car with Halliday driving and FBI agent Jim Ramey in the back seat with the suspect and hauled him back across the state to the Pinellas County Jail. Chandler already knew how the procedural world worked, and quickly withdrew his earlier permission to let police search his car. He also said he wanted a lawyer. After that, Chandler said nothing more that was important, although he chattered away as Halliday drove across Florida, telling the two officers that he was "guilty of a lot of things," such as rolling back the speedometers on cars.

They arrived at the large, dun-colored building several hours later and the FDLE and FBI agents escorted the handcuffed Chandler into the lockup about 11:40 P.M. The suspect did not like the idea that almost two dozen reporters and photographers were suddenly surrounding him, peeling away that veil of secrecy behind which he had lived for so long. As he passed one television cameraman, Chandler shouted curses and slugged him with an elbow.

Chandler was booked on the sexual battery charge

on May 15, 1989. A nine-page affidavit had been prepared to spell out the alleged crime, and the next morning, Judge Bob Barker set bail at an even one million dollars.

The following day, with Chandler finally in custody, the police moved in on his home armed with a search warrant. Debra and her child had been home when police apprehended her husband, and they swiftly escorted her to a motel in Daytona Beach. That was the beginning of what would become a long and rocky relationship between Debra Chandler and law enforcement authorities.

John Halliday, Cindy Cummings, J. J. Geoghegan, two other officers, and an identification technician approached the house with a specific shopping list. They saw an average house before them, not the lair of some monster. Toys were scattered in the yard and a piece of rope hung limply from a palm tree. But they knew that in that middle-class home had dwelled a man they believed was a multiple rapist and killer. They wanted to find the green mesh shirt the Canadian girl said was worn by the man who assaulted her, the Rogers' Nikon camera, and samples of Chandler's handwriting.

However, what they uncovered almost at the start of the search stopped them cold. Taking a description of what they discovered to a judge, they obtained a second warrant to search the place thoroughly for jewelry. A second search team, led by Jack Bislend of the FDLE and Gary Hitchcox from St. Petersburg, plunged into the house and garage the following day. As Jean Pounds, a criminal intelligence analyst, kept track of the booty on a laptop computer, the cops pulled out two trunks filled with jewelry, a kit that salesman George Eash used at shows, business cards, a briefcase, a booklet about diamond grading, an aluminum ruler, and tweezers of the sort used by jewelry experts. Rings and necklaces were found in the master bedroom. By the time they were done, the police team had recovered about $250,000 worth of jewelry that they suspected had been stolen. Pursuing one crime had solved another.

The first search team had also been successful. Not only did they find handwriting samples on a paper beneath a Nikon camera, but they also discovered videotapes of sex acts that included bondage and the bright green mesh shirt they had been hunting.

In Ohio, the *Lima News* ran the story large on September 25, beneath a banner headline that read "Floridian held in vacation killings." In the center were the three pictures of Jo, Michelle, and Christe. It said that the news had made its way through Crestview High School, where Christe would have been a junior that year. Around the farm area, faded yellow ribbons were still tied to some trees.

When Hal Rogers was notified of the arrest, he did not allow himself to be more than cautious. "I don't get too excited because I've gotten my hopes up too many times before," he said, adding, "I hope it is the guy. . . . It's been so damned long."

His reticence was understandable, but down in Florida, the investigators who had been haunted by the case for three long years were happy. They were sure they had the right guy. Not only was the hard evidence beginning to mount, but Oba Chandler was an almost perfect fit for the phantom killer described in the FBI profile. He was white, had worked in the area, was clean and neat, he was outwardly very nice, he liked to talk, he took care of his personal property. "I haven't seen anything that he doesn't fit," said Boomer Moore.

John Martin picked up the *St. Petersburg Times* and got a kick out of the story that Oba Chandler had been arrested. He telephoned Steve Segura and told him to look at the paper. Both men had been victims of Chandler's skullduggery in the 1991 marijuana bust, and were not the least bit upset that the snitch had been nailed for a big time crime, even if Martin was related to him.

Lula Harris, Chandler's sister, placed a telephone call to Cincinnati, Ohio, to talk to Kristal Mays.

"Are you sitting down?" Lula asked.

"No."

"Well, you better sit down. Your father's been arrested. He's in jail."

It was not a huge surprise for either woman.

Two days after Oba Chandler was arrested, police drove Debra Chandler back to St. Petersburg and booked her into the Pinellas County Jail, too. Oba's view of family life proved true once again.

In 1990, Chandler asked his wife, who was working for Alumco, to order some seven thousand dollars worth of aluminum for him to use in his business. The bill was never paid, although she wrote on company sales orders that her husband had paid her. So thirty-six-year-old Debra Chandler, bitter at her husband and furious with the police, was charged with grand theft but allowed to remain free upon a promise to show up for trial. The offense normally carried a price tag of twenty thousand dollars in bail, but prosecutors thought that by giving Debra a break on her first offense, she might help them on the case against her husband. It didn't work out that way.

Once Oba Chandler was in custody, new players entered the legal game, and the investigators who had been around for years changed tactics. The problem before the police now was to dig up every shred of information they could about the suspect in order to turn the case from sexual battery into a triple homicide. With the agreement of the Canadian women to testify, the prosecution felt comfortable that a conviction could be won on the rape charge, but that was not what they were after. They wanted Chandler for the murders of Jo, Michelle, and Christe Rogers. The sexual battery charge was a way station, not the final destination. "Our main emphasis was to get him off the street," said Boomer Moore.

As the news of the arrest spread, police in St. Petersburg began receiving telephone calls from other women in Ohio and throughout Florida who claimed that Chandler, or someone who looked like him, had befriended then attacked them, too, at some time in the past. Boomer Moore commented, "Apparently he did very well at making people feel at ease."

The police began building a "time line" on Chandler that would date back to his birth and bring them up to the present. Before it was complete, they had the profile of a youngster who skipped from problem to problem, a daring ex-convict with the wiles of a cat, a man who used and discarded his wives and children at whim, a liar, a thief, and most likely, a rapist and a murderer whose future probably would have been even blacker than his midnight-hued past, for there was no sign that Chandler was slowing down on his crime spree before he was arrested.

The legal battles began immediately when the Office of the Public Defender was notified to represent Chandler in his earliest hearing. Chandler's writ of insolvency, which was to clear the way for him to be represented at public expense, would not be approved by Judge Richard W. Carr until November 11, but the case was moving too fast to wait for the official paperwork to be filed with the clerk of court.

The prosecutors wanted to keep Chandler right where

he was, in the D-Wing of the Pinellas County Jail under the full-time protective watch of guards. They did not want Chandler hurting himself, nor did they want other inmates wreaking jailhouse vengeance upon him for the dreadful murders.

The task of providing the initial defense for the most notorious man in the county jail fell to Assistant Public Defender Ron Eide, a tall, muscular lawyer with a messy desk, a slight beard, and a razor-sharp mind. Born on the Jersey shore and a 1976 graduate of Rutgers University and then Stetson University Law School, his reputation was that of a hard-nosed, working-man kind of lawyer who reveled in the rough-and-tumble world of criminal courts. A child of the '60s, the idealistic Eide had landed in the PD office right after law school and was completing his fifteenth year on the job. Having served in Korea as an infantryman, Eide did not shy away from challenge.

He was the point man, but was backed up by his boss, David R. Parry, a dapper attorney who was Eide's exact opposite in many ways. Parry wore starched shirts and suspenders and was a clean-desk man with a neatly trimmed beard, a talent for smooth administration, and a dedication to representing the underdog. This "odd couple" of public defenders willingly stepped into the path of the prosecutorial freight train that was about to run over Oba Chandler. Both lawyers firmly believed in the Constitutional guarantees that are allowed defendants, neither was frightened of the people on the opposite sides of the courtroom, both knew they had many cards they could play and many investigative resources they could tap, and, anyway, they enjoyed a high-profile case.

Working in an office where first-degree felony murders, armed robberies, kidnappings, and other dreadful crimes steadily marched across their desks, the chance to work on a "big one" was enticing to everyone involved. "It was a challenge," Eide said. "It was the case of a lifetime.'' Thirty other first-degree murder cases were also in the pipeline when Chandler was arrested, but the pressure of events forced this one to the top of the stack.

Eide demonstrated immediately that he was up to the job, blistering the prosecution for wanting such a high bail set on his indigent client. After all, no matter that authorities might *think* Chandler was under arrest for the most heinous crime to hit St. Petersburg in years, no matter that he *might* be charged with something in the future, for the present he was actually only charged with sexual battery! That didn't merit a million-dollar bond. ''A million dollars? That doesn't make any sense,'' he said. ''A bond of a hundred thousand dollars on a sexual battery charge would be unusual. Remember, this guy is supposed to be presumed innocent.''

The shrewd Eide also turned the highly publicized victory of the police against them. ''This thing has been getting so hyped up for the last three years, it's been like the buildup to a big game. We're going to try this in a court of law, not in the media.'' On the side, he said that Boomer Moore ''was already starting to write his book.''

Eide didn't win the opening skirmish, and Chandler kept the million-dollar-bail figure, but the defense lawyer did have a smile on his face when he went home that night to his condominium in Pass-a-Grille, knowing he had tweaked the noses of a couple of his immediate neighbors who were also lawyers, and who worked in the office of the state attorney.

21

As hectic September came to an end, police had recovered the boat on which they believed the assaults had taken place against the Canadian victim as well as the Rogers family. It was not much to look at when compared with the hundreds of sleek craft that ply the state's waterways, for Chandler had bought it for only a hundred dollars from Wolfgang Roessel on Dalton Avenue on October 24, 1988, and later sold it for a profit on September 15, 1989—three months after the Rogers' deaths—when it became a liability, a potential link between himself and some very serious crimes. The 1976-model, blue and white Bayliner pleasure boat, twenty-one-feet-long, was put into storage so police could display it to potential witnesses and to allow the forensic experts to comb the boat from its pointed bow to the Volvo inboard-outboard engine in its flat stern. Officers were disappointed that, as the boat went through the hands of successive owners, changes and new paint had been added to alter its appearance. In an effort to pinpoint how it looked in 1989, they searched for photographs both in the Boat Trader magazine and in several photo albums that had been found by the searchers who combed Chandler's residence.

As for his houses, police discovered that a Chandler trademark seemed to be leaving his previous addresses in a mess. The Dalton Avenue home cost the new owner a substantial sum before the debris that the Chandlers had left behind was cleared. But an even more telling story, one that went to the violence of which the suspect was capable, emerged as cops tracked down Clyde Shelton, an Indiana resident who had rented a home to Chandler in Ormond Beach, just north of Daytona, for a short time. When Chandler failed to pay the rent, Shelton went to court and began eviction proceedings. In response, Chandler did two things. He decided to move from the house and take up residence in Port Orange, only a few miles away. Then he also went out and bought a hammer and smashed every marble windowsill in the house he had rented from Shelton and stole the horizontal blinds. A disgusted Shelton sued—and won—a $2,600 judgment, but was never paid because the destructive tenant vanished into thin air.

For police, it was like the old days. The telephone calls started coming in by six o'clock in the morning and continued until after midnight. Ramer of the FBI, Halliday from the FDLE, and a dozen St. Petersburg detectives and support staffers were running down the new load of leads, while at the same time putting together the incredible life story of Oba Chandler. A police bulletin was distributed nationwide to other law enforcement agencies and even more information flooded in. ''There's no end in sight,'' said a weary Cindy Cummings.

As far back as 1963, there was a possible link to Chandler and a Pinellas Park rape. The following year, there was a complaint filed that he was sexually involved with a young girl. Also, there was an attempted rape in Cincinnati in 1965, an arrest in 1971 in Cincinnati for masturbating while allegedly peeping into the windows of an apartment complex, an unreported rape in Daytona Beach in 1973, in which the victim said she kept his picture. On and on the allegations went. Two teenaged girls on a St. Pete beach said Chandler coaxed them off the sand and into his boat, made sexual advances, and returned them to the beach when they said their boyfriends had seen them get into the boat. The list of allegations grew to surprising dimensions and his public defender, Ron Eide, pointed out that the charge, at present, still remained the single sexual battery, no matter what the police and the press were saying. One night in the Eide home after the latest news bulletin linking Chandler with still some other crime, Eide's son, Jeep, cracked, "Gee, Dad, he looks like the guy who stole my bike."

Then the police uncovered a crime linked to Chandler that was certainly no laughing matter. The jewelry that had been found in the garage and house in Port Orange, plus the stolen jewelry that turned up in Ohio and Kentucky in the hands of people who said it came from Chandler, led authorities to formally file a charge of robbery with a firearm, in connection with the $750,000 heist in Pinellas Park only a few weeks before the arrest. Halliday of the FDLE went over to the county jail and re-arrested the inmate, and it was back to court. This time, Circuit Judge Richard Luce set a one-million-dollar bail on the robbery charge. "Seems to be the going rate," sniffed Eide, who noted the usual bail on such a crime more likely would have been about $25,000.

With their client now held in lieu of a two-million-dollar bail, Eide and Parry learned that police were also investigating the possibility that Chandler was involved with other murders, some not even in Florida. According to Eide, they were about to paint Chandler as a suspect in everything up to the assassination of President John Kennedy. In fact, the police did indeed view Oba Chandler as a very dangerous man, a veritable "killing machine," and the incredibly high bail set on a man who had legally declared himself a pauper meant that Chandler was going to stay in jail and not on the street.

As a precautionary measure, the defense lawyers went to court to obtain a ban on police discussing any of the other possible crimes with Chandler without his attorneys present. They didn't want the cops pumping him for information, in hopes of linking the prisoner to another case that might have some relevance to the pending charges—the rape and the robbery—and the triple-murder charge that was expected soon.

In effect, his lawyers were telling Oba Chandler to keep his mouth shut. He had done the proper thing for someone under arrest when he refused to speak without a lawyer present. Now they wanted him to maintain that silence, mindful that anything he said could be used against him.

Getting Oba Chandler to totally shut up was like trying to build a house out of Jell-O. It might be the correct shape, but would have no strength whatsoever. Chandler had spent a lifetime as a con man and his track record indicated he believed in his ability to talk himself into or out of anything. He obeyed the attorneys' instructions not to talk to the cops, but he simultaneously began a telephone campaign to family members, notably his daughter Kristal and her husband Rick, who could be damning witnesses against him. He also talked to fellow prisoners. His threatening bragging would return to haunt him when he went on trial for his life, and even then he wouldn't be able to shut up.

On the courtroom side of the story, Chandler filed an official plea of not guilty to the charges against him, even as the prosecution sought to have him declared a "career criminal" who should be tried for the existing charges with the possible penalty of a life sentence. If the prosecutors, for some reason, were unable to convict him on the murders, then with a career criminal label, they could still keep Chandler locked up tight.

Eide fought back hard, complaining to the court about both the pretrial publicity and the apparently unwillingness of the police to charge his client with murder while they were simultaneously fingering him to reporters as their chief suspect in the horrendous killings. "If they've got evidence on a triple homicide, then charge him," he said.

The background work by the police continued at a breakneck pace.

Law enforcement officials said the key link in their case was the match, proven by experts, of the handwriting and a palm print found on the Rogers' tourist brochure with Chandler's own writing style and prints. Eide countered that, even if it were true, it proved nothing beyond that his client may have met the Rogers women. The exchange of the document from his hand to theirs was not exactly a smoking gun that proved he killed anyone. Police knew they needed other evidence in the case, but were happy to be able to link the suspect in a firm way to the victims.

However, police had to endure a bit of embarrassment, too. First, they had to admit they had overlooked the importance of the brochure for months before beginning to focus on it as such an important piece of evidence. Second, they were red faced as the public learned that Oba Chandler—ensconced in jail under two-million-dollar bail—had served several federal and other police agencies as a confidential informant!

That was history, and as the police continued to dig, they came up with a couple of important facts:

They discovered that Chandler was involved in a one hundred-thousand-dollar jewel robbery in 1991, during which he used duct tape to bind the female victim.

And they heard Lula Harris, his sister, say in a deposition that Chandler saved newspaper clippings about the Rogers' deaths. Harris said Debra Chandler had also suspected his involvement and was scared because he was saving the stories. When Lula confronted Oba about it, she said he responded by saying, "Yeah, right, I killed those women," but soon retracted that by claiming, "I'm just bullshitting." Further, he had telephoned his sister shortly after his arrest and commented, "I didn't have nothing to do with those damn women."

In early November, the state's lawyers were ready to slap Chandler with official charges in the Rogers murders. A grand jury proceeding is a relatively friendly port for prosecutors, since the defense lawyers are not allowed inside the secret chamber to present opposing arguments. A grand jury impaneled in October was not given the Chandler case because prosecutors said they were not ready. By waiting the extra few weeks for the November panel to be sworn in, investigators tied up some loose ends that allowed the prosecutors the opportunity to present a solid case.

The guts of the presentation by the lawyers were affidavits from Detective Cindy Cummings, Detective Katy Connor-Dubina and Sergeant Glen Moore of the St. Petersburg Police Department, and Special Agent John Halliday of the Florida Department of Law Enforcement. The four cops spelled out in detail the numerous similarities between the rape of the Canadian student and the murders of the three Ohio tourists, that Gayle Arquette had picked Chandler out of a photo pack, and that Chandler, at the time of both crimes, owned the sort of dark four-wheel-drive vehicle and blue and white boat that had been identified by witnesses.

Then they stated, "Your Affiants believe the Rogers got lost as they arrived in Tampa and pulled onto Dale

Mabry off the Interstate where they met someone who gave them directions. Your Affiants further believe that this subject was Oba Chandler and that Chandler was the same suspect who they later met at the boat ramp and who kidnapped and murdered them.''

No one doubted that the grand jury response would be an indictment, which was required in a first-degree murder case, and it came out right on time, after less than three hours of consideration. It formally and finally accused Oba of committing the murders that rocked Tampa Bay on a summer's day in 1989.

INDICTMENT

IN THE CIRCUIT COURT FOR THE SIXTH JUDICIAL CIRCUIT OF FLORIDA, IN AND FOR PINELLAS COUNTY

Spring Term, in the year of our Lord one thousand nine hundred ninety-two

State of Florida vs. Oba Chandler

SPN 01360128

M/W; DOB: 10/11/46

SSN: 288-38-2664

IN THE NAME AND BY THE AUTHORITY FOR THE STATE OF FLORIDA:

The Grand Jurors of the State of Florida, impaneled and sworn to inquire and true charge make in and for the body of the County of Pinellas, upon their oath do charge that

OBA CHANDLER

on or between the 1st day of June and the 4th day of June, in the year of our Lord, one thousand nine hundred eighty-nine, in Pinellas County and Hillsborough County, in the State of Florida, did unlawfully and from a premeditated design to effect the death of Joan Rogers, a human being, inflict

homicidal violence upon and did asphyxiate Joan
Rogers, and by the means aforesaid and as a direct
result thereof, the said Joan Rogers died; contrary
to Chapter 782.04 (1) (a), Florida Statutes, and
against the peace and dignity of the State of Florida.

COUNT TWO

And the Grand Jurors of the State of Florida, impaneled and sworn to inquire and true charge make
in and for the body of the County of Pinellas, upon
their oath do charge that OBA CHANDLER, on or
between the 1st day of June and the 4th day of June,
in the year of our Lord, one thousand nine hundred
eighty-nine, in Pinellas County and Hillsborough
County, in the State of Florida, did unlawfully and
from a premeditated design to effect the death of
Michelle Rogers, a human being, inflict homicidal
violence upon and did asphyxiate Michelle Rogers,
and by the means aforesaid and as a direct result
thereof, the said Michelle Rogers died; contrary to
Chapter 782.04 (1) (a), Florida Statutes, and against
the peace and dignity of the State of Florida.

COUNT THREE

And the Grand Jurors of the State of Florida, impaneled and sworn to inquire and true charge make
in and for the body of the County of Pinellas, upon
their oath do charge that OBA CHANDLER, on or
between the 1st day of June and the 4th day of June,
in the year of our Lord, one thousand nine hundred
eighty-nine, in Pinellas County and Hillsborough
County, in the State of Florida, did unlawfully and
from a premeditated design to effect the death of
Christe Rogers, a human being, inflict homicidal
violence upon and did asphyxiate Christe Rogers,
and by the means aforesaid and as a direct result
thereof, the said Christe Rogers died; contrary to

Chapter 782.04 (1) (a), Florida Statutes, and against
the peace and dignity of the State of Florida.

His mother, Margaret Chandler, was shaken by the
news, telling the *St. Petersburg Times*, ''He didn't do that
murder. He didn't do it, I know he didn't. I never knowed
him to hurt a hair on anyone's head. . . . Lord knows that
isn't true.'' Her comment was indicative of the wedge
that Oba Chandler drove through his widespread family.
Many believed he was perfectly capable of doing the
crimes of which he was accused, and many others believed he was innocent. Few, if any, would change their
minds.

Circuit Court Judge Susan F. Schaeffer, a tough and
veteran jurist, drew the assignment to handle the Chandler case, and true to her reputation, wanted to put it on
a fast track. She set the robbery trial for June 15, 1993,
wanting to get it out of the way before starting the murder
trial, which would be much more complicated. Even
while she heard a plea of not guilty from Oba Chandler
and inked the murder case in to start on November 30,
1993, she acknowledged the public defenders' caution
that preparing the case might easily push the murder trial
back until 1994.

For while the police and prosecutors were quite familiar with the accumulated data in the Rogers' investigation, the defense team stared at the Wall with concern.
''It was a nightmare,'' said Eide. Each and every piece
of paper on those shelves, gathered through thousands of
police investigative hours, would have to be examined by
the defense team. The task would be daunting, to say the
least.

Schaeffer also dealt the defense a setback by agreeing
to a prosecution motion that would have Chandler appear
in a lineup in the sexual battery case. Parry argued that
Chandler's picture had been distributed nationwide by the

news media and that "everybody in the country" knew
what he looked like. The judge said Gayle Arquette
would have the opportunity to once again look at the man
she had known as Dave Posner, this time for the purpose
of locking him into a trial for raping her. Arquette flew
down for the lineup and pointed her finger straight at Oba
Chandler.

22

The year of 1993 began with Bernie McCabe becoming the new state attorney for the counties of Pinellas and Pasco, having been elected to replace his boss, James T. Russell, who had retired. One of the first items on his agenda was to shuffle his office staff and 114 lawyers. His choices would be critical, for it was within his power to change the positions of those prosecutors who had been heading the Arquette-Rogers-Chandler cases. To do so would risk major disruption.

McCabe stayed within the bounds of good sense. He appointed thirty-eight-year-old Bruce L. Bartlett, the lawyer who won the Chandler indictment, to be his executive assistant state attorney. And he left Doug Crow in his job of handling special prosecutions, which also carried the rank of executive assistant state attorney. If Oba Chandler was thinking his rocky road to justice might improve with some new prosecutors, he was disappointed, for all he got was another load of rocks. Bartlett and Crow remained as the point men, backed up by a whole team of other lawyers and special investigators.

Just across the bay, Lee Atkinson found himself out of a job on the first day of the new year. After a career that spanned twenty years of being both federal and state prosecutor, he discovered that he had finally hitched his wagon to the wrong star.

In the November elections, his boss, Hillsborough County State's Attorney Bill James, was beaten in a re-election bid by Harry Lee Coe, a former circuit judge. Unlike Bernie McCabe, who had gone for stability, the incoming top prosecutor for Hillsborough County chose to make at least one significant change in his staff.

When the new roster was complete, to the surprise of many, there was no room for Lee Atkinson. The aggressive prosecutor who had been the bane of serial killers and motorcycle gangs, fire bombers and the nude bar business—one club owner posted a sign designating Atkinson the ''Asshole of the Month''—the lawyer who dared to investigate a former state's attorney and prosecute white-collar bank fraud, was gone.

His fiery demeanor had been the stuff of legend, and his heavy cowboy boots pounding the courtroom floor in front of a jury were the sound of doom to felons, for Lee Atkinson did not lose many cases. ''There are people who think the devil sent me to Tampa to disrupt society,'' he told one reporter. But now the pit bull prosecutor was relegated to the dog pound.

Immediately after the election, Atkinson began sending out resumes to private law firms and his former employer, the federal government. The response was almost total silence. The hottest prosecutor in Hillsborough County retired himself in January to train horses on his ranch, wondering just what the hell went wrong in his life.

The necessarily vague legal wording in the murder indictments against Chandler forced a problem to the surface. It wasn't large, but it was big enough to unsettle the smooth flow of the case toward trial, because Judge Schaeffer had to deal with the possibility that the crime could have been committed in Pinellas County *and* Hillsborough County. Huge costs would be involved in preparing for a trial in Pinellas, where the bodies were discovered, and, at the last minute, Chandler might have the right to say he wanted to be tried on the Tampa side of the bay, in Hillsborough. She directed the lawyers to study precedents and get back to her. Chief Assistant Public Defender Parry knew an opening when he saw one. He said that it was much too early for the defendant to make that choice. Suddenly, having the trial held in Pinellas County no longer looked like such a sure thing.

The defense had a new ace in its hand. In the county courts building, the public defenders' offices are located on the first floor and the state's attorneys are directly above them on the second floor. The boys downstairs weren't about to give Doug Crow and Bruce Bartlett a break.

Then, out of the blue, it was learned that Eide and Parry would not be around to make the decision on location. The case was jerked out of their hands.

Oba Chandler's motormouth caused the change. He started bragging in jail about the murder, the rape, and the robbery cases, apparently not realizing that the men to whom he was talking were also prisoners who could perhaps use the information he was spewing to their own advantage.

Several of them contacted prosecutors and said they wanted to cooperate by giving testimony against Chandler. The catch was that those prisoners were also indigent and represented by the Office of the Public Defender. Since the public defender could not simultaneously represent the prison snitches and Oba Chandler, because the snitch might have to appear in court to testify on the charges against Chandler, something had to give.

On March 4, Eide and Parry appeared before Judge Schaeffer and said they were faced with "an ethical conflict . . . which precludes the further representation of the defendant.'' With that cryptic remark, they retired to the sideline, having to give up the exciting case that both of them had badly wanted to handle in the courtroom.

Chandler, therefore, was temporarily without legal representation to which he was guaranteed under law. Since that particular problem had arisen before with the public defenders, the court was ready with a backup plan. Instead of being defended by the state's lawyers, he would be handed over to a private attorney, who would be paid by the state to handle the case.

Criminal Administrative Judge Brandt Downey turned the controversial case over to Tom McCoun III, a highly regarded St. Petersburg lawyer with a reputation for good defense work on capital crimes, and McCoun would be allowed to hire a second lawyer to assist him.

The forty-two-year-old McCoun, a former prosecutor, was a Miami native who began living in St. Petersburg in 1974. A graduate of Georgia Tech and the Stetson College of Law, he had worked as an attorney for sixteen years, earning a reputation as a methodical researcher, and who was more than competent in the courtroom. McCoun was also ambitious, and only the previous November had narrowly lost a race to become a circuit judge, coming in second in a field of fifteen.

Even with his experience and reputation, the work involved in representing Oba Chandler presented a massive task. The public defenders had already been on the job for six months and now the new defense team would have to start from scratch. The Wall, containing thousands of documents, challenged McCoun and his co-counsel, Bob Dillinger. McCoun warned Judge Schaeffer that it might require at least a year for them to prepare for trial, which meant the November opening date was clearly in jeopardy.

*   *   *

That "ethical conflict" that cashiered Parry and Eide out of the case took on a more understandable form when court records outlined prison conversations that Chandler had with an anonymous inmate, who gave it all to law enforcement authorities.

"The things that went on on that boat were downright sickening," the thirty-two-year-old inmate told *Tampa Tribune* reporter William Yelverton. The prisoner, who at one time shared a cell with Chandler, said the accused killer chain-smoked and talked away for hours during the nights. "He was lonely, scared, and looking for someone to confide in," he said of Chandler.

The big surprise was that the informant claimed Chandler told him there was a second killer involved, another man on the boat. According to the informant, Chandler said the Rogers women had gotten lost and asked him for directions, saying they wanted to take a boat ride in order to snap some pictures of the Sunshine Skyway Bridge, an artistic span that serves as the southern entrance to Pinellas County. He said he would tell the court that as a contractor who roamed widely, he often gave directions to strangers.

Chandler told the informant he wrote directions to a shopping mall and to the boat ramp, where he and another man linked up with the family later that day.

The inmate related that Chandler said he struck Jo Rogers on the head with a blunt object, but did not sexually assault her, then raped and sodomized the daughters, Michelle and Christe. The second man helped Chandler tie the three women and throw them into the bay.

The prisoner who was talking to prosecutors said Chandler had removed the bloody carpet from the deck of the boat and dumped it along a lonely dirt road in Tampa. Finally the inmate said Chandler threatened him and his family if he ever talked about their conversations.

From that interview with a newspaper reporter, it was obvious that Chandler was talking to other prisoners, and by the time the trial rolled around, a significant number of them were willing to testify against him. The words of men serving jail terms normally do not carry much weight with a jury, but a story repeated over and over does, no matter who the audience.

McCoun and his assistants were getting a handle on the complex murder case, and at a monthly conference for all parties, Judge Schaeffer told the defense lawyer she wanted a decision soon from Chandler on where he wanted to stand trial. She estimated that it was going to cost Pinellas County about a hundred thousand dollars to defend Chandler, money that might not need to be spent if the case shifted to Tampa, where Hillsborough County might have to pay. Further, if the case went to Hillsborough County, a public defender there could pick up the defense of Chandler, saving Pinellas dollars not only in court costs, but in not having to pay for the expensive presence of McCoun. The decision to change would also impact whether Pinellas or Hillsborough would prosecute.

A newly passed state law allowed for judge, prosecutors, and defense counsel to follow a case that changes location, but no one yet had made use of that statute. The Chandler case would be the unprecedented first.

McCoun replied that there was no question in his mind that a change of venue would be sought, meaning the prisoner and the trial would probably shift elsewhere. However, he did not specify Tampa, which indicated he might be looking elsewhere in the state—perhaps Miami, Jacksonville, or Orlando. The judge gave them one more month to reach a decision, setting a deadline of June 30.

In a related matter, McCoun and Dillinger won a delay in the Pinellas Park robbery trial, saying they were simply not yet finished reviewing the documents and conducting interviews. The weight of the three-year investigation was bogging down the newcomers on the block.

Schaeffer grudgingly pushed the robbery trial back until August 17 and the murder trial date to November 30. Soon thereafter, another judge gave McCoun the green light to spend whatever Pinellas County funds he felt necessary in preparing the defense for the robbery charge. The cash register was beginning to strain in the defense of Oba Chandler on the least of the charges facing him. At that point, no upper limit could be estimated on how much all of the cases would cost before conclusion. "This is one of those cases—whether they like it or not—that there is not going to be any caps on spending," the attorney said.

The decision on whether to change venue came just before Schaeffer's deadline, and Chandler had his lawyers announce that he wanted to be tried across the bay, in Tampa. Citing his constitutional right to silence, he did not explain his decision. During the hearing, Schaeffer telephoned the Chief Circuit Judge in Hillsborough County, F. Dennis Alvarez, to say the prisoner was shifting jurisdictions for the murder trial. McCoun hinted that he had some other ideas, however, dodging the question of whether the trial still might be moved to some place other than Tampa, because the pretrial publicity had blanketed Tampa as well as St. Petersburg. How could there be anyone in that county to serve as an impartial juror when the newspapers and television stations had been covering the case so heavily for the past three years?

The administrative twists and turns were becoming extraordinarily confusing. Schaeffer turned down Chandler's request to keep McCoun and Dillinger as his lawyers, and said that with the change of venue, he could be represented by Public Defender Julianne Holt, who had already met with him and the current defense team.

"Once he gets lawyers in Hillsborough County, don't bill us for any more services, because you won't get paid," she said.

McCoun also said he thought Chandler should be able to keep his current defense team.

"We're happy to allow you to represent Mr. Chandler, assuming Ms. Holt wants you and you want to do it pro bono," the judge said. "I'm just telling you the taxpayers are not going to pay for that."

The decision on whether the prosecutors Bruce Bartlett and Doug Crow could follow Chandler across the causeway was cleared by Harry Lee Coe, the new Hillsborough state attorney. That guaranteed that a new prosecution team would not have to start from scratch, as would the Hillsborough public defender.

So Chandler returned to his cell with the turf change as a minor, hollow victory.

Not only was he risking the loss of his private attorneys, but during the same hearing, the nonchalant prisoner, clad in a prison uniform and Reebok sneakers, entered a plea of no contest to the charge of robbery with a firearm. Schaeffer had sentenced him to fifteen years in prison for the $750,000 Pinellas Park jewel robbery. According to prosecutor Bob Lewis, some $225,000 worth of loot had been recovered by authorities, less than half the amount that was stolen.

The conviction meant the controversial bail figures were no longer important. Since Chandler used a gun in the robbery, he would have to serve a minimum of three years, and it was unlikely he would be getting any break for good behavior. Barring an escape, Chandler would be around for the upcoming sexual battery and murder trials.

23

Judge Schaeffer modified her ruling on the site shift for the trial a short time later, saying the new law would indeed allow all of the current players, including herself and Chandler's lawyers, to follow the case to Tampa. Meanwhile, the Hillsborough Public Defender Julianne Holt researched the new venue change law and said her office did not have to take the case. So not only would the original teams stay in place, the price for defending him shifted back to Pinellas. Hillsborough, by reading the law carefully, dodged a one-hundred-thousand-dollar bullet.

Schaeffer, however, had some words of warning for the defendant, who might have been thinking he was getting a good deal with the change in cities. Recently published statistics showed that Hillsborough County juries had sent thirty-four people to the electric chair, ranking only second in the state to the fifty prisoners sentenced to death by juries in Miami's Dade County. After Hillsborough came Duval county (Jacksonville) with thirty, Broward County with twenty-three and only then, in fifth place, came Pinellas, with twenty-one prisoners on death row. With his choice of moving to Tampa, Chandler may have moved closer to the electric chair.

* * *

But move he did. And in only a few months he was
pleading with the court to let him return to Pinellas.
Schaeffer was unimpressed and media columnists had a
field day that the accused triple-murderer was not happy.

Chandler's lawyers notified Cal Henderson, the sheriff
of Hillsborough County, that their client was kept in isolation, shackled when moved, denied visitation rights,
could not reach his attorneys at reasonable times, and was
not allowed to watch television like other inmates. In St.
Petersburg, during his ten months of incarceration, he had
been allowed to mingle with other inmates, talk, play
cards, and watch TV. This mistreatment, the lawyers declared, was a violation of the prisoner's rights and could
subject the jail officials to lawsuits for "unconstitutional
and illegal confinement."

Major Steve Saunders, a ranking corrections officer,
fired back, denying most of the claims and noting that
Chandler was being held in tight custody for a couple of
reasons. One, other inmates had threatened to kill him if
they had the chance. Two, he had already escaped from
prison once in his career and Hillsborough wasn't about
to give him a second chance. "We consider him a very
high security risk, a very high escape risk. We're re-
sponding in that manner," declared Saunders, clearly unimpressed with either the prisoner's complaints or the
accompanying legal threat. And, he said, Chandler could
watch television like any other inmate.

Daniel Ruth, a columnist with the *Tampa Tribune*,
knew a good story when he saw one. His piece on August
26 skewered the man accused of three heinous murders:

Oba Chandler is upset.
OK, everybody now:
Awwwwwwww, poor snookums.

Ruth went on to write that "those big meanies over there at the jail" have caused "Good Time Oba" to become upset through such barbarian acts as not allowing him to watch TV when he wanted or to shower with other inmates.

"Oh pooh! A shower? Like it would really do any good?"

"Yeah. Yeah. He's only a suspect," added *Tribune* columnist Neil Cote. "He's not to be convicted of gagging, binding, and tossing three Ohioans into Tampa Bay a few years ago. . . . Innocent until proven guilty.

"Keep him in the Hillsborough slammer. The folks who run that place must be doing something right, as long as Oba and his attorney—failed Pinellas judicial candidate Tom McCoun—keep whining about how his constitutional rights are being flushed down the toilet."

Their sarcasm summed up the general feeling of Tampa Bay residents about the often-arrested felon complaining about his living conditions as he faced a triple-murder rap. The road in Hillsborough County was proving rougher than Chandler anticipated.

He got confirmation a short time later, when Schaeffer held the first Tampa conference on the case and ordered that the prisoner would stay right where he was. After being rebuffed on a shift back to Pinellas, the defense asked for him to be placed in a state facility. No, ruled Schaeffer, apparently growing tired of Chandler's complaints. "I have little enough control here in Hillsborough. I have absolutely zip control in (the state prison at) Starke," she said. McCoun also wanted a subpoena to interview jail officials concerning Chandler's treatment. She responded she had no intention of meddling with jail operations.

McCoun made a more successful pitch to have the trial set back, noting that he still had to interview literally hundreds of witnesses and examine ten thousand documents. He wanted three thousand dollars to hire an investigator and asked that the trial date be put off for a full year. Schaeffer trimmed the delay to nine months. She said that McCoun could ask for an extension, if necessary, closer to the new trial date in May.

That entire episode would soon become a moot point, for although no one knew it at the time, defense lawyer Tom McCoun was about to exit the Oba Chandler case in rather dramatic fashion.

Investigators tracking the movements of Oba Chandler prior to his arrest linked him with a couple of significant crimes in 1991, a robbery and a rape attempt in the Daytona area, both of which could be related to the triple murder in Pinellas County and the Madeira Beach rape. In both east coast cases, silver duct tape was used to bind the victims, just as in the St. Petersburg cases.

Police found the fifteen-year-old Daytona Beach girl who had reported that a man stopped her on the street, hauled her into a van and tied her ankles and wrists with duct tape. When she screamed for help, he pasted another strip of tape over her mouth, then after fondling her, began driving the van away. The frightened teenager managed to break free of the tape and jump from the moving vehicle, breaking a foot when she jumped. When she was shown a picture of Chandler, officers said she gave a positive response.

More importantly, the investigators made Chandler the primary suspect in the March 31, 1991, Daytona Shores robbery, in which he and an accomplice had kicked in the door of an apartment, assaulted the man and his wife who were inside, robbed them of a substantial amount of jewelry, and molested the woman, who had been bound with silver duct tape. Prosecutor Doug Crow in Pinellas County said the duct tape bore the fingerprints of none other than Oba Chandler.

Debra Chandler noted with irony that the Daytona

Shores robbery happened on her birthday, but she did not dwell on the fact. She did not really have time to worry much about her husband's plight in Daytona or Tampa or Pinellas County or anywhere else. She was having enough trouble of her own.

Accused of stealing about seven thousand dollars' worth of aluminum, the thirty-seven-year-old woman had entered a not guilty plea after her arrest, and faced a court hearing on four counts of grand theft. As a mother, there was no doubt that she was going to be dealt with leniently in the courts for the first offense, nonviolent crime of which she was accused. Her story that she shipped the aluminum to her husband indicated that he masterminded the shady deal, leaving her dangling as an accomplice. Chandler was never charged in that theft.

In September, through a court-appointed attorney, she entered a plea of no contest to the charges. Judge Craig Villanti ordered her to pay $7,593 back to her former employer in monthly payments of a hundred dollars, and placed her on three years' probation. Because it was her first offense, he also decided not to make the guilty verdict formal, which meant that Debra could legally say that she had never been convicted of a crime.

The prosecution still had hopes of persuading her to breach spousal confidentiality—and assist them in the case against her husband—but she wasn't buying into that deal. They could not even win her over by deciding not to charge her as an accessory to the Pinellas Park jewel heist, in which she had admitted driving the getaway car. Further, they also had not charged her with avoiding arrest through the use of fake names, although police searching for her had once mistakenly arrested a woman whose real name matched one of the aliases allegedly used by Debra Chandler.

Her answers to police and attorneys for the state would remain terse and subject to change throughout the inves-

tigation, and she would claim that police had been con-
sistently insensitive when dealing with her.

"Sergeant (Glen) Moore came to the apartment where
they had me and told me right in front of my daughter
that I was going to jail, never to see Whitney anymore,"
she said in a deposition. "She started crying hysterically,
clinging to me. They had to physically take her off of
me. . . . (The police) told me if I didn't answer the questions the right way, I was going to jail and I would never
see Whitney."

Her steadfast reluctance to assist law enforcement was
plainly shown during a later deposition in which she
sparred with Doug Crow, who was trying to determine
what she knew about her husband's movements on the
day of the Madeira Beach rape. He might as well have
been trying to chisel rock with a toothpick.

Q: Do you recall the events of May 15, 1989, at all?
A: No.

Q: Do you recall whether you were at home or not?
A: No.

Q: Do you recall whether your husband was home or
not?

A: I don't recall.

Q: Do you recall whether your husband was out all
night or not?

A: I don't recall.

Q: You can't tell us whether he was at home or out at
any point during the evening, night time or early morning
hours of May 15?

A: I don't recall.

Q: So you can't testify that he was or was not at home?
A: I don't remember.

Q: You don't remember whether you can testify to that
or you can't testify to that?

A: I don't remember if he was at home or not.

Q: So you can't testify if he was home?

A: I don't remember if he was home.

Q: You can't testify if he was home?

A: I don't remember if he was home.

Q: You don't choose to answer any questions?

Debra's lawyer interrupted the deposition, saying, "I think she's answered the questions. I'm going to object to that. As far as I'm concerned, she said she can't remember. If you choose to characterize her as not answering the question, that's up to you. As far as I'm concerned, it's been answered."

Crow: Are you going to answer the question?

Debra: I can't remember.

She may have outsmarted herself with her reluctance. By stonewalling, she had given the prosecutors a golden ruble, because the wife was unable to provide an alibi for her husband.

As the Rogers murder case against Oba Chandler seemed to be clearing away the legal debris and heading toward trial, possibly as early as May 1994, it again came to a jarring halt.

In late September 1993, Thomas McCoun III, who had sought delays almost from the first day he was on the case, brought it all back to the starting line through no fault of his own.

An unexpected opening had come in the judicial ranks, in the form of an empty slot for a federal magistrate for the Middle District of Florida, based in Tampa. A panel of judges had interviewed five candidates for the job and announced that their top choice was Peter Grilli, a veteran Tampa attorney. That had seemed to take care of the position, until Grilli self-destructed by admitting that he had used marijuana twenty years earlier.

Suddenly, Grilli was out and McCoun was appointed to replace him, finally giving McCoun the black judge's robe for which he had been campaigning. When McCoun went off to begin an eight-year term with an annual salary

of $122,912, he left behind a rather large piece of unfin-
ished business.

Oba Chandler, accused of the foul murders of the Ohio
family, was once again without a defense lawyer.

More than four years had elapsed since the Rogerses
were slaughtered, and Chandler, charged with the crime,
had been in jail for exactly two years awaiting trial. Now
with a new lawyer needed, someone who would have to
start from scratch on the case and deal with the thousands
of secrets imbedded in the Wall, the prospect of bringing
the case to resolution faded like paint in the hot Florida
sun.

24

Oba Chandler

Every October, the legal eagles in Pinellas County gather in St. Petersburg for an elite conference known in the trade as the Top Gun Seminar, in which prosecutors, criminal defense lawyers, public defenders, and judges get together to brainstorm the latest procedural developments in their profession. Judge Susan Schaeffer had been a headline speaker at the first Top Gun, and as she reached for the telephone in late September to find a new lawyer for Oba Chandler, she realized that the conference was right around the corner.

The Top Gun chairman for 1994 would be Fred Zinober, since the conference was his creation, and Schaeffer knew that what she was about to do would throw his plans into disarray. But for the judge trying to get Oba Chandler to trial, there was no choice. The public defenders were history, McCoun was out, and his co-counsel, Bob Dillinger, who would have handled the defense during the penalty phase of the trial, said he was also signing off because the county only paid fifty bucks an hour, a ridiculously low sum in a complex death penalty case. Even paralegals made sixty an hour!

Schaeffer had to be careful in choosing a new lawyer, for the last thing the judge wanted was for the Chandler

trial to grind to a halt again a few months down the road.
A lawyer working alone in private practice could not be
chosen, because the financial burden would be crushing.
Instead, she wanted an experienced attorney who worked
with a large firm, so the firm's other clients could offset
the lack of dollars from the county and the lawyer would
not go bankrupt while performing a public assignment.
Even the departing Tom McCoun envisioned at least a
thousand hours being expended on the case.

She discussed the dilemma with other judges and they
came up with a name—Zinober. He had the experience.
He was a partner in a large and busy law firm. Schaeffer
dialed the phone and gave him the good news: You're it.

Zinober weighed the options and it was clear from the
start that there was no logical way he should take the
Chandler case. There was the Top Gun seminar coming
up in a month, he had been putting in an incredible
amount of time on a tangled commercial case, the partners were interviewing candidates for a specialized position in the company, and he, his wife Dala, and their
three kids were getting ready to move into a new house
on Homeport Drive. Also, he felt the same about the fifty-
dollar-an-hour fee as Dillinger. His reluctance had nothing to do with whether or not Oba Chandler was guilty.
The logic was simply overwhelming; for him to take on
such a burdensome case would make no sense whatever.

Sometimes, however, defense lawyers just cannot help
themselves. Wave a good murder case at them, let them
know they will be going against the best lawyers in the
system, that the case is impossible and the pay is low.
Schaeffer was well aware that Zinober could not walk
away from a challenge. Any man that gets up at dawn to
exercise as a triathlete before going to work must consider himself rather invincible, she reasoned. Therefore,
knowing Zinober would realize the deck was stacked

against him, that even Superlawyer probably couldn't pull this one off, the judge reeled him in like a fish.

Through the process of elimination, the indigent and veteran criminal, Oba Chandler, had bounced from the care of the best lawyers in the public defender's office onto the desk of a lawyer who was so good that he was becoming a judge and finally into the hands of one of the finest defense lawyers in private practice in Florida. A reputable person facing a charge would probably have had a hard time paying the bills of the lawyers involved in the Chandler case, and in his wildest dreams, Chandler would have never envisioned the lengths that the public, which he had terrorized for a lifetime, would go to in order to insure him a fair trial.

The irony was once again heavy. In court, Zinober would be facing Crow, who had been head of special prosecutions during the four years that Zinober had been an assistant prosecutor. And as a prosecutor, Zinober had frequently found himself paired against Ron Eide, the public defender whose celebrated case he was now inheriting.

The news that Fred Zinober was taking the Chandler case spread rapidly in the legal community, but it was a minor ripple in the ocean of gossip surrounding the case compared to Zinober's first two orders of business. No one held it against Zinober that he was taking the case, since they realized that everyone is entitled to a defense. Somebody had to do it.

On the matter of money, Schaeffer and the county worked out a contract that would pay Zinober a flat fee of one hundred thousand dollars. Although that amount looked like a lot to a layman, the authorities knew that the hours required on the Chandler case—as evidenced by the lawyers who had come before Zinober—probably would make it a bargain by the time it was all done. Indeed, there was no question that the Clearwater law firm of Tew, Zinober, Barnes, Zimmet, & Unice could have earned more through Zinober's labors during the time in question by having him continue to handle the profitable practice of real estate and business disputes.

Zinober started earning his fee immediately. Having just been handed the deck, he dealt an ace of spades, face up, and made the state flinch.

In November, Lee Atkinson, the high stakes Tampa ex-prosecutor turned rancher, finally found a new job as a lawyer for the state Department of Health and Rehabilitative Services. Not exactly the high profile that he had enjoyed for the past two decades in Hillsborough County, but it was at least a steady paycheck. He had interviewed with thirty-five law firms and only four were even mildly interested, and a job was a job. The rugged Atkinson had already had a good dose of humility and knew a scrapbook full of headlines didn't pay the mortgage.

Only a week after taking the federal job, a new offer came his way, and Atkinson hurried away from the bureaucracy as fast as he could. He accepted a position as a real estate and commercial transactions attorney with a Clearwater law firm—Tew, Zinober, Barnes, Zimmet, & Unice. The former prosecutor who had piloted the Hillsborough County law enforcement team in the multi-agency conference in the first days of the investigation of the Rogers' murders would work just down the hall from Zinober, the attorney who had been hired by the state to defend the man accused of murdering the three Ohio tourists.

Zinober wasted no time in attempting to tie the talented Atkinson into a more direct role in the case. He had Chandler sign a waiver that it was okay by him to have Atkinson on the defense team, promised the state the addition of Atkinson as co-counsel would not run the bill up higher and filed a motion to allow Atkinson to be his defense co-counsel in the case, because "we are facing pretty significant odds."

The maneuver took the Pinellas prosecutorial team by surprise, but lit up the interest of other lawyers who would gladly trade a hefty personal injury fee for the chance to see Bruce Bartlett and Doug Crow go *mano-a-mano* with Fred Zinober and Lee Atkinson, with Susan Schaeffer cracking the whip in the county's most celebrated criminal trial of the decade. It would be a Top Gun conference in a real-life courtroom setting. "Where do I get tickets?" laughed one attorney. "I'm going to be on the front row."

Bartlett and Crow responded immediately. The Pinellas prosecutors had no intention of letting Atkinson's courtroom talent enter this felony murder case. They pointed out to Judge Schaeffer that Atkinson had played an important role in the early part of the investigation and if something came up to show a conflict of interest, it could taint Zinober's entire representation and might force still another change of defense lawyers.

Furthermore, they argued, Atkinson did not meet a rather antique state law that required him to have been a defense lawyer for three years in order to be qualified to represent a murder defendant in a death penalty case. The idea that Lee Atkinson, of all people, would not be qualified to assist in a murder case was ludicrous, but the law was quite clear.

Schaeffer eventually shot down Zinober's request for Atkinson to join the defense team, agreeing that a conflict of interest might be apparent to the public. She also upheld the law that Atkinson, who had spent twenty years as a prosecutor, wasn't up to the standards required of court-ordered defense lawyers because he had not spent three years in that role. During the Chandler trial, Atkinson, whose expertise was criminal trials, would remain on the sidelines.

Although successful in torpedoing Atkinson, the prosecutors, interestingly enough, had not objected earlier on
the grounds of conflict when one of the St. Petersburg
detectives who worked on the early stages of the Rogers
case turned up, after retirement, as an investigator for the
public defender's office when it was representing Chandler.

Schaeffer also acknowledged the inevitable, that the
scheduled May 1994 start date for the Chandler trial was
no longer possible. It would be more likely, she said, for
the trial to take place a year from now—September 12,
1994. Maybe.

As Fred Zinober began chipping away at the tens of
thousands of documents lining the Wall, time did not
stop.

Chandler was moving again, heading under guard back
to Volusia County for a one-day arraignment on the
charges connected with the Daytona Shores robbery. Police there had released information that matched remarkably with Chandler's preferred methods of operation. One
victim was bound with duct tape and plastic wire ties,
and Chandler's fingerprints were lifted from the tape. In
court in Daytona Beach, Chandler entered a plea of not
guilty, but the judge in that case decided not to set an
immediate trial date, pending the outcome of the triple-
murder case in Tampa. After the brief round-trip across
Florida, Chandler was brought back to his detested private cell in Hillsborough County. The hearing had taken
all of two minutes. Oba Chandler, facing so many
charges in so many places, was single-handedly clogging
the court system.

The ongoing delay in the case, however, was not necessarily working to Chandler's benefit, for it allowed police
and state investigators more time to conduct interviews,

hunt for inconsistencies in his statements, track his life-time of crime, plug holes, and generally solidify the evidence.

One thing that had not changed was that he would be tried on circumstantial evidence—there were no eyewitnesses to the crimes with which he was charged, and no one was able to stand up in court to testify even that he had been out on the water the night the three Rogers women had been killed.

The prosecutors had a lot of evidence, but as Zinober said as 1993 came to a close, "They still didn't have the Silver Bullet."

25

One crucial element of the Chandler trial was that it was a capital case, in which the defendant, if declared guilty by the jury, could face the ultimate penalty under law—execution by the state of Florida in the electric chair.

Therefore, in compiling the defense of Oba Chandler, Fred Zinober opened a secondary front: He launched an assault on Florida's death penalty statutes. If he could overturn those controversial laws, then even if his client was convicted, the maximum sentence would be life in prison instead of a possible death by electrocution.

There is no doubt that the actual process of execution is horrid, and Zinober filed with the court an extraordinary document that was published by the *Tallahassee Democrat* on September 25, 1977, that gave readers a step-by-step, macabre description of an electrocution.

Sometime after dawn on the condemned man's last day, the hair will be shaved from his right calf. A priest or minister will be with him. The Bible will be read and there will be prayer.

A clear, greasy substance will be smeared on the top and back of his scalp. The ointment looks like petroleum jelly. Its purpose is to help conduct electricity and reduce the burning of human flesh.

The prisoner will be told it is time to go. Most men walk to their death, quietly and without a struggle. Some cry. Some have to be helped.

The writer described how guards quickly place the man in the chair and buckle a two-inch-wide strap across the chest and upper arms, attach another over the lap, and buckle one more on each arm and leg.

The electrician's assistant will buckle a crude device to the right calf. This is a wide strap lined with a thin sheet of lead that has a screw protruding from it. A wire will be bolted to the screw.

Then the electrician will retrieve the sponge from the bucket. The salt water had made it an efficient conductor of electricity. He will squeeze it out and prepare the death cap. Onto that sponge is sewn a piece of heavy copper wire mesh. To that is welded another screw.

When the condemned man has been prepared, there is a final check to see if the governor has issued a last-minute pardon, and if not, then the signal is given.

This is the final moment in a ritual that began when the man in the chair broke the law, once or many times, was caught and convicted and could show no defect in his passage through the American system of justice.

The costs to this point come to millions. Police, lawyers, courts, prisons, mountains of paper and years, all leading to this moment when the man sits there in darkness, waiting.

The automated machine can produce three thousand volts, which is the force behind the current, and twenty amps, the current that actually will do the damage. The executioner, who is paid $150 for his work, watches for the signal, and when it is given, he turns the switch to the left. "There is a loud click which the dying man never hears," the newspaper stated.

The powerful equipment surges through four cycles, beginning at 2,250 volts and cycling down to six hundred, during the next two and a half minutes.

The body will lurch upward and backward. It will stiffen and tremble in convulsions. The arms and legs and chest will strain at the straps as the muscles contract tighter than they ever have before.

Muscle tissue will break, and the body will bleed inside. The massive jolt will explode the mind, and the temperature of the brain will rise.

Then the power will cycle down to 600 volts. The muscles will relax and the body will sag slightly. Then the power goes up again and the violent convulsions return. Then it sags again. This goes on for four cycles, for more than two minutes.

To avoid the skin burning, the newspaper reports that giving the man a lot of liquids before the execution allows it to proceed more smoothly.

Sometimes the man in the black mask is signaled to turn the machine off early if the skin begins to burn too much. Always there is burned flesh. The stench in the death chamber is sickening.

Steam rises from the wet sponge within the death cap, and usually white smoke is given off by the scorching of human flesh. A large blister usually forms on the head.

The heart usually stops immediately. A doctor steps forward and listens and pronounces the man dead. But the heart doesn't always stop immediately.

At times, it has been necessary to reset the machine, flip the switch again and send a second jolt to stop the heart. Almost invariably, when the mask is removed, the man's eyes are found to be open.

The astonishing account ended by noting that the electricity required to execute a man actually only costs three or four cents. A veteran court clerk in St. Petersburg read the document with amazement. "I had no idea," he whispered.

The legal pleadings that surrounded that motion would be voluminous but would bring no relief. The death penalty would stand in the Oba Chandler case, lurking like a dark curtain behind the legal civilities that were unfolding in the courts.

Prosecutors brushed aside the attack on the death penalty as legal boilerplate, a routine motion that was attempted in every first-degree murder case. St. Petersburg police agreed that what happened on the morning of an execution, as described by the Tallahassee newspaper, was a deadly and awful thing. However, in their view, it was mild in comparison to the vicious sexual assault of three members of a tourist family, the tying of concrete blocks around their necks and dumping them into Tampa Bay. One officer would later say he wished the punishment could not only match the crime in this case, but replicate it. He wanted to take a fully alert Oba Chandler out in a motorboat, tie him up, slap duct tape over his mouth, and toss him, alive, into the dark water of Tampa Bay to slowly drown in panic.

As the trial began to take shape in early 1994, Judge Schaeffer had to make a major decision. Since the Rogers murders had been the subject of massive amounts of media attention in the Tampa Bay area, she could not brush aside the proposition made by Zinober to have the trial moved to some other city because of pretrial publicity.

In his motion, Zinober claimed that everyone in the Tampa Bay area was familiar with both the crime and the lengthy manhunt that followed, and any potential juror already possessed "an infected state of mind against the defendant." Zinober contended that the police had actually used the media as an investigative tool and that national television broadcasts about the murders had inflamed the local community to the point where his client could not obtain a fair trial.

That the area had been drenched by publicity about the deaths over the years was undeniable, thus opening the possibility of still another move for the case—from Pinellas where Chandler had been charged, to Hillsborough where he had chosen to stand trial, and, now, to some other location yet to be determined.

A new law passed by the legislature in Tallahassee promised some relief in this difficult course to bring Chandler into a courtroom. It originated with another Tampa area crime, in which two men were charged with setting a New York tourist on fire. When it came time for trial, attorneys were unable to find anyone for jury duty who had not heard about the heinous crime. The judge attempted to bring in jurors from outside the area but was overturned by an appeals court, so the entire trial was moved to Palm Beach County, costing Hillsborough County, which had to pay for the out-of-town trial, about a hundred thousand dollars. A state representative from Tampa, Ron Glickman, introduced a law that would allow jury importation in certain instances and it won legislative approval.

The law became effective in June of 1994, and less than a week later it was cited for the first time by a judge—Susan F. Schaeffer. Instead of picking a new trial site, she only had to pick a county that was similar in demographic makeup to Pinellas and Hillsborough. Working out the details with Zinober, Bartlett, and Crow, she ruled that the jurors who would hear the Chandler case would be drawn from Orlando, halfway across Florida, but close enough that the jurors could drive over. It was cheaper to pay room and board for a dozen jurors and a few alternates than come up with the money to transport the defendant, all lawyers, the judge and her court staff, and witnesses.

This decision was followed by another that finally got Chandler out of the Hillsborough County Jail. He had not grown any fonder of Tampa's spartan accommodations in the passing months, and when Schaeffer moved to keep things as simple as possible, she also opened the door for shifting the trial back to the more familiar environment of Pinellas County.

In February, Schaeffer had firmly turned down Zinober's request for moving the defendant back to Pinellas, commenting, "I'm not going to have Mr. Chandler in a position of being transported back and forth." With the decision to import a jury from Orlando, there was an opportunity to relocate the trial again. The judge only needed the okay from the prisoner, who had asked to be tried in Hillsborough. Tired of the Hillsborough brand of jail time, Chandler couldn't give his permission fast enough to the Schaeffer plan.

It was a Pinellas case. It would be tried in Pinellas.

26

After the sudden starts and jarring stops, detours to other cities and countless hours of preparation, the trial of Oba Chandler for the murders of Jo, Michelle, and Christe Rogers finally neared the launch point in the second week of September 1994.

Schaeffer had realized from the start that this one would require a lot of physical space, and roamed the halls of the Pinellas County Courthouse to solve the logistics problem. She needed not only a large courtroom, but had to determine the best facilities for a jury that would be sequestered for the trial, and an appropriate space for the growing press corps covering the case. Reporters were coming in from Ohio and elsewhere in Florida, and even Court-TV wanted coverage for its national audience.

She eventually made a deal with Judge Douglas Baird, who normally presided in Courtroom M on the fourth floor of the large building. The court was a vast chamber, the largest in the building, and could hold up to 150 people on its two wide rows of benches. Every seat would be needed when Oba Chandler was brought before the bar, and Baird swiftly agreed to lend it to his colleague for the duration. A single television camera would broadcast the proceedings to a press room elsewhere in the building, and provide a feed to the local television stations.

This case had the potential to become a circus, but attorneys who knew Schaeffer were confident that she would not let it spin out of control. At the age of fifty-two, Schaeffer had been a lawyer since 1971, when she graduated from the Stetson University College of Law, following her undergraduate degree at Florida State University. As a circuit judge, her reputation was for her quick legal mind, swift and sure decisions, and a track record that supporters thought might some day propel her to the Florida State Supreme Court. She was unafraid of handling big trials and equally unafraid of handling top lawyers who, to win a case, were never more than a step behind any boundary the court may set. If anybody could keep a lid on the Chandler trial, it was Susan Schaeffer.

She needed fourteen people in the jury box—twelve jurors and two alternates—and the judge hauled the prosecution and defense teams over to Orlando to find them. In a suffocatingly tiny courtroom that could hold only thirty-five people at a time, Schaeffer began interviewing a list of 324 potential jurors.

Even before the prosecution or defense attorneys began their questioning of the potential jurors, the judge had to weed out those who would be unable to serve. Asking someone to put his or her life on hold, to be almost totally severed from contact with the outside world for four consecutive weeks, was not a task undertaken lightly. It would do no good to have people in the jury box who were drafted over their protests. Although the law actually permits hauling jurors in off the street if the case demands, Schaeffer wanted volunteers and was totally honest with them.

Her pitch was more negative than positive, since she

wasn't trying to sell them on anything other than hard-time public duty. There was no rose garden, no pot of gold at the end of the rainbow, she told them, only hard but vitally important work. Family visits would be allowed only on Sundays, telephone calls would be scrutinized, recreation limited, and comings and goings strictly controlled. Anyone chosen for the jury would be locked away in either a Pinellas hotel or the county courthouse for a month and work six days a week. The pay would be a lousy thirty bucks a day and fringe benefits would be board games, crossword puzzles, and videotapes of movies.

Schaeffer was obviously anxious to get the trial underway and her manner of interviewing the potential jurors signaled to everyone that the judge was putting the case, which had stumbled along for months, onto a lightning fast track. She spoke to each and every one of the 324 listed prospects before lunchtime of the first day.

Thirty-three said they could do a stint of jury duty in Pinellas County. The lawyers and the judge pared that list down to a final fourteen people, all of them middle class whose professional affiliations cut across economic lines. Among the occupations represented were an apartment house maintenance man and a missile mechanic, a minister's wife and a postal worker, a soda salesman and two school bus drivers, a banquet server and the manager of two Holiday Inns.

The following morning, Schaeffer spoke briefly with another 250 prospects and excused them all, including more than a dozen volunteers. By that afternoon, she and the opposing lawyers carefully examined those making the final cut.

Assistant State Attorney Robert Lewis emphasized to the jurors that the case was not some television detective show. "This is not something that was contrived to entertain you. The victims in this case are really dead. They won't appear later on some other show.''

Zinober also gave them a stern warning that they were going to encounter rough personal moments when they entered the courtroom to decide a case where the death penalty could be imposed. ''It's going to be an emotional case, I can tell you that right now. I cannot prepare you for the emotions when you see these pictures,'' he warned. In fact, he had fought to suppress the use of the photographs of the three victims, claiming such gruesome pictures would prevent his client from receiving a fair trial. He lost that bid.

Knowing that the jurors would be automatically sympathetic toward the victims, Zinober underlined their duty, explaining that the defendant in the American system of justice does not have to prove his innocence. It would be the job of the state to prove guilt beyond a reasonable doubt, Zinober said. Put personal feelings aside, he said, and make a decision just on the evidence, whether or not you hate his guts.

The winnowing process was done in almost record time, and the judge commented she could not have picked a jury faster in St. Petersburg. An entire week had been set aside by Schaeffer to cull through the Orange County jury list. She finished in less than two days, giving the nine women and five men who were picked one last chance to back away from taking a ticket for this nightmarish journey that lay ahead. When no one accepted her final offer, the judge folded her papers. ''Now you belong to me,'' she intoned. ''It's not optional anymore. You have got to go, or I will come and find you.'' Not a person in court had a doubt that she would do exactly what she said.

Court watchers said the end result was already a victory for the state. Much of the case would center on Oba Chandler's assaults on women, his poor relationships with them, his multiple marriages, the mistreatment of his daughter in Ohio, and the sexual bondage pornography found in his home. And more than half the jury was female.

If Chandler thought the Orange County Jail was going to be a nice break from his detested incarceration in Hillsborough, he learned quickly that he was not a welcome guest. By the time he came into the courtroom to watch jury selection, he bitterly complained that he had been given only a sack lunch the night before, not a hot meal, and that he was not allowed to shower until 1 A.M., only three hours before he had to get up at 4 A.M. to prepare for the court's 9 A.M. starting time. The people who ran the jail, he thought, were treating him like a criminal.

The decision to bring in jurors from another county turned out to be a wise one, for in the middle months of 1994, leading up to the trial, a number of pretrial motions and newsworthy developments came to light and received major play by both the print and broadcast media around Tampa Bay. It was as if Zinober and Crow were involved in a peculiar match of legal tennis, batting motions back and forth, and each play added more extraordinary detail to the upcoming trial of Oba Chandler.

The defense attorney filed one motion to quash the charge of murder during the commission of a felony, claiming that the doctor who performed the autopsies on the water-ruined bodies found no evidence that the victims had been raped. The prosecution pointed out that the time the bodies had spent in the water had washed away such evidence as semen, and that the manner in which they had been tied and partially stripped spoke loudly of sexual assault. Schaeffer dismissed the defense motion.

A week later, Zinober was back with the suggestion that the knots that bound the victims were tied in significantly different manners, indicating that possibly more than one person tied them. He wanted the state to hire an expert in knot-tying for him. The judge refused. "The state may not care if it's one person or two people," Schaeffer said, "as long as one of them is your client."

A few things became very clear. Zinober, whose business before had been concentrating on complex financial deals that generated tons of paperwork, was not intimidated by the thousands of documents contained in the Wall of black binders. Also, the public was getting its money's worth by providing Chandler with a stubborn and savvy defense lawyer. The motions that Zinober was filing resembled a relentless probing of an enemy line as he searched for a weakness in the prosecution's case. Any victory, however minor, would help him, while a loss on any of the motions would do little harm. Therefore, the motions kept coming from the defense camp.

He scored a body blow against the prosecution in late July when he attacked their plan to use as many as fourteen witnesses who had been cellmates or served time in the same jails as Chandler. Oba's big mouth had not been stilled by his arrest, and the torrent of words was coming back to haunt his lawyer. The state wanted to trot out the prisoners as witnesses, hoping that jurors could look past the fact that the inmates were criminals themselves. Zinober wanted to show that crooks lie.

Their stories had been logged into depositions for the court and in combing through the papers, Zinober pulled out the strange tale of Dennis Rowe, a convicted bank robber from Clearwater, who had good news and bad news for both sides in the case. Rowe, who once shared a cell with Chandler, said Chandler admitted raping and killing the mother and her two daughters, but said he didn't do it alone. Chandler had an accomplice aboard the boat that night, claimed Rowe.

In the papers filed with the court, Rowe said Chandler told him during their interminable conversations that he met the family when they were looking for a mall. "The younger girl had a camera and was having trouble getting the film in. He helped her with it. The mother walked up and they started talking." When Jo Rogers mentioned she was from Ohio, Chandler said that was also his home. "They told him they planned on going to the beach to get photos of the sunset for their dad," Rowe had told the prosecution team in his sworn deposition. Then, Chandler offered to take them out on the boat.

When the Rogers family showed up at the boat ramp on the Courtney Campbell Parkway about 5 P.M., Chandler assisted them in loading two bags and an ice chest aboard his boat. "His buddy was hiding aboard the boat," Rowe said.

Already, the jailhouse informant was slipping in veracity. Police knew the boat in question very well, in fact, they now *owned* the craft and there was absolutely no way someone could have hidden aboard. The only possible place for a person to be kept out of view was in the cramped forward hold, and only a tiny contortionist could fit in there. In addition, two other inmates had given depositions claiming that Chandler denied the rapes.

But the overall content of the story Chandler allegedly related to Rowe was too important to police for them to throw it away over such a discrepancy. The decision to listen to Rowe's comments opened the possibility for Zinober to use the damaging idea that a second person was on board that fateful evening.

Chandler's comments to Rowe soon overcame any idea that Zinober might be able to employ the popular S.O.D.D.I.—Some Other Dude Did It—defense. For Rowe continued, saying Chandler told him that when his "buddy" appeared once they were on the water, Jo became upset. "At some point Chandler said he slapped one of the girls on the ass and Joan became upset to the point where Chandler struck her and knocked her out."

With Jo unconscious, Chandler told Rowe he used a sharp knife to keep the two daughters under control while he raped Christe, the youngest.

The coldest part of the prisoner's recitation was Chandler's comment on what followed the rapes. His words would ring like some horrible chime throughout the rest of the case. Rowe said in his sworn deposition that Chandler told him he bound and gagged the three of them, tied the heavy concrete blocks to their necks and then threw them off of the boat and told them, "Swim for it."

Rowe added that Chandler threatened to kill him if he ever told of the conversation.

The result of Rowe's statement was an admission of guilt by Chandler that he was actually on the water and in the boat with the women, if not that he actually raped and killed them. The downside, for the prosecution, was that Chandler said a mysterious unknown partner was with him that day and the testimony of a bank robber was not the strongest sort of evidence to bring before a jury.

27

*S*wim for it.
      Prosecutors and police would never forget that phrase and never forgive Oba Chandler for saying it. The intense vision of assault, rape, and murder that the three words provoked steadied the nerves of every investigator and prosecuting lawyer in the case. They wanted Oba Chandler to pay, big time, for his callous and brutal attacks on Jo, Michelle, and Christe Rogers.

Swim for it.

A month before the trial began, those intentions became absolutely clear in papers filed with the court in which the prosecutors stated flatly they now had enough evidence to convict Chandler of felony murder in the first degree. Under Florida law, the state does not have to prove premeditation to obtain a first-degree murder verdict if the victim dies during the commission of a narrow range of violent crimes, such as robbery, kidnap, and rape.

Assistant State Attorney Robert Lewis, while not letting the defense glimpse the actual strategy the prosecution planned, wrote in the legal brief that Chandler could fall into either of those categories. "The defendant hog-tied and duct-taped the children, along with their mother, and . . . he threw them off the boat, telling them to 'Swim for it.' "

He argued that there was evidence that robbery was committed because a necklace and camera belonging to the victims were never found. As for the charge of kidnapping, they said Chandler had admitted to other people that he had used a knife—which the lawyers termed a deadly weapon—to keep the women under control. "One can commit kidnapping by confining a person to terrorize or inflict bodily harm upon them or to commit or facilitate the commission of a felony," wrote Lewis.

"Witnesses have testified that the defendant admitted committing the murders of these three victims . . . admitted taking the three victims out on his boat . . . (and) admitted using a deadly weapon to hold them at bay," he concluded. It was, Lewis said, a "terror-filled experience."

Zinober attempted to brush over the sharp attack, claiming that the alleged admission by Chandler was based primarily on the "unreliable" testimony of a jailhouse snitch. The perjorative term was not welcomed by the informant who had provided the information, and he began researching how to file lawsuits for libel.

Fred Zinober's biggest hurdle was not the prosecution team that he would face in court. The major problem was that Oba Chandler wouldn't keep his mouth closed.

Had the state only been able to bring forth the stained and self-serving testimony of a bunch of convicts, Zinober could have had a field day challenging them. It is relatively simple to make a jury suspicious of a prison inmate who tells his story to authorities. The conclusion can be proposed that the tale is told in order to win better treatment behind bars or a shortened sentence.

Chandler, however, had access to a telephone in the county jails where he was lodged.

His beleaguered daughter and son-in-law, Kristal and Rick Mays, had been surprised when workmen from utility companies had shown up at their home in Cincinnati to take away their meter and their gas and electric services. Even more of a surprise was a telephone call a few days later from Oba Chandler, locked up in Florida, who said it was all his doing. "Well, I guess you know what I've done by now," he told Kristal. She said he told her that if they talked to police about his involvement in any Florida crimes, Rick would end up, in Chandler's words, "rotting in jail."

Kristal had had just about enough of her father's deviousness. "I said if Rick does go to jail, he'll eventually get out and I'll be here when he gets out," she told him.

Oba then called Rick, with the not-so-veiled threat that "I can make the balls bounce," even while he was in prison for serious crimes.

Rick also had gotten his fill of his father-in-law. "I said the ball is in your court," he told police. "That was when my trouble started."

Chandler, having learned through those preparing his defense that Kristal and Rick had cooperated with police, began telephoning the Mays' home in Cincinnati every day. "I think the message he was trying to send us was that he was going to get even," she said in a deposition. To add to the insult, the calls were collect. Kristal and Rick Mays had to pay to listen to Oba's diatribe.

The troubled woman who had hired a detective years earlier to find her missing dad in hopes of establishing a loving relationship finally recognized that the guy was a snake. "I'm ashamed to say that he's my father," she said.

They were so outraged by his continuing threats that they contacted police again, and gave permission to have wiretaps put on their telephones. Thereafter, when Chandler called Cincinnati, a police tape recorder switched on, storing his every word.

In one call, Oba asked Kristal if she recalled what they had discussed when he visited suddenly in 1989. "And I said yes, I remember. And he said, well, what we talked about when I was up there, when I stayed at the motel, you don't have to tell anyone about that."

He hinted that he would get some eight thousand dollars to them if they remained silent and that she was asked not to tell anyone that he had confessed to "killing some women." Chandler also tried to dodge around what he had told the Mays couple several years earlier by saying, "I know I've had a lot of problems with my life. I know I've done things that I shouldn't have done, but I have never physically hurt no human being in my life. Never."

To Rick, he said, "I never admitted committing any crime. Did I?"

But in another segment of the conversation, he told Kristal, "I can't turn back history. It's over with now and there's nothing I can do. I mean I can't change it. All I can try to do now, honey, is just make it work for the best."

The tape recorder caught the damning conversations before Chandler realized that someone might be listening to a conversation he had assumed was private. The smart guy wasn't smart enough to realize that Kristal and Rick had absolutely no reason in the world to want to help him. As far as they were concerned, Oba Chandler behind bars was the kind of Oba Chandler they liked. They had no qualms about helping authorities, vividly recalling all of the trouble that Chandler had visited upon them. They could not forget him driving away one evening, leaving

Rick in the clutches of a biker gang that was furious about being stiffed by Chandler in a drug deal. They remembered his words at the time: *Family don't mean shit to me.*

Now it was payback time for that remark. Kristal and Rick let Oba tie a noose of magnetic tape around his neck.

The Mays' depositions threw a whole new light onto the prosecution's case. Having to rely upon jailbird informers was one thing, but to have the defendant's own words on tape and the solid testimony of a couple of relatives was pure gold. It was bad enough for the defense that Kristal and Rick were going to testify themselves, but the tapes of Chandler's voice could be critical.

Zinober recognized the threat and filed a motion to suppress the tape recordings, claiming that Chandler's rights under the fifth and sixth amendments of the Constitution had been violated because he had been unaware the calls were being taped. He also said Chandler had signed a form that acknowledged his right to remain silent. Prosecutors contended that as long as the Mays couple knew of the taping of their telephone, it was a legitimate piece of evidence. Schaeffer agreed to hold a hearing on the issue, but two days before the trial was to begin, Zinober withdrew his motion, claiming that if the court ruled in his favor, the prosecutors might seek to delay the case.

That was a bit of defense sleight-of-hand legalese. It was highly unlikely that Schaeffer was going to give the ruling Zinober wanted, although she had said from the bench that the clandestine recording didn't seem right to her. So it was time to clear away the loose paper and concentrate on issues where he had a better chance. With the defense decision to surrender on the issue, the vital tape recordings were put on the list of evidence that could be brought into the trial.

Both sides of the case seemed to move into overdrive in the last few weeks before Schaeffer began the trial, filing motions, gathering still more depositions, maneuvering through the system in strange strategies designed to obtain every legal advantage possible.

Defense attorney Zinober was outraged that the prosecution came up with a list of sixty-five new witnesses with less than a month to go before the trial began. He said he had been interviewing witnesses almost nonstop since being assigned the case and was working hard to prepare his defense. He wanted all of the new witnesses barred from testimony, particularly Chandler's stepson and a man who would testify that Chandler told him he was with the victims the day before the Rogers women vanished. Crow denied that the names could come as a surprise to Zinober, and Schaeffer ruled against the defense lawyer.

Then it was the prosecution's turn to hit the panic button.

Fred Zinober filed a defense motion that claimed that the rape of Gayle Arquette, the linchpin in proving the case against Oba Chandler, should be dismissed because the attack had not even happened within the jurisdiction of the state of Florida. The very idea was a novel concept and, once again, the result of a good defense lawyer exploring every avenue available to his client. While filing a flurry of motions that, at most, had annoyance value, this one was serious. Without being able to bring the Arquette attack into court to show the similarities between the attacks on her and on the Rogers women, the case against Chandler would be seriously jeopardized. Doug Crow admitted that the sexual assault was a crucial part of their case. In fact, it was considered so important that if Schaeffer approved the motion for the defense, the trial might have to be put on hold while the state appealed that decision.

Zinober's reasoning hinged on Arquette's statement that she did not know exactly how far out in the Gulf of Mexico she was when Chandler assaulted her in 1989, two weeks before the Rogers' bodies were found. Therefore, the boat could well have been beyond the offshore jurisdictional limit of nine nautical miles from the state's edge. If prosecutors could not prove the attack happened within that legal boundary, Zinober said, then the important charge of sexual battery should be dismissed.

This was the sort of thing for which Zinober had made a reputation—finding a twist of phrase, a small detail, a tiny inconsistency and blowing it up into a case-threatening situation. Chandler, listening to the motion, seemed to be perking up now that he was back in Pinellas County and his lawyer was throwing hard pitches in court. During idle time at the defense table, Chandler would flash his impish grin while joking with lawyers.

Robert Lewis, answering the motion, poured cold water on the Zinober idea. He responded that Arquette also said she saw people on shore when the sun went down and that she had heard the clanging of a bell at the time of the attack. People on the beach could be seen by someone in a boat no further than a mile offshore, he said, and the bell was probably the one on the John's Pass buoy, which is anchored one mile offshore and can be heard only at a distance of a half mile. That meant, if the arithmetic was correct, the boat was no more than a mile and a half from shore when the attack took place— well within the jurisdictional limit.

Schaeffer dealt with the motion swiftly, denying Zinober's unique attempt to disqualify the Arquette evidence. This decision sent the defense team off on an entirely new tangent that would result in a peculiar strategy move that would manifest itself in the coming opening statements, due in only a few weeks.

Then, just as it appeared that the decks were finally clear of problems, up popped Donald Gary Adkinson and things immediately started to fall apart again.

The prosecution wasn't the only team with a jailhouse informant. Adkinson was a former inmate at the Allen Correctional Institution in Ohio, where he had served time with none other than John Rogers, who had pled guilty to another crime and dodged facing charges that he sexually abused his niece Michelle.

Adkinson, according to defense lawyer Fred Zinober, was ready to testify that John Rogers and a partner were involved with a drug and pornography scheme, that Hal and Joan Rogers knew all about it and even participated in the operation, and that the illicit profits were pumped back into the family farm.

Police had already talked to Adkinson several times during their investigation to discover whether there were any links to the murders that could be traced back to Ohio. They found none.

But when Zinober added Adkinson to the witness list only a few days before trial, the prosecutors were suddenly beside themselves with indignation and concern. Did the police miss something? Was there new evidence in what he had to say? "Adkinson indicated that John Rogers had traveled to Miami to courier drugs in rental vehicles and that Hal and Joan participated in the scheme," said Doug Crow.

While lashing out that the Adkinson story was nothing more than a bizarre ruse to switch the blame away from Chandler, Crow went so far as to ask Judge Schaeffer to postpone the trial to allow investigators more time to look into what the former inmate had to say.

Zinober countered that the state had had years to prepare its case and had interviewed Adkinson three times, and that any delay would be unfair to his client.

Adkinson, according to court records, was claiming that he had actually talked with the mysterious partner, down in Miami, after John Rogers had placed the call from a prison pay telephone. In addition, Adkinson said he even had the partner's photograph and address in Miami. When authorities called his hand on that statement, Adkinson said he no longer was in possession of those articles.

Judge Schaeffer ruled quickly on the admissibility of this latest alleged evidence, refusing to let the prosecutors stop the case in its tracks. But if Zinober had won the point, it was clear from the judge's statements in the hearing on the motion that the defense lawyer should not think that it would be easy to bring in Adkinson and John Rogers in order to create an alternate theory of the murders in the minds of the jurors.

"This is just not Mister Credible Guy," she told the courtroom filled with lawyers. The state already had a good idea of Adkinson's story, had previously investigated him, and had time to pursue further investigation before he could ever reach the witness stand. And the whole thing might just be a futile exercise for Zinober, she warned.

"You've got trouble," she told him. "You've got problems. You've got a lot of stuff you want to come in, but it's not coming in." Turning to the prosecutors gathered before her, Judge Schaeffer indicated they were getting upset over nothing. "I have a real hard time believing he's going to try to sell this Adkinson story to a jury."

Zinober was running out of bombs to drop on the prosecution, but got a last-minute piece of bad news himself.

Nothing important, just enough to make another hair turn gray.

On the comic relief front, convicted bank robber Dennis Rowe, outraged over being termed a ''jailhouse snitch'' by Zinober, filed a lawsuit for slander and defamation of his good name. He claimed that he should be paid two million dollars by the lawyer, because he was not a snitch, but a ''confidential informant to the cause.'' Rowe also wanted the judge to give him another name to use in court and bar the news media from photographing his ''current facial features.'' Since lawyers are normally exempt from civil liability for things they argue in a court, the suit was only of nuisance value.

Finally the pieces were all in place. There were no more bodies to identify, no fugitives to find, no more motions, no more legal issues to settle, no more surprise witnesses to depose, no more patience from the judge, and no more time. The trial was ready to start.

28

Opening statements were given on Monday, September 19, 1994. More than five long years had passed since the bodies of Jo, Michelle, and Christe Rogers were recovered from Tampa Bay. Finally, with eight women and four men from Orange County seated in the jury box of Courtroom M. Judge Schaeffer's gavel was ready to fall to begin the trial of Oba Chandler, accused of murdering the mother and her daughters from Ohio.

It had been one of the costliest investigations in the history of Pinellas County, with the taxpayers having the added burden of paying the expensive legal defense bills for the defendant. In addition to the flat hundred-thousand-dollar fee to Zinober, another $36,000 had been spent to cover his expenses that ranged from expert analysts to copies of the thousands of papers in the Wall.

Some 420 witnesses, an incredible number that included almost two dozen who had to be flown in, one all the way from Taiwan, and housed during the trial, were listed by the prosecutors as potential visitors to the witness stand. Zinober listed more than 150 for the defense. Down in the clerk's office on the first floor, there were thirty-eight volumes of documents on file, and the paperwork stored in the Wall had finally topped out at

63,000 pieces. The state attorney's office had never prosecuted a case that involved so much paper.

Five prosecutors had worked on the case several months, supported by their own team of investigators and the continuing work of the St. Petersburg Police Department and the database spewed out by the H.O.L.M.E.S. computer. Twenty-eight different law enforcement agencies had contributed to the case. The lawyers and their seasoned investigators, who had divided up the case in order to keep it manageable, spent the last weekend before trial huddled around a table, hammering out a final plan of attack and polishing the chronology of their courtroom presentation.

Were they absolutely certain that after all that time and investigation the case against Oba Chandler would lead to a slam-dunk conviction? No. Around the table on the final weekend, Chief Assistant State Attorney Bruce Bartlett said there was a sense that everything had to fall just right in order for them to win. "I don't think there was a minute in this case that we were not concerned. We had a very tall mountain to climb," admitted Bartlett. "We were extremely nervous." They had reason to be nervous, since there were no eye witnesses to the crime, there was no medical evidence of any sexual assault, no DNA or blood evidence to link the victims with Chandler, and some of their best witnesses were prison inmates. But the case had been transformed in the two years since it had been turned over to them by the police. They might not have a Silver Bullet, but they had some important telephone records now. They could put Oba Chandler on the water.

The forty-five-year-old Doug Crow had come full circle. He had drawn the duty of overseeing the recovery of the bodies, refused to part with the case during the intervening years, and he was at the prosecution table, going through his notes a final time, ready to give his opening statement. To say he was motivated would be an understatement. In order to maintain his energy level, he had been drinking immense amounts of colas and coffee. "I was running on a constant flow of caffeine in my system," he recalled. While he was ready for the fray to come, his compatriots felt some sympathy for the defense witnesses that Crow would grill. "Doug has a way of pissing people off," laughed one attorney.

Getting his papers ready at the defense desk was Zinober, who still had a few surprises up his sleeve.

For starters, while the prosecution had H.O.L.M.E.S., Zinober had a Stevie. Stephen A. duQuesnay, a legal assistant from Jamaica at Zinober's firm, had created a computer program that would allow him, from his seat in the courtroom, to call up information on any piece of evidence or any piece of paper among the thousands logged in the case at the touch of a key. Now he warmed up his speedy 486 portable computer terminal that was linked to a hard disk on which the mass of information was stored, opened a thick black notebook that held the indexed codes, and prepared to do computerized battle with Sherlock Holmes.

Zinober was barely able to contain his excitement at going against five of the best lawyers in the county prosecutor's office. As preparation for the trial neared its climax, he had been sleeping only four hours a night and forcing early morning time for a strenuous physical workout to stay in shape. He counted on his athletic endurance to pay off in the exhausting ordeal that would begin in a few moments. To him, the prosecutors, despite all of their talent and expertise, were still heading into trial with in his words, "a bare bones case." All he had to do was convince one juror—not all twelve—that Crow, Bartlett, and their team failed to prove beyond a reasonable doubt that Oba Chandler committed the crimes of which he was accused. That was all. One would be enough.

Also at the table with Zinober was Oba Chandler, fatter than when he had been arrested so many months ago, and wearing khaki pants and a casual shirt open at the neck. He showed little emotion as he listened to the opening phase of his trial, almost as if he were just one more spectator in the packed courtroom. Each morning in his cell at the county jail, he would change from his prison garb to civilian clothes, then be escorted through the "tube" that linked the jail with the courthouse.

One indication that officials believed there was a possibility that a disturbance might erupt during the trial of the infamous prisoner was the presence of four uniformed bailiffs in the court instead of the normal two.

The prosecution had been right in its belief not to try to guess in advance the kind of case Fred Zinober would present. He startled everyone immediately.

The opposing sides had fought long and hard over the use of Gayle Arquette's testimony against Oba Chandler. Zinober had insisted it wasn't relevant, while Crow had claimed that the similarities between the Arquette and Rogers cases were overwhelming. Zinober, prior to trial, had done everything in his power to get the Canadian girl out of the picture.

As he made his opening statement, he changed course 180 degrees, catching everyone off balance with a totally unexpected strategy. He admitted his client had had forcible sex with Gayle Arquette. "Ladies and gentlemen, the state is going to be able to prove to you a Madeira Beach rape," Zinober told the jury.

The stunned Crow and Bartlett turned and stared at each other in disbelief, as if saying, "Did we hear what we think we just heard?" They had been prepared for a battle in order to get the Canadian woman's testimony on the record, but Zinober had chosen to hand it to them on a silver platter. Their case, based solely on circumstantial evidence, began looking stronger.

The defense attorney told the jurors, however, that while things "got out of hand" when Chandler took Arquette for an evening boat ride, he never threatened her. And, Zinober added, the rape of Arquette on May 15, 1989, did not prove that his client had killed three other women two weeks later. "It's a different situation entirely," he said.

He also stipulated that Chandler had met Jo, Michelle, and Christe Rogers in Tampa one day when he helpfully gave them directions. And his client was indeed out on the boat the night of the murders, because he was a fisherman who often went out at night. Again, there was quite a jump from a nighttime fishing trip to a triple murder. This, too, was an admission from the defense lawyer that Chandler was at least out on the water during the night in question.

He also revealed that Chandler would take the witness stand in his own defense, something else for which the prosecutors had been praying, since a defendant was under no obligation to testify and open himself to a rugged cross-examination. "He's going to tell you from that witness stand, 'It's not me. They were not on my boat.' " It was Chandler, not his lawyer, who had the last word in whether or not to go on the stand, and Oba was not known for keeping silent, despite the risks.

Zinober told the jurors that police had gone out on a limb to link the Canadian woman's assault with the murder of the Rogers family members. The case was so hard to solve that police had eventually even had broadcast on the NBC television show *Unsolved Mysteries*.

"When all the evidence is in, you're going to conclude that this is still an unsolved mystery," he said.

When Zinober was done, he had, in the view of other

lawyers, painted himself into a corner by saying his man was a rapist. That was not something to which a jury would take kindly, but Zinober realized that, however distasteful the sexual battery charge was, Chandler was not being tried for the rape of Gayle Arquette. Better, he probably reasoned, to admit it up front and pull the shock value away from the jurors before the issue came up during the trial when Gayle Arquette took the witness stand.

"He gave away a very important piece of evidence in leaving her (Arquette) unchallenged," said one observing attorney. "There are many ways that it could have been argued, where the victim could have been challenged—the fact she went out on the boat a couple of times, the fact she was a pretty girl. . . . Maybe she wasn't as difficult or against this as she appeared. It would have challenged her credibility."

Crow struck immediately on the issue of the rape when he rose to make his own opening argument. It was the Madeira Beach attack, he told the jury, that ultimately led police to connect Oba Chandler to the murders of which he stood accused.

There was, for instance, the fact that after chance meetings with both Gayle Arquette and her friend, he had lured her onto his boat for a "beautiful sunset" cruise in Tampa Bay. During the assault, he had asked her, "Is sex something worth losing your life for?" The similarities with the Rogers killings were overwhelming, the prosecutor said, as the promise of a sunset cruise ended with a crime.

And when police finally came up with a description of the Madeira Beach assailant, Chandler took off. "Long before police made the connection, he made the connection himself," Crow declared.

Crow also made absolutely certain the jury knew what they were in the court to hear. He spelled out in graphic detail how Jo, Michelle, and Christe had been abducted on a boat on which the "crime could be committed in darkness and without the possibility of escape."

Then he summarized the horrible manner of the deaths—the duct tape around the mouth, but not over the eyes; the tight knots that bit into their flesh; the sexual assaults on a helpless woman and two children who had been stripped from the waist down; the heavy concrete blocks that were tied to their necks; and finally, the way they were thrown overboard, one at a time, until all sank in the dark water.

If points were given for opening statements, the aggressive Crow probably would have been scored the winner. That wasn't due so much to his overwhelming presentation, but rather it was because of the ringing surprises from Zinober. The defense lawyer had admitted Oba met the Rogers women, that he had raped Gayle Arquette, that he was out on his boat with no witnesses to corroborate what he was doing on the night of the murders. Since that had all been given away on the first day, Zinober was going to need a long ladder to climb out of the hole.

When Crow and Zinober were done with their first presentation to the jury, the dozen visitors from Orange County realized they were in for a bumpy ride. They had no idea just how bumpy things would get.

29

I f the jury was jarred by the opening statements that painted in horrendous detail the type of crime with which they were dealing, its members were thoroughly shaken by photographs of the victims that were the centerpiece of the testimony of Dr. Edward Corcoran, an associate medical examiner. The heavily damaged bodies depicted in the pictures that he personally showed to each nervous juror had been in the water for several days before being recovered. Clearly evident were the tightly knotted ropes that bound each, and the concrete blocks that had pulled two of them down.

He explained that his decision to say the three had died of "homicidal violence/asphyxia" covered both the possibility of drowning or strangulation. There were no other signs of injury.

Corcoran said the time in the water rendered useless any search for semen that might have determined if they had been sexually assaulted because the shifting tides would have washed away all traces of bodily fluids. He ventured, however, to let the jury add two plus two when he said the clothing that was missing below the waists of all three victims could not possibly have been naturally removed by the water.

The medical examiner was only one of twenty witnesses who marched into court on that first day of trial. Having opposing sides deliver opening arguments can occupy a full day in most trials, but completing both statements and handling twenty witnesses during the very first court session proved to everyone just how fast Schaeffer was going to push this. There would be no time for loose ends. When she asked a question, she wanted an answer, and her temper would flare at the slightest sign of legalistic tap dancing that did not move things forward at a quick march.

The rapid-fire presentation resumed the next day, when the jurors—having been made familiar with the scene of the murders and the nature of the victims—were faced with the sad visage of Hal Rogers, the quiet Ohio dairy farmer who had endured the violent loss of his wife and two daughters by a maniac.

Thin, gaunt, Rogers wore a gray suit of western cut, cowboy boots, and heavily tinted eyeglasses for his appearance in court. He had been watching the first part of the trial from Bruce Bartlett's office on the second floor, where the proceedings were brought in by cable to a pair of television sets. He was handled gently by Doug Crow. The official reason Rogers was on the stand was to testify to the fact that his wife and daughters had taken some personal belongings on their trip that were never found, including Jo's purse, the girls' wallets, all of their shorts and shoes and a Nikon One-Touch camera. That would indicate that the victims were also robbed, establishing one element of the charges against Chandler.

But the real purpose for the appearance of Rogers, a standard tactic in any murder trial, was to let the prosecution play a major sympathy card with the jury. Photos of victims were still somewhat abstract in this age of televised mayhem. Hal Rogers was real. Although he had worked his way through the mist of pain that had gripped

him for so many months, the man was obviously still
grief stricken. A juror would have to be stone cold not
to reach out in sympathy for the hurting husband and
father.

He slowly identified photographs of "my wife, Jo,
right there, a day or two before Mother's Day 1989" and
his girls, Michelle and Christe. Twice during his testimony, he slipped and referred to Jo in the present tense.
It was a habit. When he was working alone on the farm
during the long years that had passed since her murder,
he would often find himself talking to Jo as if she were
right beside him.

If Crow handled Hal Rogers with soft gloves, Fred Zinober had the onerous task of being harsh with the witness. In fact, he had tried to bar Rogers's appearance,
declaring that anything Hal had to say would be irrele-
vant because he had been in Ohio when his family vanished in Florida. That motion didn't stand a chance and
Schaeffer slapped it down.

Zinober, forced to deal with Rogers, chose to use him
as a gateway to the sordid tale of John Rogers's rape of
Michelle before the jury. That might establish the idea
that someone other than Oba Chandler had a reason for
killing the three Rogers women. But as soon as he
brought up the suggestion, Schaeffer stopped the defense
lawyer in his tracks.

She sent the jury out of the courtroom before allowing
Zinober to continue questioning Hal about the rape of
Michelle. The judge would decide, she said, about
whether to let the testimony be heard, only after she had
a preview.

Rogers answered Zinober's questions with a quiet dignity, saying that he put no pressure on his daughter Michelle to leave Ohio to avoid confronting his brother John
in a court. "Whatever she decided was fine with me,"

he said. Anyway, before they left on vacation, John had already pleaded no contest to the rape charges filed in connection with another woman, rather than take his chances in court on the rape counts involving Michelle. By the time the family went to Florida, the standoff had been resolved, John was imprisoned, and they could enjoy their holiday without the black cloud of the Ohio proceedings hanging over them.

Zinober also confronted Hal Rogers with the internal strain that had developed among other members of his family concerning the attacks on Michelle. "There was friction between my mother and me because a mother believes her son, and I got stuck in the middle of it," Hal revealed about his mother's strong defense of John. "I was in a no-win situation no matter what I did."

Zinober pressed his idea—still out of the jury's hearing—that the rape of Michelle had left the Rogers women so shaken that they simply never would have taken a boat ride in Florida with a stranger.

Okay, interrupted Schaeffer. That was enough supposition. If they didn't get on the boat with Chandler, who was the mysterious person with whom they went for their fatal cruise? She wanted a name.

"I don't specifically know who the person is. Whoever did this is someone that they know," Zinober waffled. In the past, he had repeatedly tried to suggest that John Rogers had hired someone to kill his relatives.

Not good enough. A lawyer making a statement is not proof, and Schaeffer was not buying. "You just want to get that rape in front of the jury," she declared. She ruled that the jurors would not be allowed to learn the details of the assault on Michelle, nor the unproven defense theory of a conspiracy guided by the hand of a man in a faraway prison cell.

When Hal stepped down from the witness box, a thin smile played at the corners of his angular face. Schaeffer had agreed to allow him to sit inside the courtroom and observe the remainder of the trial of the man accused of killing his family. He would only stay a few days, just long enough to get a sense in his own mind that the person who murdered his wife and girls was indeed the defendant, a man who was pale and pudgy from his time in prison.

The fast tempo continued. The second day beat the first day's pace as twenty-five more witnesses, including Hal Rogers, came to the stand.

A feisty Jo Ann Steffey described how she had become so suspicious of her neighbor, Oba Chandler, that she clipped out a police drawing of the man wanted for the Madeira Beach rape and kept it under a magnet on her refrigerator. She also described how she and Mo Smith had matched up the handwriting samples published by the police with the contract Chandler had written.

Backing her up were a series of investigators and experts who told the jury that the defendant's distinctive handwriting style proved Chandler jotted the directions for the Rogers family in Tampa. Others described how the tourist brochure had been found in Jo's abandoned automobile. It was a direct and solid link between the victims and Chandler.

In one of the more clever pieces of investigative procedure, Crow was able to show how experts had dissected a photo found on the undeveloped roll of film in the Days Inn room. By analyzing the angle of the sun and the shadows it cast, they determined the photo was taken between 6:20 P.M. and 8:20 P.M. on June 1, 1989. A guest testified that they had been seen eating in the motel restaurant that evening about 7:30 P.M. That pegged an exact time of their disappearance.

Further examining handwriting samples, experts identified Jo's writing on the motel stationery, where she had scribbled "blue w/wht." Freida Schwierterman, a co-worker of Jo's at the distribution warehouse in Indiana, said Jo habitually noted the colors of products by abbreviations, with the predominant color listed first. The color scheme that could be interpreted from her note matched the way Oba Chandler's boat was painted.

Day three of the triple-murder trial dumped an even heavier load of evidence on Oba Chandler. His own daughter Kristal Mays took the witness stand and related the terrible story he had told her on the unforgettable stormy evening in her home years before. The jurors listened with rapt attention as the blond woman spoke carefully, trying unsuccessfully to keep her soft voice level. "I can't go back to Florida because the police are looking for me because I killed some women," she said Oba told her husband, Rick.

The statement was forceful and simple, but was a sledgehammer blow to Chandler. His daughter told the jury her father had admitted murder!

Whatever tenuous bond that might have been left between them was severed. Kristal told the television show *Hard Copy*, "I'm ashamed to say that man is my father. . . . I wish that I had never found him." Chandler would later fire back on the *Maury Povich Show*, telling his first child that her conception was nothing but "an accident."

A second heavy blow in testimony came from Kristal's sister Valerie Lynn Troxell, another of Oba's children. Oba had also seen her in Cincinnati when he was on the run and she testified that when she asked him why he was acting so strangely, continually smoking cigarettes and not carrying any extra clothing, her father's reply, Valerie told the court, was "he had to get rid of a woman in Florida. . . . She was trying to say that he raped her."

Rick Mays joined the damning choir and testified that,

during a visit to Florida, his father-in-law drove him past the piers at John's Pass and related that he "once had forcible sex with a lady there."

Rick had more. He said that Oba had used the phrase that police were searching for him in connection with "the rapes of these women," but later repeated the sentence with a slightly different wording, saying he was wanted for "the murders" of some women. "The way he talked, he actually did it," Rick Mays affirmed in answer to Doug Crow's questions.

One. Two. Three. The jury did not need the combined intellect of a team of rocket scientists to figure out by now what Oba Chandler was talking about. Doug Crow and the prosecution team were painting a big red arrow of evidence that pointed straight at Oba Chandler, who busily scribbled notes while his daughters spoke. It was becoming clear that he genuinely did not like Kristal, the daughter who had once hired a detective to find the father who abandoned her as a baby. His anger toward her had to be kept under wraps in court, but would eventually blaze full on national television.

Meanwhile, Fred Zinober had to challenge these witnesses and their testimony. He had told the jury during his opening statement of the run-ins that Chandler had with Rick and Kristal and now he hinted that all of the things to which they had testified were predicated on getting even with him. "Paybacks are hell," Zinober had said in the opening. But he didn't have much with which to work and could not shake Kristal from her comments, even when he chided her for allowing the police to tap her telephone calls from her jailed father. He asked if she had done that in hopes that Chandler would admit the crimes and she nodded in the affirmative, without hesitation. "Yes," she said. "That's what I did. Yes."

In fact, the harder he pressed, the deeper Kristal dug in her heels and the better witness she became. Zinober brought up the dope deal double-cross that Chandler had engineered, which ended with Rick being severely beaten.

"You were upset with your father for doing that," he said.

"I was upset with my father," she confirmed.

Hanging in the air between the daughter on the witness stand and her blazer-clad father writing at the defense table were the unforgettable words he had spoken—*Family don't mean shit to me*!

30

Rollins Cooper of Odessa, Florida, had a deeply lined face, long dark hair that was gathered at the back and fell below his shoulders, a mustache, a goatee, and a story to tell the jury.

Cooper testified that he had worked with Oba Chandler for five days in 1989 as a subcontractor on an aluminum insulation job, although he was paid for only three. He never paid much attention to what Chandler would say, he had told police, because, he said, "[Chandler] was just such a bullshitter, that's all he was."

Bruce Bartlett, the chief assistant state attorney, carefully led Cooper through the events of June 1, 1989—the day the Rogers women vanished. Bartlett was one day shy of his fortieth birthday and could think of no better present to himself than hammering another legal spike into the heart of Oba Chandler. Like the other lawyers, the strain was telling on Bartlett, and, like the rest of the prosecuting team, he was getting only four hours of sleep a night. "It was like I was on a treadmill, and while I might try to turn off the power, it kept on running," he said.

Therefore, he enjoyed the testimony of Rollins Cooper. It was potentially devastating material, for Cooper claimed that Chandler showed up at the work site between 11 A.M. and noon, and seemed to be very nervous as he handed over a roll of screen wire.

"He was in a hurry. I asked him why he was in such a hurry. He told me he had a date with three women." The comment was only the first part of a one-two punch, and Bartlett smoothly had Cooper recount the very next time he saw the defendant.

It was the next morning, about 7 A.M., when Chandler drove up to a Tampa location to give Cooper a ride to the job. When Cooper looked at the man, he was surprised, for Chandler had always seemed clean and well shaven. That morning, however, Cooper said, "He was kind of grubby. He said he was out in the boat all night." Chandler even had a stubble of beard and was once again jittery and anxious.

Cooper's comments bore a lot of weight, for while he was not an eyewitness to the crime, the jury could deduce that Chandler specifically telling Cooper that he had a date with three women one afternoon and admitting the next morning he was on his boat all night certainly could tie in neatly with what they already knew about the crime.

Fred Zinober recognized the danger and moved forcefully to destroy Cooper's credibility. Under sharp questioning, Cooper confirmed that he had met with police eighteen times before mentioning the comment about having the date. Lamely, Cooper said the memory had come to him only recently when he suddenly awoke in the middle of the night.

"That's the first time you remembered about a date with three women." Zinober's voice was sarcastic, lumping the witness into the realm of people who have imaginary visions.

"That's not the first time I remembered it," protested Cooper. "It's the first time I mentioned it."

"You woke up in the middle of the night in a cold sweat and remembered he said he had a date with three women."

"I'm not sure about the cold sweat. I woke up . . . I wasn't dreaming. I was wide awake."

Zinober attacked the witness's history of drinking and asked if he had been drinking the night he remembered the comment. Cooper thought carefully and said he didn't think so. When the defense attorney finished grilling Cooper, he had won only minor points. Although he had made Cooper look somewhat dotty, he had not destroyed the damning recollection of Chandler's comments to his coworker.

The first week of the trial was drawing to an end and the prosecution was almost through with its presentation. The defense had yet to present its side of the story, which would be followed by prosecution rebuttal. Although it had seemed unlikely to succeed at first, Schaeffer's plan to hurry the trial along was paying off.

The team of prosecutors, led by Bartlett and Crow, now played another major card as their case soared toward a climax, almost as if a legal symphony was playing a complex piece. The prelude was done and now a thumping wrap-up was needed to keep the state's version of the story locked firmly into the minds of the jurors.

The jury knew that all the victims had been bound in a peculiar manner and apparently had been lured out onto a boat. By now, they also presumed it was Chandler behind the deadly scheme. While the prosecution could not specifically spell out the details of the attack on Jo, Michelle, and Christe Rogers, they were about to unroll the blueprint of a very similar crime.

Through the door and to the witness box calmly strolled Gayle Arquette, who had flown down from Canada to settle an old score with the man she knew as Dave

Posner, the man who had viciously attacked, raped, and threatened to kill her five years earlier.

The jury was immediately taken by the very pretty young woman whose coiffed brown hair was a perfect complement to her cream suit. It was time to get even for her terrifying voyage. Months ago when investigators had shown her Chandler's picture, she identified it and then asked the police to place it face down on the table during their conversation because it disturbed her so much. There was no sign that she was nervous on the witness stand. She was no longer a frightened college student, but a confident thirty-year-old who held a job as a social worker in Canada.

Fred Zinober had already said in his opening statement that he would not contest the fact that his client had raped her. The jury knew exactly who Gayle Arquette was when she began to describe her ordeal of May 15, 1989.

Doug Crow let her tell her story, interjecting questions only when necessary. He asked her if the man who raped her was in court and Arquette nodded. "Right there," she said, pointing a scarlet fingernail straight at him. He showed no emotion.

The Canadian woman described how they met and how he smoothly played the role of a caring good Samaritan who volunteered to ferry her and a friend out of what he said was a high-crime area, but was really just the parking lot of a convenience store in a beach town. "He sort of drew me into him. He seemed very concerned about us," she testified.

The mask of concern fell when he had her alone on the boat that night, when he ripped off her shorts, raped her three times, and at one point threatened to stifle her screams with a gag of duct tape.

"He said, 'You are going to have sex with me. There's no way around it. What are you going to do? Jump off the boat?' " Although strong in her testimony, reliving the frightening night on the water twice brought her to tears, forcing the judge to clear the jury from the court until the witness could regain her composure, snuffling into a tissue handed to her by a bailiff.

Arquette also described his response when she threatened to report him for rape. "He seemed to think that was ridiculous. I believe I was screaming at that point and he said, 'Do you think somebody is going to hear you?' "

"I was screaming and screaming," she testified. "He said, 'Shut up! Shut up! If you don't shut the fuck up I'm going to tape your mouth. Do you want me to tape your mouth?' "

He pointed to the silvery roll of duct tape as he asked her, "Is sex worth losing your life over?"

Crow interjected a question. How did she interpret Chandler's comment?

Gayle Arquette looked at the lawyer as if he could not understand plain English. She had only one interpretation. "I was going to lose my life if I didn't cooperate."

Her story was supported by the testimony of her friend, Linda Lyle, who recalled that Chandler had been in her words, "very, very friendly, very jovial, very gentlemanlike" during their initial meeting. She had refused to go along on the trip and Gayle testified that Chandler was perturbed when she showed up alone for the second part of her sunset cruise on the Gulf of Mexico.

Although Zinober's opening statement plainly said that the state could prove the rape of Gayle Arquette, he could not let this vital testimony pass unchallenged. Unfolding his tall frame and walking toward her, the defense attorney hoped to show the jury that perhaps things were not as bleak as the witness had described.

He did not challenge her identification of Chandler, nor did he attack the basic elements of her story, although he stressed that she apparently had enjoyed her time with

Chandler so much during the afternoon that she had voluntarily returned for a second cruise that evening. While the prosecution claimed the pattern of the Arquette rape matched the style of the Rogers' murders, Zinober pointed out differences.

Did she ever see ropes or concrete blocks on the boat? No.

Did Chandler ever brandish a weapon? No.

Tie her up? No.

Threaten to throw her off the boat? No.

It was a nice effort by Zinober to regain some ground, but it simply didn't work. The jury obviously believed every word that Gayle Arquette had to say and could not fail to recognize the similarities between her assault and the way, according to police and prosecutors, the Rogers family had been murdered. "She was one of the best sexual assault witnesses I've ever seen," observed one lawyer close to the case.

For its final major piece of evidence, the state of Florida's lawyers gave the jurors proof that Oba Chandler was indeed out on the dark waters of Tampa Bay on the night in question five years ago.

It came about through some dogged detective work and more than a little luck.

Chandler had told police that he had telephoned his home from the boat, but that had not yet come into evidence. Since his story might very well change if he testified, and certainly he was not going to help the prosecution if he could avoid it, a paper trail was needed. Did he call from the boat? Who had he called? When? Police had some records of telephone calls, but not all of them, particularly for the estimated time of the murders.

The task of solving that critical part of the puzzle was handed to a pair of particularly stubborn investigators for the state's attorney's office, Steve Porter and Scott Hopkins. Their overall assignment had been to verify every piece of evidence, read every document, track down every witness, and get the case ready for trial. Hopkins likened the investigation to crossing a bridge to a different world. After two years of hard work, they had delivered to the lawyers almost everything they wanted. Almost. Only weeks before the trial was to start, the telephone records were still missing.

Subpoenas were issued in April 1994 to General Telephone for the phone records of Chandler's home and boat during the months of May, June, and July of 1989. In this technological age, it would seem that such a list could be coughed up by simply tapping a few computer keys. Not so. The word came back from GTE that any such records, since they were more than two years old, had been purged long ago.

That could have torpedoed the search right there but for the relentless probing of the two investigators. They refused to let the issue terminate at a dead end, not only because the records were important evidence but also because Porter and Hopkins harbored deep personal dislikes for Oba Chandler. During the two years leading up to the trial, the two men had worked on no other case and had grown to detest the defendant so much that they pinned his picture to the wall of their office to remind them daily of the savage murders of the Rogers family. The defendant was a big guy who might be able to intimidate a woman imprisoned on his boat, but the two lanky investigators were not impressed. In fact, they would have welcomed the opportunity to go one-on-one with him, but their badges kept them in the law-and-order camp. "The guy is garbage," sneered Porter. Scott said they were determined to put Chandler away for ever because, he said, "He's not just a killer, he's a killing machine." To them, Oba Chandler looked not like some super villain, but just an overweight, horrible Elmer Fudd.

So they persisted with their investigation and found a couple of friendly allies in the persons of a former FBI agent who was working for the telephone company and researcher Jenny White. They eventually tracked down boxes of microfilm containing old telephone records stored in a warehouse. In one of those boxes, Jenny White found the vital pieces of paper that put Oba Chandler on the water the nights of both the Madeira Beach rape and the Rogers murders.

The telephone number 223–0000, the fictitious number assigned by the marine operator to calls being made by radio-telephone from boats in Tampa Bay, showed up just where they could have best helped the prosecution.

The records stated that on May 15, 1989, the Monday that Gayle Arquette was raped, Chandler made a call from his boat to his home. The call was logged with the time code of 1749, military time for 5:49 P.M. That was consistent with the time the victim was dropped off for dinner prior to the assault.

Starting early in the morning hours of June 2, 1989, the records showed Chandler made three collect radio-telephone calls through the operator from his boat to his home in Tampa Shores between 1:12 A.M. and 1:38 A.M. Two more such calls were made after daybreak, the last one at 9:52 A.M. The person who made the calls, reversing the charges, identified the boat to the operator as the *Zigeuner*, or the *Gypsy I*, and on at least one occasion gave the operator the name of Obi or Oba.

Although the locations from which the calls were made could not be pinpointed, the value of the records was immense. For the first time, the prosecution was able to prove that Oba Chandler was out on the water on the dates in question. The two investigators and the five lawyers were elated, but knew that finding the records had been a close-run thing. Through luck and hard work, Porter said, "We got twelve shots out of a six-shooter."

When the records came to light in June, they forced an important admission from the defense. The calls clearly showed Chandler was not at home during the crucial hours right after the triple murder or the rape of Gayle Arquette, and indeed had called his house from his boat!

Since Fred Zinober could not dispute the data, Chandler was forced to concoct a story about why he was on the water that night. Without the records, there probably would have been no such admission and the defendant could have said he was in Topeka or Toronto as easily as Tampa. Now, however, everyone knew exactly where he had been at some extremely important dates and times.

Doug Crow brought the prosecution's argument to a close late Friday afternoon. Of the 420 witnesses listed by the prosecution for possible use in the trial, eighty-seven actually had taken the stand in the five swift days of testimony. Judge Schaeffer had kept the throttle wide open on the first part of the trial and there was no indication she would lighten up, as the defense readied for its turn in a rare weekend session. Fred Zinober was to take center stage at 9 A.M. Saturday morning.

31

If anyone was expecting Fred Zinober to pluck a rabbit out of a hat or magically make the case against Oba Chandler vanish, they would be disappointed. In fact, Zinober seemed busy rearranging the deck chairs on his slowly sinking ship. He had no rabbits. None at all.

Still, a surprisingly large number of courtroom observers felt that as the defense came to bat, the prosecution might have been a few points shy of victory. The case was still a bare bones, circumstantial one, despite the fire and thunder of Doug Crow and Bruce Bartlett. Had they proven that Chandler was guilty beyond a reasonable doubt? Some, including a few members of the jury, thought there were still some loose ends.

Zinober led off his case by bringing Detective Sergeant Greg "Boomer" Moore, the ramrod of the police investigation that led to the capture of Oba Chandler, to the witness stand. Almost as if he were testifying for the prosecution instead of the defense, Moore outlined how the police investigation had developed over the years, talked about the thousands of documents that were collected, the witnesses interviewed, and the use of the H.O.L.M.E.S. computer to track details.

Finally, he discussed the police realization that the brochure containing the handwriting—in their possession from the first day—might hold a significant clue. "It was looked at from then on as an important piece of the case," Moore said.

Publication of the handwriting in the newspaper and on billboards led to the tips that broke the case, he said.

Zinober had taken the risky move of using Boomer Moore as his lead witness to demonstrate a theory that once the police obtained Chandler's name and matched it to the unknown handwriting, they ceased looking for other suspects.

It didn't work out that way. In Doug Crow's cross-examination, he punctured the defense balloon. He asked Moore if anyone else ever came forward to admit giving the directions to the women. No, replied Moore.

"Did that affect your decision and make you think that perhaps that person was culpable?"

"Yes."

Saturday saw Zinober call to the witness stand two clerks who testified that they had seen Jo Rogers and her daughters shortly before they were slain with a man and a child at a Tampa shopping center.

Dorothy Lewis, a clerk at the Maas Brothers' department store in the West Shore Plaza, said Michelle Rogers was looking for a bathing suit on the morning of June 1, 1989, but the three tourists just bought a single blouse. A man walked up with a child while they were checking out and showed a package to Christe, who asked the clerk the location of the children's department. "He decided to go up, and Jo went with him and Michelle followed. Christe waited a few minutes, thanking me for helping her," the witness said. Lewis added that the three tourists kept shopping in the store for another hour.

Rose Ann Fuchs Upton, another clerk, encountered

them in the junior's section, she testified, and she sold a cloth bracelet to Christe Rogers. A man accompanied by a child between eight and ten years old came into the department at the same time, and the tourists left the store in the company of the unidentified man and child.

Assistant State Attorney Robert Lewis handled the cross-examination and made quick work of the two witnesses. Neither could identify the mysterious man they saw as Chandler, the bracelet Upton said was sold to Christe was not the same one found on her body, Lewis waited six months before coming forward with her information, and the witnesses both admitted that their identification of the Rogers women were based, not on their recollections, but on photographs published in the media.

No rabbits there.

When court was over for the week, Schaeffer having adjourned until Monday morning, the prosecution team breathed a sigh of relief. They had been very concerned that Zinober might use the Saturday session "to roll out a hand grenade" of extraordinary testimony or evidence. That way, the sequestered jurors would have all day Sunday and Monday morning, prior to the resumption of the trial, to consider that perhaps the prosecution case had holes in it.

But just as Zinober had no rabbits to pull from a hat, he had no hand grenades either. As one observer later said, "He (Zinober) really didn't have any witnesses."

That was underlined the very next trial day, Monday, when Zinober quickly exhausted his supply of witnesses, probably not a moment too soon, since they kept blowing up in his face.

James Jackson, who worked at the Days Inn at Rocky Point, had said in depositions that he saw a boat matching the description of Chandler's there about seven o'clock in the morning the day after the murders. On the stand, he said he didn't remember that, but he did remember seeing Christe at the motel swimming pool about 2 P.M. on June 1.

Zinober introduced a large fishing rod into evidence to bolster the claim that his client was simply out fishing, his favorite pastime, that night. Don Fulton, who lived across the canal from Chandler's house, was brought on to support that claim. Instead, he testified that whenever Fulton caught a big fish from the dock in back of his house, many neighbors would emerge to look at it. Chandler, who lived directly across the creek, would not be among the spectators and evidenced no interest in fishing, said Fulton.

Mildred Worsham testified she saw Christe Rogers in the window of a car at the boat ramp on June 1, about the same time Jackson—another defense witness—had said Christe was at the motel swimming pool. With his own witnesses stumbling over their testimony, things were not going smoothly for the defense lawyer.

Still another witness testified that Chandler bought a roll of screen wire a few days before the murders, testimony that supported the damaging claims of Rollins Cooper. About the only win for Zinober on Tuesday was the word of a Tampa traffic enforcement police officer, Richard Pemberton, who said the Rogers' car was not at the boat ramp on June 7 because on that day, he wrote a ticket for a car parked in the space where the Oldsmobile was discovered on June 8. Earlier, another policeman had testified that the car had been there for some time.

As if to illustrate just how rocky a road was being traveled by Zinober, one of his scheduled witnesses—Gary Adkinson, the former Ohio prisoner with things to say about John Rogers—managed to get himself arrested for stealing a car on Tuesday. The judge refused to allow him to take the stand, claiming his comments were hearsay at best.

All along, Zinober had planned to put Oba Chandler on the stand near the end of his list of witnesses. But with Schaeffer trying to keep the trial moving, the defense lawyer, who had been moving extraordinarily slow compared to the prosecution, used up all of the witnesses he had scheduled for Tuesday around 2:30 P.M. An annoyed Judge Schaeffer refused to allow him extra time to round up new ones that could be heard that afternoon. The trial, she ordered, would go forward.

Zinober bought some extra time only by agreeing to a bargain. To avoid having to put Chandler on the stand immediately, he had to agree to let the prosecution team interview Chandler's wife, Debra, about the mysterious calls Chandler had made to Debra during those times cited in the telephone records. The defense had never waived the spousal privilege that could prevent a wife from testifying against her husband, and Debra Chandler was stubborn when answering prosecuters' questions, so Zinober did not have to worry that she might end up testifying against her husband. And in fact, nothing happened, just as he had guessed.

It was a very small victory, however, for the next day provided the highlight of the trial. Oba Chandler finally took the witness stand in his own defense.

Meanwhile, back in Ohio, people were following the trial as best they could. Television and newspapers gave their accounts, but Colleen Etzler in Convoy would bump into someone in a market who would have information that she had not heard. Hal Rogers was working his dairy farm, trying to push the trial in Florida into the back of his mind until it was all over. He had seen his hopes soar and crash too many times during the past five years and would not let himself become excited until he heard the final verdict.

Colleen was frustrated that the family was not being kept updated by the authorities in Florida, but was infuriated at something happening closer to home. An insensitive teacher at Crestview High decided the trial would be an excellent lesson in the way government works, and during a classroom discussion asked his students, "How many of you think Oba Chandler is guilty?" Sitting in the class was Colleen Etzler's daughter, Mandy, the cousin and close friend of Michelle and Christe Rogers. Mandy came home that day in tears.

Wearing khaki pants, a blue blazer, and a tie, and with his half-lens reading glasses at hand, Chandler seemed to be a rather normal fellow. His words were crisp, the manner confident, and the answers came fast. The jury was entranced. They had heard dozens of people talk about him, now the man accused of a triple murder was right there before them, finally speaking his piece, answering in public the questions that he had refused to comment on—except to his various lawyers—for two years. About one hundred people jammed into Courtroom M for the occasion.

In criminal cases, the defendant has access to all of the evidence and documents that the prosecution will use at the trial. It is not unusual for them to spend their days, weeks, months and years in jail while awaiting trial dreaming up a scenario that would logically cover all major points, without indicating any criminal wrongdoing. "Chandler would admit the obvious, lie about the unknown, and conveniently forget the rest," said one detective.

Zinober had him describe for the jury how he had met the three Rogers women. Chandler said he was returning from giving an estimate for a construction job when he stopped for gas and cigarettes on Interstate 4 and 50th Street in Tampa. As he came out of the store, a puzzled Michelle was there and asked him the location of the Days Inn on Route 60. "Well, I just turned around, there's a Days Inn right there and 60 is only a couple of blocks down from where we was at, and I just turned around to look at a sign and Christe stuck her head out the window, yelling 'Rocky Point! Rocky Point!' That's when I told her you don't want this one, you want the one on the Courtney Campbell Parkway. So I just gave them directions and that was it. I mean, there was nothing spectacular about it. Total conversation, two minutes." He added that they had a brochure and that he had printed directions to the motel on it.

"Did you see these people again at any time?"

"No sir."

"Did you kill them?"

"No, I did not."

"Did you ever take them on your boat?"

"No, they never went on my boat."

Zinober, stepping as lightly as in a mine field, brought forth the chronology and Chandler's version of events. Chandler said it was not unusual for him to be out on his boat at night and that he was fishing by the Gandy Bridge over Tampa Bay when he made the calls home on his radio-telephone.

"Did you kill anybody that night?"

"Of course not."

Chandler then added some embroidery to his answer, not knowing that fate was waiting just a few words away.

"It was nine thirty or ten," he said, smoothly. "The tide was running. I like to catch the tide changing; it's the best time to fish. Uh, you know when the water is still and its high tide, it's not good fishing. Fishing is best when the tide is moving. About nine-thirty or ten, we went out fishing, get out there, fishing, started for home, started the engine up, started pulling the anchor in and the engine died. I tried to start it again, it ran for a second and stopped. Uh, couldn't really figure it out, got my big spotlight out, and looking to see what the problem was. Started smelling gas, pulled my hatch away from the engine area and I could smell gas in my bilge area. My bilge had been pumping gas and I had a broken hose. I was totally out of gas.''

Two floors below the courtroom, Assistant State Attorney Glenn Martin was watching the trial on cable television in Doug Crow's office. He was intentionally not in the courtroom so that he could act as well as listen. When he heard Chandler's story about the loss of gas, it rang a bell and he started scribbling notes. The owner of a boat himself, Martin thought, ''It's impossible to lose forty gallons of gas like that.''

While Chandler was still testifying, Martin telephoned Butch Hensley of the Florida Marine Patrol, an expert engine mechanic. ''Drop what you're doing and go take a look at that engine,'' Martin said. Both thought there was an antisiphon valve on the Volvo engine, which would have prevented the gas from escaping as Chandler had just described.

Zinober, however, was blindsided by the explanation. His sports were swimming, biking, and running. Triathletes who happen to also be busy lawyers simply don't have time to learn about boats. Therefore, he had taken Chandler's word as truth and had no idea that the prosecution mill was suddenly in high gear again.

Zinober led Chandler onward, explaining the telephone calls. The defendant said that he was calling for help because he was stranded in the bay. ''I was stuck on the boat. It came daylight and I gave a call home, said I'll be home. . . . Well, the Coast Guard came by. I flagged

them down. They said they would come back and give
me some assistance if they could. They couldn't. Another
boat came by, I said, 'Can you give me a tow to the
mooring?' By that time, I figured out what the problem
was and proceeded to tape my hose where it was leaking.
It did okay. Two guys gave me a tow to Gandy Marina
where I bought five bucks worth of gas and went back
home.''

"Did you kill these ladies?''

"I never killed no one in my whole life. It's ludicrous.
It's ridiculous.''

He sounded sincere, an innocent man wrongly condemned. Of course, he had just tripped over his own
words again. Downstairs, investigators Porter and Hopkins were already getting in touch with the Coast Guard,
which kept meticulous logs for each of their ships and
boats. Chandler said he flagged down a Coast Guard
boat? Let's see if it checks out.

Zinober walked back to the defense table, finished with
his presentation. Chandler's story sounded solid enough,
perhaps enough to raise reasonable doubt in the mind of
a single juror. That was all he needed. One juror.

32

The cross-examination of Oba Chandler began on Tuesday, September 27, as Doug Crow rose from the prosecution table to question the man whose deeds had haunted the lawyer for five years. Tension almost crackled between the tenacious prosecutor and the glib defendant.

It was evident that it was going to be a brawl from the start, when Crow had Chandler confirm that he met the Rogers family.

"Approximately what time?" asked Crow.

"I don't remember," Chandler replied.

"Give me your best estimate."

"I don't remember."

Crow pressed harder. "Was it morning?"

"I don't remember."

"Was it afternoon?"

"I don't remember."

"What were you doing?"

"I don't remember."

The two men genuinely did not like each other, and the relationship would deteriorate further as the abrasive Crow picked at Chandler's story.

* * *

Crow had the defendant explain why he fled the area after the victims' pictures were published with stories linking their deaths to the rape of Gayle Arquette. "Did you flee the state?" the prosecutor asked.

"Yes, I did, because I was afraid of the Madeira Beach case. . . . It worried me. But I figured you guys would find out who did it."

Crow shot back, "Perhaps we have, Mr. Chandler. That's why we're here." Laughter rang out in the court, causing Schaeffer to bang her gavel for order. Chandler stewed in embarrassment, realizing there was little for him to gain by verbally sparring with such an experienced trial attorney. Schaeffer warned both men to keep on the subject and Chandler glanced over at Doug Crow, who was pacing up and down, then turned to the judge and said, "He gets under my skin."

He continued to be vague and evasive, particularly when Crow battered him about the rape of the Canadian tourist only eighteen days before the murders. Sixteen times, on every attempt Crow made to get him to talk about the rape, Chandler invoked his Fifth Amendment right against self-incrimination. "I'm not answering no questions about the rape trial," he said.

"On what grounds?" Crow questioned

"The case is still pending."

"So you're afraid your answers might incriminate you?"

"No. I invoke my Fifth Amendment on the rape case."

Crow needled him further, counting on the man being unable to contain his growing anger. When he directly asked Chandler if he had threatened the tourist that she could either submit to sex or "swim for it," Chandler shot back an answer. "No!" Crow followed by asking if he threatened to use duct tape as a gag to stop her screams, and Chandler again snapped, "No!"

Schaeffer pulled him back to reality, reminding him that he could either talk about the rape case, as he had started to do in replying to Crow's questions, or he could stand on his constitutional right of silence. You cannot have it both ways, she explained. "I plead the Fifth all the way," he responded.

Crow also slowly led the defendant through his story of being stranded in the bay on the night of June 1, and Chandler again told how he could smell leaking gasoline in the boat, but could not find the problem in the darkness, so he just went to sleep. After the sun came up, he patched the leaking gas line with tape and tried to flag down a passing Coast Guard inflatable, but the three people aboard said they were on their way to recover a body from the rocks and would come back later to help. Then he hitched a tow from a boat to get gas at a marina. Crow particularly was interested in having Chandler describe the problem in detail for the jury. Chandler said he was not a master mechanic, but Crow knew he had exactly such an expert now waiting in the wings.

Finally, Crow was satisfied. He had not even tried to break Chandler's alibi. In fact, he *wanted* the burly defendant to not only stick with his story, but even to embellish it, to dig in his heels on the details. And the talkative Chandler did exactly that, unknowingly tying a noose around his own neck.

On Wednesday, with the defense having rested its case, the prosecution called James A. Hensley and Robert Shidner, a former Coast Guard coxswain, to the stand. Normally, witnesses have to be listed far enough in advance to allow opposing counsel an opportunity to quiz them. Since the prosecution did not know what Chandler was going to say in advance, however, Schaeffer allowed the use of the last-minute expert witnesses.

Zinober, at this time, did not have the slightest idea where this was leading. He certainly did not have an expert mechanic that he could summon on a moment's notice. He grabbed at the only straw available. His teen-aged son, Luke, was studying marine mechanics at school and hurried to court from class. He sat in the front row behind Zinober, providing some last minute mechanical tips, and at one point drawing a barb from Judge Schaeffer, who asked Zinober if he wanted "a family moment" with his son.

Shidner, the Coast Guardsman, was put on the stand first. Chandler had said a couple of things of interest involving the Coast Guard—that a Coast Guard inflatable had bypassed his call for help that morning in Tampa Bay, and that there were three crewmen aboard that craft.

With Bob Lewis taking over the questioning for the state, Shidner said the only station patrolling that area would have been the St. Petersburg base, and the logs showed that the single inflatable boat at that station did not go out at all that day, and no area station had dispatched a boat to recover a body from any rocks. Further, the boat only carried a two-person crew. The only time three people would be in the boat would be if it were sent to recover a body or some task requiring extra lifting help. Photographs of the recovery of the Rogers' bodies had shown three crewmen in the Coast Guard inflatable boat. Chandler had apparently thought they always carried three when he wove that detail into his story. He was wrong on the crew size and he was wrong about a Coast Guard boat being out on the bay that morning. The information was so solid that Zinober did not bother to cross examine Shidner. Jurors had to wonder what else Oba might be wrong about.

They soon found out. The Florida Department of Law

Enforcement had become owner of the Bayliner, having paid $7,500 for the vessel in order to have it as evidence. It was some of the state's best-spent money of the trial, for by having it available in an FDLE storage warehouse, Hensley, the Florida Marine Patrol expert, was literally able to examine it from stem to stern. When he was done, he could demonstrate that Oba Chandler was a liar. After a detailed examination of the Volvo engine on the boat, Hensley said it was impossible for a fuel line leak to have drained the gasoline tank as the defendant had claimed.

A special antisiphon valve would not permit such a leak, and even if the valve malfunctioned, all vital connections—including the fuel line—were at the top of the engine. Therefore, since fluids do not flow uphill, the gasoline in the tank could not have leaked out of the line. "The engine would quit operating, but the fuel would remain in the tank."

Lewis then had Hensley describe the solenoid starter switch on the boat, and how sparks from the switch could cause a fire if they contacted an exposed puddle of gasoline.

"Let's assume by some miracle you've got forty gallons of fuel in the bilge and try to crank the boat," Lewis asked.

Hensley volunteered that with such a scenario, "You'd have a serious problem."

"You might not be here?"

"Yes, sir."

With that, the jury had no doubt. Chandler had been lying through his teeth on the witness stand. One attorney who watched the trial on television put the damage done to the defendant in clear but very unlawyerlike terms. "When the gasoline leak excuse went down, he was fucked."

Zinober made an emergency rescue attempt, but Schaeffer refused to extend the trial to allow him to obtain a rebuttal expert witness whom he had contacted in another city. He had earlier protested having the prosecution spring an expert witness on him, but Schaeffer had agreed with Crow. Chandler himself had opened this can of worms in his testimony.

"It seems Mr. Zinober made the mistake of taking the accuracy of his client's statements without checking them out. If there's a trap that he's caught in, it's of his client's own making," the prosecutor argued. The judge agreed.

The two expert witnesses had knocked huge holes in Oba Chandler's story, and his case, never watertight, began sinking before his eyes. There was nothing his lawyer, to whom he had lied, could do about it. His face had turned beet red during Hensley's testimony.

Closing statements came on Thursday, September 29, and they seemed anticlimactic, after the short but intense trial of Oba Chandler.

Fred Zinober gave it his best shot, and had to realize there was little chance for a victory at this point. The case had always been circumstantial, and perhaps there had even been hope for a hung jury, but then his client went on the witness stand and lied. Zinober could do little more than sweep up the ashes.

He attempted to cling to the idea that it was all just a strange and horrid case of circumstances and coincidences. He went through his list again—no witnesses, no weapons, no sign of sexual assault, nothing to directly link his client to the murders. "Ladies and gentlemen, where's the evidence? Where is the conclusive evidence that this guy took three women out on a boat, tied them up, put duct tape on their mouths, then tied concrete blocks around their necks?" Zinober asked.

There was one piece of evidence connecting Chandler to the Rogers victims, the handwriting on the brochure. But that was evidence only that he had written the direc-

tions, Zinober argued; it did not mean he had killed anyone. As for the earlier rape that involved so many
similarities, it was nothing but ill-starred chance. "Based
on this horrible coincidence, they're trying to convict this
man of first-degree murder," the defense lawyer declared.

"It hurts to think that we'll never know what happened," he said. "Don't hang it on someone who didn't
do it."

In the jury box, Patricia Pittman watched Chandler and
listened to his lawyer, thinking, "He should have stayed
off the stand." Her fellow jurors were feeling much the
same.

Bruce Bartlett, in his part of the closing statements,
took them again through the crime, then step-by-step
through the investigation and gathering of evidence, then
through the relevant testimony of witnesses.

Doug Crow then summed up, relating the murders to
the rape of Gayle Arquette and telling the jurors that they
should not pay attention to Chandler's tale from the witness stand. "Almost everything that came out of his
mouth . . . was a lie," he said.

He called Chandler a "chameleon" who charmed
women by posing as "an ingratiating stranger and then,
when he has them under his control, (he) becomes a brutal rapist or a conscienceless murderer."

The rape of Gayle Arquette provided the jury with "a
narrow window into the malevolent inner workings of
Oba Chandler's brain." By looking through the window,
they could understand his guile and ruthless operations.

"He puts a knife to Christe's throat, or a gun to Michelle's head, and he orders their mother to lie down on the
deck and says, 'You don't move and you don't say anything or your daughter's dead,' Crow said, brushing
aside the theory that three women could have over-
powered such a brute. "A mother will suffer anything,

endure any pain, to save the most precious thing to them on the planet, the life of their daughter.''

Before he ended his summation, he reminded the jurors one last time of Chandler's threat to his Canadian rape victim. ''Is sex worth losing your life over? The Rogers women know the answer to that,'' Crow said, looking intently at the jury but thinking about three bodies he saw on a pier five years ago. ''They lost their lives.''

The jurors stayed out only long enough to make it seem that perhaps somebody may have asked a few questions about something that happened during the nine days of trial in which they listened to 160 witnesses, seen 141 pieces of evidence, heard various lawyers make logical arguments, and endured the testimony of Oba Chandler. Surely, at least a few issues needed to be examined. Not so. An hour and twenty minutes after being given the case at the end of closing arguments, they were back in court, decisions made.

They were quick and they were unanimous. Oba Chandler, they announced, was guilty of first-degree murder three times, for the deaths of Jo, Michelle, and Christe Rogers.

The jury's work wasn't quite done, and they returned on Friday, the last day of September 1994 to debate whether Chandler should be given the ultimate punishment Florida had available for his crime—death in the electric chair.

Zinober had one last chance. He could no longer argue that his client was innocent, but he could challenge the death statute. He showed the jury pictures of little Whitney and produced telephone records that indicated Chandler telephoned his mother eighty-five times in a single month from his jail cell. This proved Oba Chandler was not a worthless creature, Zinober claimed. And, he said, the defendant was forty-seven years of age as he sat in the courtroom that day, and that sending Chandler to prison on a life sentence with no chance of parole for the first twenty-five years was the same as a death verdict, for he would most likely grow old and die behind bars anyway.

It was about the only sort of argument he could make, a plaintive plea for pity.

Judge Schaeffer kept her trial moving even in these critical closing moments, not giving either side extra time for their presentations. The prosecution, which had excelled in making their points, stumbled in trying to fly in a late witness. From the courtroom window, they could see the airport and pointed to a Sheriff's Department airplane that was touching down as they pleaded with Schaeffer for a just a few more moments. Reluctantly, she allowed the time.

Weighed against Zinober's request for mercy was the emotional presentation of Assistant State Attorney Jim Hellickson. To demonstrate Chandler's legacy of violence, he called several witnesses who had been robbed by the defendant.

Peggy Harrington broke down crying while recounting her terror when Chandler, shouting obscenities, put a pistol in her face while robbing her of $750,000 worth of jewelry in a Pinellas Park motel parking lot.

Robert Plemmons, from Daytona Beach, told the jury of the 1976 robbery when Chandler and a pal burst through his front door, knocked him unconscious, stripped his girlfriend from the waist down before molesting her, and robbed them of cash and guns. As Plemmons left the court, he glared at Chandler with unmitigated hatred on his face.

Hellickson countered Zinober's call for a life term for Chandler by saying that would be just too easy a fate for

a man who routinely dealt out cruelty to others. He gave
a blow-by-blow account of what probably happened
aboard that small boat on a dark night in Tampa Bay.

"He couldn't throw them over the side all at the same
time. He had to throw them over the side one at a time.
That means he threw one over the side—which one, we
don't know, but somebody was first. Was it the mother
. . . the daughter . . . the sister?"

While Chandler was carrying out the first murder, he
said, "The other two watched. Their eyes weren't taped.
And they heard. Their ears weren't taped. And they
smelled. Their noses weren't taped. And at that point,
they knew they'd be next.

"Nothing could be more horrendous, more atrocious,
more cruel and unmitigated than that. . . . He deserves to
pay the ultimate price," Hellickson said.

The jurors, who had been almost unseemly in their haste
the previous day when they returned the verdict of guilty,
left the court again to deliberate the life-or-death issue.
This time, instead of eighty minutes, they required only
thirty minutes. The eight men and four women were
unanimous in calling for the death penalty. Chandler
heard the verdict while wearing a slight grin, and was
quickly led from court. One juror said she had wanted to
walk over and slap the smirk off his face.

Judge Schaeffer set the official sentencing for November 4, one month away.

During the intervening month, Chandler actually won a
case. He was found not guilty of the March 1991 armed
robbery in Daytona Beach, in which a jewelry sales-
woman was robbed of about $140,000 after her assailant
used duct tape to seal her mouth, cover her eyes, and
bind her arms and legs. The turning point was that she
said her attacker had freckles on his hands. Chandler's

lawyer in that case, Bennet Ford, pointed out to the jury that Chandler did not have freckles, and they acquitted him. His murder convictions were not allowed to be introduced in the Daytona Beach case. The acquittal was shocking to the men and women in Pinellas County, particularly the vital item about the lack of freckles. Bruce Bartlett pointed to a color photo of Oba Chandler taped to his file cabinet. It shows a smiling man standing in the cockpit of a boat, wearing sunglasses. His arms and hands are covered with freckles. Between the time the Daytona Beach robbery took place and Chandler was actually tried for it, he had been in jail for several years and his entire skin had paled almost fishbelly white. Without exposure to sunlight, the freckles on his always light skin simply vanished.

On November 4, with Hal Rogers present, finally able to believe that his nightmare was coming to an end, Judge Schaeffer convened her court in Pinellas County for the final time in the tragic triple-murder case. After going through all of the necessary legalities, she had the defendant stand and face her verdict, and he rose with a frown.

"Oba Chandler, you have not only forfeited your right to live among us, but under the laws of the state of Florida, you have forfeited your right to live at all," she pronounced in a clear and unequivocal voice.

The judge gave a final summation of the crime, of how he met the three innocent vacationers from Ohio, lured them onto his boat for a sunset cruise, and attacked them when the sun went down. He tied them, taped their mouths closed, stripped off their shorts and underwear, assaulted them sexually, tied concrete blocks to their necks, and threw them into the water, she recounted. There was not a shred of sympathy in her voice.

"Imagine the fear and anxiety of each victim, with her hands and feet tied, her mouth bound by tape and a rope

around her neck being pulled tight, until blessed uncon-
sciousness takes over,'' said the judge.

"One victim was first. Two watched. Imagine the fear.
One victim was second. One watched. Imagine the horror. Finally, the last victim, who had seen the other two
disappear over the side, was lifted up and thrown overboard. Imagine the terror.''

As Chandler was led away for the last time, Hal Rogers slipped quickly and quietly out of the courtroom. The
satisfaction of watching the monster sentenced to death
helped ease his soul, but it would not bring back his
family. Nothing would.

EPILOGUE

Oba Chandler now wears prisoner number 056979 as he occupies a cell on death row at the Union Correctional Institution in Raiford, Florida. In several interviews since the death penalty was handed down, he has shown not the slightest sign of remorse. To this day, he claims that he is innocent and just another victim in the case.

But a warped sense of self-importance allows him to gloat over the fact that all the other prisoners know his name and his crime, as if the opinions of other felons are important. He has used his moment of celebrity during interviews to attack family members, mostly his daughter Kristal, and harbors a particular hatred for prosecutor Doug Crow, who doggedly led the way to conviction. Chandler says Crow is a weasel, and he mocks Judge Schaeffer as "that broad."

The bellicose prisoner told one interviewer that he wasn't bothered that the death penalty was handed down against him. "What am I supposed to do, fall down and scream?" he asked.

If all of the expected appeals are turned down in coming years, and Chandler is eventually strapped into Florida's electric chair, he has sworn that his last words to the world will be: "Kiss my rosy red ass!" From a man such as Oba Chandler, that is just about what one would expect.

The twenty-thousand-dollar reward that was posted for information leading to the arrest and conviction of the person who murdered Jo, Michelle, and Christe Rogers turned out to be one more sad chapter in the Chandler episode.

Jo Ann Steffey was given fifteen thousand dollars. Her sister, Connie Dickson, was awarded five thousand dollars. Mozelle Smith and her daughter, Dale Curtis, each received $2,500. Protests erupted over who deserved what amount and led to such strong, angry feelings that, months later, Jo Ann was not on speaking terms with any of them.

Hal Rogers survived a tragedy that would have sent anyone into a personal tailspin. As time passed, he conquered the demons that had beset him in the long night hours, without losing his sanity, or becoming an alcoholic or a recluse. He endured, knowing that he would never be able to forget. Years later, the quiet dairy farmer began making plans to marry a charming woman.

Though his girls are gone from him, they are never really far away.

Dark marble tablets mark the final resting places of Jo, Michelle, and Christe in the church graveyard. The markers are in the midst of dozens of others, the graves of former area residents, and it seems as if they just moved from one family into another.

The cycle of life is repeated all around them in the verdant growth of the flat Ohio farmland. They are home.